SPECIAL EDUCATIONAL NEEDS IN THE EARLY YEARS

2nd Edition

Ruth A. Wilson

RoutledgeFalmer
Taylor & Francis Group
LONDON AND NEW YORK

First published 2003
by RoutledgeFalmer
11 New Fetter Lane, London EC4P 4EE

Simultaneously published in the USA and Canada
by RoutledgeFalmer
29 West 35th Street, New York, NY 10001

RoutledgeFalmer is an imprint of the Taylor & Francis Group

Typeset in Palatino by
Keystroke, Jacaranda Lodge, Wolverhampton
Printed and bound in Great Britain by
TJ International Ltd, Padstow, Cornwall

British Library Cataloguing in Publication Data
A catalogue record for this book is available from the British Library

Library of Congress Cataloguing in Publication Data
Wilson, Ruth A., 1943–
Special educational needs in the early years / Ruth A. Wilson.—2nd ed.
p. cm. — (Teaching and learning in the early years)
Includes bibliographical references and index.
1. Children with disabilities—Education (Early childhood)—Case studies.
2. Special education—Case studies. I. Title. II. Series.

LC4019.3 .W55 2003
371.9′0472—dc21 2002036957

ISBN 0–415–30346–X (hbk)
ISBN 0–415–30347–8 (pbk)

SPECIAL EDUCATIONAL NEEDS IN THE EARLY YEARS 2ND EDITION

This book is a practical and accessible guide to teaching young children with special educational needs. At the heart of the book is the belief that the focus should be on the child as an active learner, rather than on his or her disability.

This fully revised and updated edition takes into account current changes in educational policy to provide the reader with comprehensive information about understanding and working with young children with special needs. The author addresses key issues such as the nature and causes of specific disabilities, intervention and assessment, working with families, planning individualized objectives, and instructional strategies. There are also new sections on emotional competence, early literacy concerns, and discussion of the emotional implications of brain research. Case study examples and practical suggestions are included throughout.

The book will be a valuable resource for all early years practitioners, primary teachers, student teachers and learning support assistants.

Ruth A. Wilson is Professor Emeritus at Bowling Green State University, Ohio.

TEACHING AND LEARNING IN THE EARLY YEARS
Series Editor *Joy Palmer*

This innovatory and up-to-date series is concerned specifically with curriculum practice in the first three years of school. Each book includes guidance on:

- subject content
- planning and organization
- assessment and record-keeping
- in-service training

This practical advice is placed in the context of the National Curriculum and the latest theoretical work on how children learn at this age and what experiences they bring to their early years in the classroom.

Other books in the series:

GEOGRAPHY IN THE EARLY YEARS
Joy Palmer

HISTORY IN THE EARLY YEARS, 2ND EDITION
Hilary Cooper

MATHEMATICS IN THE EARLY YEARS
Wendy Clemson and David Clemson

MUSIC IN THE EARLY YEARS
Aelwyn Pugh and Lesley Pugh

PHYSICAL EDUCATION IN THE EARLY YEARS
Pauline Wetton

RE EDUCATION IN THE EARLY YEARS
Elizabeth Ashton

FOR ALL YOUNG CHILDREN
WITH THE JOY AND POSSIBILITIES
THEY OFFER TO THE WORLD.

CONTENTS

ILLUSTRATIONS

Figures

Table

Boxes

FOREWORD

I am pleased to welcome the second edition of this book as a valuable addition to UK texts on the early years/special educational needs scene.

Ruth Wilson is Professor Emeritus in the Department of Special Education at Bowling Green State University, Bowling Green, Ohio, USA, and her book demonstrates her sound and extensive knowledge and experience of early years development as well as of the equally specialist area of early years special needs.

Ruth's writing style is clear and accessible, and jargon is explained with a supporting glossary and list of abbreviations. Readers will find a wealth of references/further reading as well as many helpful tables. The many case studies graphically illustrate the points and messages contained in each chapter and also serve to show the concerns and issues dealt with by our counterparts across the Atlantic Ocean, many of which are so similar to our own. Indeed such commonalities transcend other cultural and educational differences and confirm that, for identified problems, there are solutions that we can relate to in the UK.

Practitioners will welcome the practical content of the book to support their pursuit of the requisite pedagogic and curriculum goals.

There is one profound principle pursued throughout the book which I greatly welcome – namely promotion of the idea of integration or 'reconciliation' between regular early years educators and special needs educators. This is a message well worth reiterating for a UK readership of early years and SEN practitioners and policy makers, at a time when co-operative working is being urged.

Ruth often contextualises her material by reference to significant recent developments in the UK such as Early Learning Goals, Early Years Development and Childcare Partnerships, Sure Start and the revised Special Educational Needs Code of Practice.

Other welcome additions to this second edition are sections on considering children's views, brain research and implications for early years practice, literacy, and an emphasis upon inclusive approaches.

Overall I commend this book for its blend of research and evidence-based practice.

Professor Sheila Wolfendale,
London

SERIES EDITOR'S PREFACE

Each book in this series focuses on a specific curriculum area. The series relates relevant learning theory or a rationale for early years learning to the practical development and implementation of subject-based topics and classroom activities at the infant level (i.e., Reception, Year 1, Year 2). It seems that the majority of existing books on primary education and the primary curriculum focus on pupils aged 7–11 years. It is hoped that this series presents a refreshing and much needed change in that it specifically addresses the first three years in school.

Each volume is intended to be an up-to-date, judicious mix of theory and practical classroom application, offering a wealth of background information, ideas and advice to all concerned with planning, implementing, monitoring and evaluating teaching and learning in the first three years in school. Theoretical perspectives are presented in a lively and interesting way, drawing upon recent classroom research findings wherever possible. Case studies and activities from a range of classrooms and schools illuminate many of the substantial issues related to the subject area in question.

Readers will find a similar pattern of contents in all the books in the series. Each discusses the early learning environment, transition from home- to school-based learning, and addresses the key questions of what this means for the early years teacher and the curriculum. Such discussion inevitably incorporates ideas on the knowledge which young children may have of subjects and an overview of the subject matter itself which is under scrutiny. As the thrust of the series is towards young children learning subjects, albeit in a holistic way, no doubt readers will wish to consider what is an appropriate content or rationale for the subject in the early years. Having considered young children as learners, what they are bringing into school in terms of prior knowledge, the teacher's task and the subject matter itself, each book then turns its attention to appropriate methods of planning, organising, implementing and evaluating teaching and learning activities. Crucial matters such as assessment, evaluation and record-keeping are dealt with in their own right, and are also referred to and discussed in ongoing examples of good practice. Each book concludes with useful suggestions for further staffroom discussion/INSET activities and advice on resources.

As a whole, the series aims to be inspirational and forward-looking. As all readers know so well, the National Curriculum is not 'written in concrete'. Education is a dynamic process. While taking due account of the essential National Curriculum framework, authors go far beyond the level of description of rigid content guidelines to highlight *principles* for teaching and learning. Furthermore, they incorporate two key messages which surely underpin successful, reflective education, namely 'vision' and 'enthusiasm'. It is hoped that students and teachers will be inspired and assisted in their task of implementing successful and progressive plans which help young learners to make sense of their world and the key areas of knowledge within it.

Joy A. Palmer

ACKNOWLEDGEMENTS

A special thank you to Dr Sheila Wolfendale for all the support and suggestions she provided.

ABBREVIATIONS

ADD	Attention deficit disorder
ADHD	Attention deficit hyperactivity disorder
APA	American Psychological Association
CP	Cerebral palsy
DAP	Developmentally appropriate practices
DCD	Developmental co-ordination disorder
DfES	Department for Education and Skills
EI	Early intervention
EYDCP	Early Years, Development and Childcare Partnerships
FAS	Foetal alcohol syndrome
LEA	Local education authorities
LRE	Least restrictive environment
LSA	Learning support assistant
NSPCC	National Society for the Prevention of Cruelty to Children
SEN	Special education needs
SOME scale	Social Observation for Mainstreamed Environments
TBA	Traumatic brain injury
TPBA	Transdisciplinary play-based assessment
UK	United Kingdom
UN	United Nations
UNICEF	United Nations International Children's Emergency Fund
USA	United States of America

University of Chichester

Borrowed Items 08/12/2015 23:51
XXXX1050

Item Title	Due Date
* Children with speech and language difficulties	18/01/2016
* Special educational needs : the key concepts	18/01/2016
* Special educational needs in the early years	18/01/2016
* Special educational needs and disability in education : a legal guide	18/01/2016
* Educating special children : an introduction to provision for pupils with di	15/12/2015
* Supporting language and literacy development in the early years	18/01/2016
Addressing pupils' behaviour : responses at district, school and individual	18/01/2016

* Indicates items borrowed today

INTRODUCTION

Since the publication of the first edition of *Special Educational Needs in the Early Years*, there have been some exciting developments in the field, especially in the areas of brain research, emotional competence, early literacy development, and inclusive practices. This second edition incorporates new information and insights in these and other areas while retaining the overall tone and format of the previous work. Connections between knowledge and practice are provided throughout the text and presented in the form of examples, guidelines, case studies, and practical suggestions for teachers and other professionals working with young children with special educational needs.

In this second edition, several new sections and approximately 100 recent references have been added. In addition, some of the material has been reorganized, especially in Part II where major areas of child development are specifically addressed. These revisions are consistent with the four areas of development outlined in the National SEN Specialist Standards published in 1999. This second edition is also consistent with the provisions outlined in the SEN revised Code of Practice (DfES, 2001a). Inclusion and the importance of working from a developmental perspective are emphasized in both editions.

Overview of the book

This book is divided into four major parts. Part I establishes a theoretical framework for understanding and working with young children with special needs; Part II presents some of the major issues and concerns related to atypical development and programming for children with special needs, followed by Part III devoted to the intervention team, and Part IV to the individual child. Case studies and/or programme examples, as well as a discussion of relevant research and theory relating to the early years classrooms, are woven into each of the chapters.

This book is written primarily for teachers and teachers in training. Others who may find this book helpful include school administrators, other professionals in non-teaching roles, parents and the general public. The book is written in the hope that individuals will come away from the reading with a deeper understanding of young children with special needs, and ways in which their needs may be met in their early years of school. This understanding is crucial to becoming partners with the children in developing competence and confidence on their individualized paths to learning.

The understanding that young children with special educational needs are both alike and different from their same-age peers is one of the primary principles, or beliefs, running as a basic theme throughout this book. This understanding calls for services that are both integrated (i.e. provided in a mainstream environment) and individualized. It also calls for professional expertise in both typical and atypical child development. In terms of curriculum and programme planning, this belief translates into a merging of developmentally appropriate practices and exceptionality appropriate practices in inclusive settings.

Philosophy of early intervention

Special Educational Needs in the Early Years is based on the understanding that early intervention for young children with special needs is crucial to their growth and development in terms of current functioning and future capabilities. *Special Educational Needs in the Early Years* is also based on the understanding that young children with disabilities need the same type of learning experiences as their typically developing peers – that is, experiences involving play and meaningful interactions with people and objects in their environment. As young children with disabilities often lack the skills and/or motivation to engage in play-based activities and to interact with the world around them (Guralnick, 2000; Linn *et al.*, 2000), intervention is required to make the channels of learning more readily available to them. A major goal, then, of early intervention (EI) for young children with special needs during the first three years of school is to remove or side-step the barriers to learning that disabilities often impose. The primary focus of early intervention, however, should be on the development of skills rather than on the treatment of deficits. Unfortunately, this is not always the case.

There is a tendency for programmes serving young children with special needs to focus on the disability or deficit areas and to lose sight of what is most important for learning and development during the early childhood years – that is, opportunities to engage successfully in a variety of playful interactions with people and objects in one's environment. Because there is little evidence to support the idea that play in any form is educational (Kohler *et al.*, 2001), it is critical for adults working with young children to understand which types of play are optimal for development. This understanding becomes especially critical when working with young children with disabilities, as they are more dependent than typically developing children on the intervention of adults to make play situations meaningful and valuable to their growth and development.

Play that is optimal for development is play that reflects or slightly stretches the current abilities of the child (Kohler *et al.*, 2001). Given interesting and appropriate materials and a supportive environment, typically developing children tend to create the kind of play situations that are a good match for their abilities and potential. They enjoy the excitement of challenge and accept with gusto problems to be solved or feats to be accomplished. Can I move this heavy rock all by myself? Can I figure out how to use these blocks to build a bridge over that road we just made in the sandbox? Can I throw the ball over the fence or run faster than Scotty the dog? Can I paint a picture of a dragon or dinosaur, and can I write my own name at the top of the paper? Young children with disabilities, however, often have a great deal of trouble envisioning such feats and, with a history of failure and frustration, little incentive to try.

To be successful in play, young children need to manipulate objects, look for challenges in using materials, and engage in social interactions. Most children with disabilities have trouble in one or more of these areas. Some lack the motor skills to hold or control objects; others, due to vision or attention deficits, may not even notice the objects available to them. For other children, social and communication deficits may be the primary obstacles to engaging in play and other types of learning situations. Such children may not know how to join a group activity already in progress. They may also have difficulty inviting or involving other children in a play/learning initiative of their own. The aggressive behaviour of some children may cause them to be disliked and shunned by their peers. For other children, cognitive delays may create developmental differences between them and their peers, resulting in widely differing interests and abilities. Due to such differences and disabilities, it is not surprising to find that young children with special needs, when served in programmes with typically developing children, are often isolated and not engaged in play and other learning activities with their peers (Odom, 2000; Odom and McLean, 1996).

Approaches to intervention

One approach to intervention might be to focus on the disability or deficit in an attempt to 'fix it'. This approach, however, has very limited potential for success. Many disabilities cannot be 'fixed'. The child who is blind, for example, may never be able to see. The child with a physical disability – perhaps due to cerebral palsy or a missing limb – may never be able to kick a ball or walk independently. While, at times, some deficit-related behaviours can be taught (such as using a spoon for feeding or saying 'please' to get a second biscuit), the benefits of this 'fix-it' approach to more generalized learning situations are usually minimal. Because young children's learning is so closely tied to competence in play and widely varying interactions with people and objects in their environment, the 'fix-it' approach to intervention (which tends to focus on narrowly defined goals and activities) is not recommended.

The recommended approach to intervention focuses on removing or circumventing the barriers young children with special needs often experience in their attempts at play and interactions with their physical and social environment. Circumventing these barriers is accomplished by developing competencies in the overlapping areas of play, social interactions and exploration of the environment. It is this competency-based approach to serving young children with special education needs (SEN) that is presented in this book.

Intervention with a competency-based approach looks at the child holistically versus focusing on deficits of disabilities. The primary thrust of this approach is on building competence and confidence in the young child and minimizing any negative impact the disability may have on development and learning. This competency-based approach therefore looks at the child in terms of strengths as well as areas of need. It works from the premise that all children can learn and that a major part of our challenge is figuring out how each child learns the best.

This competency-based approach also views children as learners who construct knowledge versus receiving such knowledge from adults. This approach recognizes all children as being competent to construct their own knowledge, as long as major barriers to interacting with the environment are removed or circumvented.

A competency-based approach to intervention involves creating a vision for the child. By viewing the child in terms of competencies and strengths, we acknowledge the child's potential for the future. Obviously, a vision for the child's future cannot be developed without a consideration of the child's interests and special abilities. It is the vision for the child's future which should be a major determining factor in developing and planning educational experiences for the young child. In addition to involving the family in developing a vision for the child, the competency-based approach to intervention also works in partnership with the family to make the vision become reality. The vision for the child's future cannot be realized without the family's involvement, as it is with the family that children spend most of their time from birth to adulthood. The family provides the context and continuity for the ongoing development of the life and learning goals for the child.

Uniqueness of the field

The field of early intervention for young children with special needs is unique in a number of ways. First, a close look at the field (sometimes referred to as early childhood special education) indicates that it is relatively new and still in its early stage of development. What we currently know as 'best practices' in the field is likely to grow and change over time. Our knowledge in early childhood special education will continue to evolve, and values and conditions in society will continue to change. Thus practices considered 'best' today may not be considered such even just a few years from now. With this in mind, the term 'recommended practices' versus 'best practices' will be used throughout this book.

The field of early childhood special education is also unique in that it reflects a blend of practices and values from several different disciplines, primarily early childhood education and special education. Compensatory education, which overlaps with both early childhood education and special education, certainly plays a role as well. This role will be discussed in Chapter 1 in relation to the historical roots of the field. A brief overview of the two other contributing areas (i.e. early childhood education and special education) follows. It should be evident from this discussion that these two areas differ considerably in their major areas of emphases. A special challenge of the field is to merge these two disciplines in a way that retains the integrity of each. This challenge is discussed in greater detail in Chapter 2.

Early childhood education, or education during the early years, usually emphasizes creative play, social skill development, 'pre-academics' (i.e. early skills in English, maths, reading and science), and the development of basic understandings about the natural and built environment. Curriculum during the early years is often planned around themes (e.g. neighbourhoods, animals in our backyard) which combine concepts across different subjects such as maths and science. Because young children learn best when they are curious and interested in what they are doing, a large portion of the day in many early childhood classrooms is devoted to child-initiated, child-directed and teacher-supported play activities.

While early child education is usually planned around children's interests and natural curiosity, special education is more typically planned around individual needs and areas of weaknesses or deficits. One of the cornerstones of special education is an 'individual education plan', which must be drawn up for each child identified as having special needs. The nature of the child's learning difficulties, as well as performance targets to be achieved in a given time, are essential components of this individual plan. This individualized focus with specified targets often results in a more teacher-directed versus child-initiated curriculum. For many children with special needs, a special educator is involved in teaching the child directly or supporting the classroom teacher in implementing the child's individual education plan.

In the literature, as well as in recent practices, early childhood education and special education have followed separate and quite differing paths. Today, a merging of these disciplines is considered recommended practice. Such a merging brings with it not only a great deal of potential benefits for young children and their families, but also some special challenges for professionals working with young children during their first three years of school. Both the potential benefits and the challenges of this merging are discussed in subsequent chapters of this book.

Part I

ESTABLISHING THE FRAMEWORK

The discussion in Part I of this book emphasizes the twofold mission of early intervention services – that of providing successful learning experiences for young children with special needs, and providing effective and timely intervention before a handicap or at-risk condition undermines the development and future capabilities of these children. Specific topics addressed in Part I include an overview of who, what, where and how early intervention services are provided. Also presented is a discussion of why early intervention for young children with special needs is important and what data we have to support effectiveness claims relating to early intervention services. A brief historical overview is also provided, as well as some information about social and legal support for early intervention services. Finally, some basic understandings and recommended practices are presented.

1

SURVEY OF THE FIELD

Who is served?

Special education during the early years is not about an intervention system or a special curricular model. Special education during the early years is about children who have special needs. Such children cannot be categorized, or thought of, as an homogeneous group. Children with special needs vary tremendously. Not only do they have the same type of variances as the general population (e.g. different interests, likes, dislikes, temperaments, abilities), they also vary by type and extent of disability.

A concept often stated and rarely challenged is that 'no two people are alike'. While we all know and accept this statement to be true, we still seem, in some ways, to be troubled by the notion of 'differences'. Once differences are identified, we tend to think in terms of 'we' versus 'them' and begin judging individuals in relation to 'better' and 'worse'. While some lip-service is given to 'celebrating differences', many of our attitudes and behaviours fail to reflect this orientation.

It is true that people with disabilities are, in some ways, different from those who do not have disabilities. These differences challenge not only the people with disabilities, but everyone else as well, including parents, teachers, programme planners, school administrators, architects, playground designers and peers. Rising to the challenge often requires an understanding of the conditions causing, or relating to, the disability. Rising to the challenge also requires an understanding of the potential impact of the disability on the child's overall development and learning. It is this potential impact that gives special urgency to early intervention for children with disabilities.

Teachers of children in the early years serve a wide range of students. Some of these children have obvious disabilities or handicaps, some may be developmentally delayed, and others are at risk of future academic failure. While the needs of these children differ widely, as a group they are sometimes referred to as 'children with special educational needs' and require an educational programme customized to their unique needs. It is estimated that approximately 20 per cent of children will have some form of special educational need at some time. In England, according to the revised *Special Educational Needs Code of Practice*, children are considered to have special educational needs if they have a learning difficulty which calls for special educational provision to be made for them (Department for Education and Skills, 2001a). The learning difficulty is manifested when children (1) have a significantly greater difficulty in learning than the majority of children of the same age; or (2) have a disability which prevents or hinders them from making use of educational facilities of a kind generally provided for children of the same age in schools within the area of the local education authority, and (3) are under compulsory school and fall within the definition at (1) or (2) above or would do so if special educational provision was not made for them (Department for Education and Skills, 2001a).

For some children, their exceptionalities, or special needs, are readily apparent; for others, their special needs are not immediately obvious. Many children with cerebral palsy have motor difficulties which prohibit or greatly hinder walking; thus their disability would soon be obvious to any observer. Conversely, however, the disability of a 6-year-old who is developmentally delayed and functioning at a 4-year-old level may not be noticed immediately by a visitor to the classroom.

Whether obvious or not, it is to the young child's advantage to have his or her disability identified and understood. However, it is also crucially important to recognize that a child with a disability is first a young child who is more like his or her typically developing peers than different. It is for this reason that 'person-first' language should be used when referring to children with disabilities. 'Person-first' language puts the child first and the disability second. Instead of saying 'deaf child', the preferred terminology would be 'child who is deaf'; likewise, instead of saying 'disabled child', the preferred terminology would be 'child with a disability'.

Another important understanding in relation to terminology has to do with the terms 'disability' and 'handicap'. While the general public tends to use these terms interchangeably, they have distinctly different meanings. Referring to a child as having a disability indicates that he or she is unable to do something in a certain way. A disability, then, is an inability to perform as other children do because of an impairment in some area(s) of functioning (e.g. physical, cognitive, sensory). A handicap, on the other hand, refers to the problem an individual with a disability encounters when attempting to function and interact in the environment. While attention to the quality of the environment is important in all educational programmes for young children, it is particularly significant for children with disabilities, in that the quality of the environment determines, in large part, the extent to which a disability becomes handicapping.

A disability may or may not be a handicap, depending upon the specific circumstances or demands of the environment. For example, a 7-year-old child with cerebral palsy may have a great deal of difficulty standing by a blackboard to draw or write. When seated at a table with support for balance, however, his or her creativity and talents may be easily expressed and recognized. In this instance, the child experiences a handicap at the blackboard but not at the table. One major goal of intervention is to minimize the extent to which a disability puts the child in a handicapping situation. For educators to provide such intervention, however, they need some understanding of the different types of disabilities and the ways the disabling conditions may impact on development and learning. Discussions throughout this book are designed to help educators develop and/or deepen this understanding.

Some people believe that all children have special needs, in that each child, regardless of abilities and background, has unique needs and deserves special adult attention. The term 'special needs', however, refers generally to children with disabilities or developmental delays. In this book, the terms 'children with special needs' and 'children with special educational needs' (SEN) will be used interchangeably with 'children with disabilities'. These terms will refer to those children whose well-being, development and learning are compromised if special intervention is not provided.

As stated above, children with disabilities are similar in many ways to their typically developing peers; yet many children with disabilities also have special needs that children without disabilities do not have. These needs include: (1) environments that are arranged specifically to minimize the impact of the disabilities, and (2) professionals who are competent in promoting learning and the use of skills critical to the specific needs of children with disabilities.

A discussion of who is served in early intervention cannot be complete without some reference to the families involved. All families play a critical role in the early development of a child and are faced with many challenges in the process. These demands and challenges, however, certainly escalate when the child has a disability. Thus while the child is usually considered to be the focus of educational programmes designed for children and youth, for children with disabilities such programmes should also focus on the family. This is especially necessary during the first few years of the child's schooling.

Who provides services?

Early intervention services are provided in a wide variety of settings, representing both public and private providers and diverse disciplines (e.g. education, medicine, psychology, social work). This means that the formal education system (i.e. the schools) represents just one of the providers of services for children with disabilities. While the school's focus is on the educational needs of the children served, other needs (e.g. medical, recreational) and various forms of intervention (e.g. medication, therapies) certainly impact on a child's growth and development. Educators, then, need to be aware of who else is involved in providing services for young children with special needs and should be entitled to receive the necessary training to work as effective members of interdisciplinary and interagency teams. Because of its importance to meeting the special educational needs of young children with disabilities, an entire section of this book (Part III) is devoted to the issue of teaming. The following discussion addresses some of the current thinking and concerns related to who provides services in early intervention.

Early intervention, according to Dunst (2000), is an environmental variable. He says that 'children and their parents and families are the recipients of many different kinds of social support that can and often do function as a form of early intervention' (Dunst, 2000, p. 95). According to this perspective, the information and guidance needed by parents for promoting child learning and development come from both informal and formal social support network members. Thus, according to Dunst, 'interventions should emphasize mobilization of supports from informal network members rather than relying solely or primarily on formal supports from professionals and professional help-giving agencies' (ibid.). This perspective leads to a resource-based versus service-based model of early intervention, in that the emphasis is on access to desired resources rather than the provision of services which may or may not be consistent with family and child priorities.

For many young children (with or without a disability), childcare is considered one of the most important and frequently used community service providers. While educators have, at times, worked in relative isolation from childcare providers, it is becoming increasingly clear that the education of a young child is not confined to what takes place in the classroom. This understanding has led to relatively intense interest in 'partnering' with childcare providers to enhance the learning opportunities for young children with special needs. This interest is reflected in the network of Early Years, Development and Childcare Partnerships (EYDCPs) recently established in England. EYDCPs bring together private, voluntary and independent settings which receive government funding to provide early education with Local Education Authorities (LEAs), Social Services departments, health services and parent representatives in the planning and provision of early intervention services (Department for Education and Skills, 2001a). Local EYDCPs must include in their plans how children with SEN will be cared for both within childcare and early education (Wolfendale, 2000). The UK Schools Standards and Framework Act 1998 also outlines a statutory framework for ensuring a coherent and equitable provision of early education and childcare services for children under 5.

Schools in the UK generally take four-year-olds into Reception classes on either a part-time or full-time basis. Government policy is for EYDCPs to expand preschool services across all sectors with the private, maintained and voluntary sector providers as 'genuine' partners (Sestini, 2001). The UK government Green Paper *Meeting the Childcare Challenge* (May 1998) established a 'National Child Care Strategy' and proposed inclusive provision where possible for children with special needs (Sestini, 2001). It is becoming increasingly common in many communities for early education and childcare to be carried out by the same institution. Such combined services should be made accessible and appropriate for all children, including children with special educational needs.

Where and how are services provided?

In the educational realm, services for young children with special needs are typically provided in a classroom or playgroup setting – whether in a formal school programme or a more informal childcare programme. Today, best practices recommend the provision of services in inclusive settings – that is in programmes serving typically developing children, along with children with special educational needs. Not all children with disabilities are served in inclusive settings, however. Separate programming may be due to lack of access to inclusive settings or lack of community support for the inclusive model of intervention.

The different instructional approaches used in programmes serving young children with disabilities usually take some form of either activity-based instruction or didactic instruction. Activity-based instruction, designed to be conducted across the day in the context of ongoing activities and routines, is often described as a natural approach to intervention (e.g. teaching based on child interest, using child-selected materials, and using natural reinforcement). Didactic instruction, on the other hand, is usually conducted over a specified period of time and focuses on the acquisition of very specific skills (e.g. responding to a two-part command, asking for assistance, buttoning a shirt).

According to many experts (as outlined by Hemmeter, 2000), 'successful and meaningful inclusion depends on the implementation of effective interventions in the context of ongoing classroom activities and routines to teach functional and developmentally appropriate skills to children with disabilities' (pp. 58–59) – that is, activity-based instruction. Activity-based interventions are considered to be valuable tools in inclusive settings because they do not require teachers to step out of their role as leaders to conduct a separate individual or small group activity (Odom, 2000).

There are, however, some concerns associated with activity-based instruction. In addition to the fact that research has not provided conclusive evidence that this approach is more effective or efficient than more didactic approaches, studies indicate that it is also difficult to train teachers to use activity-based approaches to intervention (Hemmeter, 2000). These and other concerns relating to how services are provided for young children with special educational needs are discussed in Chapter 2.

What are the goals?

The term 'goals', when used in an educational context, usually refers to desired outcomes. Goals in early intervention represent desired outcomes for the child as well as of the programme itself. For the child, the goals are typically determined on an individual basis and usually relate to specific assessment results – that is, the child's individual needs and strengths. Working from individualized goals and objectives is one of the major tenets of special education. There are some more global and long-term goals of early intervention, however, that should be considered for every child with special needs. Such goals include (1) preparing young children with disabilities for participation in life in the community (Odom, 2000), and (2) developing social competence and effective learning strategies (Hemmeter, 2000). These more global goals represent several of the desired outcomes for the child as well as of the programme itself. Other programme goals include minimizing the negative impact of a disability on the overall growth and development of the children involved, decreasing the need for ongoing special education services for these children, and enhancing parental competence and confidence in promoting their children's learning and development.

In England, additional goals have been outlined. These goals, referred to as 'Early Learning Goals', address six areas of development (Qualifications and Curriculum Authority, 2000). The following is a list of these areas along with a brief description of the types of goal associated with each area.

1 *Personal, social and emotional development*: covers aspects of personal, social, emotional, moral and spiritual development, including the development of personal values and an understanding of self and others.
2 *Communication, language and literacy*: covers important aspects of language development and the foundation for literacy, including competence in talking, listening, and becoming readers and writers.
3 *Mathematical development*: covers important aspects of mathematical understanding and the foundation for numeracy.
4 *Knowledge and understanding of the world*: focuses on children's

developing knowledge and understanding of their environment, including other people and features of the natural and human-made environment.

5 *Physical development*: focuses on children's developing physical control, mobility, awareness of space and manipulative skills in indoor and outdoor environments.

6 *Creative development*: focuses on the development of children's imagination and their ability to communicate and to express ideas and feelings in creative ways.

The early learning goals establish expectations for most children to reach before the age of 6. While they are not a curriculum in themselves, the early learning goals provide a basis for planning throughout the early years so that children will have a secure foundation for future learning. It is understood that some children will exceed these goals before the age of 6, while others will still be working towards some or all of the goals – particularly those with special educational needs (SEN) and those learning English as an additional language. It is expected that all early childhood educators will be aware of these goals and that they will plan the curriculum with these goals in mind.

Historical perspectives

Young children with special needs have not always been served in educational programmes. In fact, there was a time when children with special needs were excluded from public schools. It was felt that since the curriculum was not appropriate to the children, the children did not belong in the programme. The understanding today is that all children do, indeed, belong in school and that they have a right to an educational programme which is appropriate to their individual needs. This understanding, however, is relatively recent. Over the past twenty years there has been a dramatic increase in awareness, services and opportunities for young children with special needs. Factors supporting this growth include legislative initiatives, litigation, public policy and the efforts of various advocacy groups.

Historical roots of the rapidly emerging field of early childhood special education may be traced to trends and developments in early childhood education, special education, and compensatory programmes for children at environmental risk. Several early contributors to the concept of compensatory programmes warrant special mention, notably John Locke and Robert Owen.

John Locke (1632–1704), a seventeenth-century English physician and philosopher, was an early contributor to our understanding of the importance of the early years for later development. Locke was a strong advocate of an environmental point of view and introduced the notion that, at birth, children resemble a blank slate (*tabula rasa*). According to this view, what children learn is a direct result of experiences, activities and sensations; and what children become is determined by the type and quality of experiences they have, especially during their early years.

Locke's belief in the powerful influence of the child's environment and early experiences is reflected in compensatory education programmes for young children living in poverty. These compensatory programmes are designed to 'make up' for the disadvantages experienced by children living in deprived environments.

Robert Owen (1771–1858) was another important contributor to early childhood and compensatory education. Owen, a manager of a textile mill in Scotland, was concerned about the living and working conditions of the children and their parents. He prohibited very young children from working at all and limited the number of working hours for older children. Believing that the early years represented the best time to influence a child's development, Owen established an infant school for children between the ages of 3 and 10. This infant school and others that soon followed were noted for an emphasis on basic academics (e.g. reading, maths and science), creative experiences (e.g. music and dance), and mutual respect between teacher and learner. These schools were also seen as a way of compensating children of poverty for the deprived conditions they experienced at home. Owen's work was based, in large part, on the premise that poverty could be eliminated by educating and socializing young children from poor families.

The establishment of compensatory programmes indicated that the belief that early intervention can make a difference in a child's development and learning was becoming understood and accepted more readily. In compensatory education, early intervention usually takes the form of 'make up' or equivalent experiences which are designed to offset, or make amends, for the poverty conditions experienced at home. The rationale for special education takes this concept one step further. Maria Montessori (1870–1952) played a major role in laying the foundation for this step.

In the late 1800s, Montessori worked as a physician in a psychiatric clinic in Rome, Italy, where she had the opportunity to closely observe 'idiot children', or children with mental retardation. At the time, mental retardation was viewed as indistinguishable from insanity. From her observations, Montessori concluded that educational intervention rather than medical treatment would be a more effective strategy in working with these children. This phenomenon of 'physician becoming educator' is representative of the historical tradition upon which special education is built.

Montessori's work with children with mental retardation was based on the premise that intelligence is not static or fixed, but can be influenced by experiences. To provide enriching experiences for the children, Montessori developed an innovative, activity-based sensory education programme involving didactic, or teaching, materials. This programme proved to be highly effective. Children who were believed originally to be incapable of learning, after participating in the intervention programme, performed successfully on various academic achievement measures.

Over time, Montessori expanded her educational programme, and in 1907 opened the Casa dei Bambini or 'children's home' in one of the slum districts of Rome. Here, she worked with children between the ages of 30 months and 7 years, who in today's terminology would be considered environmentally at risk. Montessori based her educational programme on the belief that children have a natural tendency to explore and understand their world and that they learn best by direct sensory experiences. While she envisioned child development as a process of natural unfolding, she also believed that environmental influences play a crucial role in how and when the unfolding takes place.

Montessori's programme emphasized three major components considered to be important in developing the child's independence, responsibility and productivity. These three components are: (1) practical life experiences, (2) sensory education, and (3) academic education. These same three components are often found in intervention programmes for children with disabilities. There follows a brief discussion of each.

- *Practical life experiences*, as outlined by Montessori, focus on personal hygiene and self-help (e.g. eating, dressing), motor development (e.g. walking, grasping), and responsibility for the natural and built environment (e.g. sweeping the floor, raking leaves, caring for plants and animals).
- *Sensory education* focuses on developing the student's various senses (i.e. seeing, hearing, feeling) and is based on the educational belief that cognitive development is dependent on sensory experiences. Montessori's sensory educational materials are designed to lead the students from concrete to abstract (i.e. real to representational) learning experiences.
- *Academic education* introduces the child to English, maths and science in developmentally appropriate ways. Formal or teacher-directed academic instruction is avoided. The emphasis is on self-chosen didactic (i.e. 'teaching') materials and activities. The didactic materials are designed to be used independently by the children and are self-correcting, in that the children discover that there is only one correct way to use them.

Other important aspects of the Montessori programme which have critical implications for children with special needs include: (1) an emphasis on individual student activities rather than group work, and (2) the practice of modifying the curriculum to meet the unique, individual needs of each child. Children in a Montessori programme work at their own pace, selecting learning materials of their choice. These materials are displayed on low shelves in an organized manner to encourage independent use. Montessori believed in allowing children to do things for themselves and was convinced that children are capable of teaching themselves through interaction with a carefully planned learning environment. The teacher's role in this environment is to foster the development of independence in the children. For some children, this means breaking down ideas and/or tasks into small, sequential steps that build on current levels of development and relate to previous experiences.

As is evident from the above discussion, the field of early childhood special education reflects valuable contributions from early childhood education, special education and compensatory education. It also reflects a changing view of young children with special needs and their potential for development and learning. Rather than 'writing them off' as uneducable, ignoring their special educational needs or suggesting that they wait until they 'outgrow' their learning problems, we now view young children with special needs as capable of learning, as responsive to the types of environments we provide for them, and as individuals with a unique potential for achieving the vision of their future. For individuals with disabilities, such a vision can neither be developed nor attained without support. Teachers and co-professionals have a crucial role to play in this process.

Rationale and effectiveness of early intervention

The primary goals of early intervention, as outlined by Wolfendale (2000, p. 4), are as follows:

- to help families support their children's development;
- to promote children's development in key domains (cognitive, social, physical, emotional, linguistic);
- to promote children's coping competence;
- to prevent the emergence of future problems.

One of the key concepts relating to the goals of early intervention is the need to provide successful learning experiences for young children with special needs in an effective and timely manner so as to prevent or minimize the handicapping or at-risk condition from undermining the development and future capabilities of these children. As is evident from this understanding, early intervention may be viewed as being both remedial and preventive in nature – i.e. remediating existing developmental problems and preventing the occurrence of additional ones (Council for Exceptional Children, 1988).

But does it work? Is early intervention effective in accomplishing its goals? As stated by Wolfendale (2000), 'the interventions should manifestly *make a difference*' (p. 4). Before going into specific studies addressing this issue, a broader perspective is discussed. This perspective focuses on the relationship between early experiences and development.

Both theoretical arguments and empirical evidence relate to the significance of early environmental influences on later development. In the early 1960s, this significance was brought to the attention of the professional community in Hunt's notable book *Intelligence and Experience*. After presenting a convincing argument for the impact of the early years on later development, Hunt (1961) recommends that young children be provided with optimal environments as a way of increasing their intellectual development. Hunt's argument lends strong theoretical support to early intervention in that it clearly links developmental outcomes to early experiences.

Empirical evidence in support of early intervention was provided by a number of landmark studies, including investigations by Skeels and Dye (1939) and Skeels (1966). In Skeels and Dye's study, a group of children living in an orphanage were transferred to a ward housing women with mental retardation. These women showered the children with a great deal of attention and care. Follow-up testing indicated that the children who received such attention showed impressive IQ gains when compared with children who had not been transferred to this women's ward.

The new environment clearly provided more stimulation and richer learning experiences for the children and resulted in increased intellectual functioning. Approximately twenty-five years later, Skeels (1966) did a follow-up study of these same children. He found that differences remained between the group of children who had been transferred to the women's ward and the group who were not transferred. As adults, the individuals who had been transferred (and thus received a more stimulating environment) showed higher academic education levels and more advanced levels of occupational achievement. Thus not only theory, but also research data support the concept that developmental outcomes can be effected by early experiences.

A major premise of early intervention is that the stimulation provided through such programmes will result in higher levels of functioning for individuals with disabilities than would have been achieved without such intervention. In essence, the argument for early intervention is that it does make a difference. As stated above, both theory and research support this argument.

The rationale for early intervention also relates to societal needs and the fact that such services are cost-effective. Special education is more intensive (i.e. involving more individualized programming, more professionals and so on) and is thus more costly than regular education. However, because children who receive early intervention services are more likely to go on to regular education later in their academic career, the net result is considerable savings in educational costs.

A number of studies indicate that these cost-saving arguments for early intervention are based on more than theory. Research relating to the Perry Preschool Project is perhaps the most impressive. The long-term follow-up of the Perry Preschool Project found that children who participated in the preschool experience were less likely to require more costly and intensive special education services in later years and that the projected lifetime earnings for programme participants were greater than those of the control group of children who did not have the preschool experience. Projected benefits were estimated to be in excess of $14,000 per child over his or her life span (Schweinhart *et al.*, 1993). Other studies focusing on the economic benefits of early intervention have arrived at similar or greater estimates of cost savings. See Bricker (1989) and The Council for Exceptional Children (1988) for a review of such studies.

Societal benefits, however, extend beyond cost savings and improved academic outcomes for children. Early intervention services also provide benefits for families of children with disabilities. Positive outcomes for such families include improved mother–child interactions and decreased parental stress (Mahoney *et al.*, 1999). Such outcomes tend to increase the child's and the family's chances of developing their full potential (Hanson and Lynch, 1995).

Today, legal support also provides incentives for early intervention services. In the United Kingdom, *The Special Educational Needs and Disability Act 2001* (Learning and Skills Council, 2002) specifies that the needs of all students who may have special educational needs must be addressed. In response to this mandate and to provide guidance on how to implement it, the Department for Education and Skills (DfES) developed the Special Educational Needs Code of Practice (DfES, 2001a). This Code of Practice clearly indicates that Local Education Authorities (LEAs) are responsible for identifying and assessing children with special educational needs as early as possible (even before the age of 2) and for providing them with the greatest possible access to a broad and balanced education.

Basic understandings and recommended practices

During the early history of special education, it was common practice for intervention services to be provided in separate classrooms or facilities. Today, the recommended practice, supported by theory, research and public mandate, is to educate children with special educational needs alongside their peers in inclusive classrooms.

In addition to the concept of inclusion, the following 'basic understandings' also help establish the framework around which recommended practices in the field of early childhood special education are developed.

- Young children with disabilities are viewed as active learners who are capable of constructing their own knowledge in environments offering alternative ways (when necessary) to explore and experience the world around them.
- Children with special educational needs differ widely from one another and thus require individualized plans for intervention.
- Individualized instructional goals should be fostered in the context of a developmentally appropriate curriculum.
- Instructional materials and daily activities should reflect an understanding and appreciation of diversity in various dimensions of the human community (e.g. gender, race, culture).
- The interests, priorities and resources of the community should be reflected in instructional materials and daily activities.
- Children with special educational needs should be identified and assessed as early as possible.
- Child assessment should be an individualized process and should be shaped by a child's characteristics and diagnostic concerns, as well as by family priorities and information needs.
- An ongoing process should be used to identify needs, strengths and resources, and to monitor the development of each child with special educational needs.
- Intervention programmes should address the needs of the whole child versus being focused on the deficit area(s).
- A specific diagnosis rarely results in precise prescriptions for educational practices. While the diagnosis of a specific disability may suggest the need for certain broad categories of interventions, the precise nature of the interventions should be tied to a variety of other considerations, including the child's current abilities and interests, the influence of specific environmental factors and instructional strategies on the child's learning, as well as the family's goals, priorities and resources.
- In addition to focusing on the child with special education needs, early intervention must also focus on providing support and assistance to the family and offer varied opportunities for their meaningful involvement. Throughout this process, parents should be recognized as full partners in educational planning and decision making.
- Meeting the needs of young children with disabilities requires a team approach and necessarily involves several disciplines. Co-ordination

across agencies is also required. Teaming skills should thus be addressed in pre-service and in-service teacher preparation programmes and should focus on the transdisciplinary (versus multidisciplinary or interdisciplinary) model.

- Careful planning should guide the process of transitioning a child from home to school and from one educational setting to another.
- Early intervention services should encompass prevention as well as adaptation and remediation. The goal of prevention is to prevent disabling conditions from happening in the first place and/or to minimize the impact of a disabling condition. As such, preventive efforts should focus on the health, safety and optimal development of young children.

Case Study – Patrick

Background information

Patrick's first few years of life were quite unstable. His mother, Tammy, had just turned 16 when he was born about eight weeks prematurely. Patrick's father, Chuck, who was 17, had dropped out of school the previous year and now worked as a car mechanic in his uncle's garage. Chuck seemed pleased and proud to be a father. Tammy, however, wanted nothing to do with Chuck. She considered giving up the baby for adoption but was hampered by Chuck's opposition. Chuck indicated that he would never consent to the baby's adoption and would raise the baby on his own if necessary.

Patrick lived with Tammy and her mother (i.e. the maternal grandmother) for the first eight months. Tammy tried going back to school after Patrick was 6 weeks old. Childcare, however, was a constant concern. Tammy's mother was often too intoxicated to be left alone with the baby. Chuck was constantly angry about the situation. While he wanted to be more involved in his son's care, he was almost helpless to do so. His own parents believed that Patrick should have been given up for adoption and vowed to offer absolutely no financial or emotional support. They refused to even see the baby and demanded that as long as Chuck chose to be involved with his son, he could not live with them.

Chuck moved to a small apartment where two of his 'buddies' lived. He tried, at times, to care for his son in this apartment, but conditions there were very unhealthy for an infant, including inadequate bedroom, bathroom and kitchen facilities and loud parties lasting late into the night. Tammy talked to a social worker about these conditions; the social worker agreed that Chuck's apartment was not suitable for an infant. After repeated instances of inadequate care for Patrick – such as being left alone with Tammy's mother while she was intoxicated or spending considerable time in Chuck's apartment – Patrick was placed in a foster home. He was now 8 months old.

One of the first things his foster-parents noticed was that Patrick was not demonstrating the skills expected of an infant of his age. He could not sit up independently, did not make babbling sounds, showed little interest in toys and other objects presented to him, and did not reach out to adults for comfort or social interaction. Developmental assessments requested by his foster-parents indicated that Patrick was considerably developmentally delayed and was showing signs of serious mental retardation. Patrick's foster-parents had never cared for a child with special needs before and requested that Patrick be moved to a different foster home.

By the time Patrick was 4 years old, he had lived in three different foster homes and had only sporadic contact with his mother. Chuck, now 21, finally won custody of his son. Chuck was engaged to Annmarie, who agreed to care for Patrick while Chuck was at work. Chuck and Annmarie were planning to get married in about six months.

Since his initial assessment requested by his first foster-parents, Patrick's progress was being monitored by the local education authority, and a home-based learning programme was provided. Chuck had had some involvement with this intervention programme, but foster-parents had been the primary contacts for the early intervention team. Now that Patrick was 4 years old, he was to be enrolled in a reception class at his local school. Special education services were to be provided in the context of the mainstream class. Chuck was feeling very optimistic that by having custody, stable childcare and enrolment in a school programme Patrick would make great progress.

At this time, Patrick was walking independently but had balance and co-ordination problems, would occasionally look at a book but could not turn the pages one at a time, was using two-word utterances but usually relied on gestures and cries to express his feelings and needs, was naming a few body parts and familiar objects, was using the toilet with assistance but only when prompted, and was showing very little interest in playing with other children.

Information about Patrick was shared with the teacher prior to his first day of attendance at reception class, and arrangements were made for a special education resource teacher to assist in developing and implementing an individualized education plan for Patrick. The plan that was developed outlined three stages to be implemented sequentially. During the first stage, the emphasis would be on increasing independence in self-help skills: eating, dressing and toileting. The second stage would focus on language and basic concept development (e.g. colours, numbers, sizes, shapes). The third stage would focus on making friends and playing co-operatively with others. The special education resource teacher would provide direct assistance in the classroom for at least two hours per week.

The first day of school was traumatic for Patrick, his father and the classroom teacher. Patrick clung to his father, screamed, kicked the teacher, threw the toys that were offered to him to the floor, and fell against a table while trying to run out of the classroom. Patrick's head hit the table, resulting in a small gash over his right eye. The teacher suggested that Chuck take Patrick to the emergency room to see if stitches were necessary. Not having medical insurance to cover the expense, Chuck resisted, and suggested that he should take Patrick home and monitor him closely. As Chuck had to go to work, Annmarie agreed to watch Patrick during the day. Patrick cried for most of the day and refused to eat.

The following day, Annmarie went with Chuck to take Patrick to school. Again, there was a great deal of crying, hitting and screaming. The teacher and the other children in the classroom all seemed frightened. Annmarie agreed to stay at school with Patrick while Chuck went to work. A call to the special education resource teacher brought her to the classroom in the early afternoon. Patrick was still crying and refusing to eat or play. Annmarie held him and tried to comfort him throughout the morning. After consulting with the special education teacher, the decision was made to provide services to Patrick at home (primarily with Annmarie) until he developed some of the independence and social skills specified on his individual education plan.

Discussion

Patrick's case is an example of a child at risk for special education needs even prior to his birth. His parents were young, unmarried, estranged, and had little financial or social support to raise a child.

Patrick was also at risk due to a premature birth. Observation and formal assessment results indicated that Patrick was developmentally delayed and showed signs of mental retardation. Because he had significantly greater difficulty learning than other children his age, Patrick qualified for special education services. Such services commenced while he was still an infant.

Unfortunately, due in part to his inconsistent home situations, the early intervention services provided did not prepare Patrick or his family for the transition to a school-based setting. In addition, the three-stage instructional plan developed for Patrick failed to prioritize goals in relation to the educational setting. For Patrick to succeed in a mainstream classroom, he would need to feel comfortable in that setting and would need at least some social skills in relating to peers and unfamiliar adults. Yet, according to the plan, social interaction skills would not be emphasized until after satisfactory self-help and cognitively related and language skills were in place.

The experience for Patrick might have been different if the transition had been carefully planned and more support provided during the initial entrance to school. If support had been provided on a more-to-least schedule (i.e. more at first with gradual withdrawal), Patrick may have been able to adjust to the classroom setting. By starting with a minimum of support and little attention to the social aspects of integration, Patrick did not have much chance of succeeding.

The three-stage instructional plan developed for Patrick represents a deficit-versus competency-based approach to intervention. Patrick's deficit areas (i.e. self-help, cognitive, language and social) dictated the nature of the plan. A competency-based approach might have started with a recognition of Patrick's positive response to his father. In most situations, Chuck was able to calm and comfort Patrick. Patrick also enjoyed playing simple games with Chuck. Thus two of Patrick's 'competencies' were calming in response to his father's attention and interacting socially with a familiar adult. Building on these competencies, initial goals for Patrick could have been to respond positively to other adults (e.g. the classroom teacher and Annmarie) and to interact socially with other adults and peers.

Instead of 'one giant step' into the mainstream environment, smaller steps might have included one or several classroom visits with Chuck and Annmarie, with just the teacher present. Gradually, Patrick could have developed a sense of familiarity and comfort with the setting and the teacher. After that, the teacher, with one or two peers, could have played the games Patrick engaged in with his father. This gradual approach to integration would represent adaptations to the social environment. Rather than placing the demands of the environment on Patrick, the environment would be adapted to meet the needs of Patrick. The gradual approach to integration and a focus on competencies versus deficits would also reflect attention to the needs of the whole child (i.e. emotional, psychological, social) versus focusing on the more narrow self-help and academic needs. Patrick's negative experience with integration in a mainstream classroom may have been avoided – or at least minimized – if recommended practices had been followed.

2

SPECIAL CONCERNS AND CHALLENGES

The field of early intervention continues to experience challenges in connecting theory and practice and translating recommendations into action. This chapter will address some of the special concerns and challenges facing the profession today, especially as these relate to (1) merging early childhood education and special education, (2) issues related to inclusion, (3) the expanded role of the teacher, (4) identification and assessment issues, and (5) working with families. While these 'challenges' are discussed as separate sections in this chapter, in reality there is considerable overlap between them.

Merging early childhood education and special education

The field of early intervention evolved from a medical or therapeutic model rather than from educational perspectives. As such, its focus has often been on the remediation of skill deficits in children who are not developing normally on their own (i.e. without special intervention). In an effort to help the child with delays to catch up with their typically developing peers, special education teachers have often used highly directive teaching methods, including drill or rote learning, and the teaching of isolated skills (Niemeyer *et al.*, 1999).

This direct teaching approach is in conflict with the philosophy and practices of most early childhood programmes where learning through child-initiated activities and discovery is emphasized. These philosophical and instructional differences produce inevitable conflict when attempts are made to embed early intervention services in typical early childhood classrooms. Such conflict may be viewed either as a formidable road-block to effective programming or as a healthy challenge with potential benefits to all involved.

Many of the challenges associated with merging early childhood education and special education involve the integration of developmentally appropriate practices with exceptionality appropriate practices

(Niemeyer *et al.*, 1999). Developmentally appropriate practices (DAPs) are characterized, in large part, by active exploration and interactions with learning activities and materials that are concrete, real and relevant to young children (Bredekamp and Copple, 1997). Such activities and materials are designed to be both age appropriate and individually appropriate – i.e. both chronological age and developmental age are given consideration in planning activities and providing materials. Other considerations in a DAP programme include children's interests, cultural backgrounds and special abilities. DAP settings tend to de-emphasize teacher-directed activities and direct instruction. A major goal of DAP is to enable children to construct their own knowledge versus transmitting a body of knowledge to them.

The DAP approach is considered a good context in which intervention for children with disabilities can be provided (Brown *et al.*, 2000; Davis *et al.*, 1998). To effectively meet the needs of children with disabilities, however, the DAP approach must, at times, be integrated with exceptionality appropriate practices. This means that, for some children, the DAP guidelines may require adaptation or modification. It also means that, at times, 'children's experiences will need to be facilitated using strategies and adult behaviors not described in the [DAP] guidelines' (Wolery, 1994a, pp. 100–101). Such behaviours sometimes include direct instruction.

One of the primary responsibilities of early childhood personnel when working with children with disabilities is to adapt the environment in ways which will motivate them to explore the environment and to experience success in doing so. This requires close observation of children interacting with their environment over time and in multiple settings (e.g. classroom, home, clinic). It also requires talking with others, especially parents, about their observations of how children interact with their environment, and being attentive to their concerns and suggestions about how to foster their children's competence and confidence in exploring the environment.

In the classroom, the early childhood teacher needs to facilitate the interactions children have with toys, materials, activities, peers and adults. Such interactions, if successful, develop understandings about the world and the way it works, and help children gain feelings of self-worth and competency. Such experiences also help children to enjoy learning and provide incentives for further explorations. By supporting and facilitating the interaction between children with special educational needs with their environment, the teacher, in essence, combines the roles of early childhood educator and special educator. The teacher uses information about the child's disability and his or her developmental level to determine the degree to which intervention is necessary to facilitate the child–environment interaction.

While the curriculum in a DAP programme is both child initiated and teacher directed, the extent of teacher directedness is often greater for the child with special needs than for his or her typically developing peers. The degree of teacher direction or direct instruction appropriate for any one child depends on that child's need for adult support. Children vary considerably in their ability to interact meaningfully with their environment and to assume increasingly more responsibility for their own learning. Direct instruction, when used appropriately, does not negate the DAP approach; it augments it. Adjusting the curriculum and environment to meet a child's special educational needs is what exceptionality appropriate practices are all about.

Another concern associated with the merging of early childhood education with special education relates to intensity of instruction. Inclusive intervention models which rely primarily on the regular education teacher for day-to-day implementation are sometimes criticized for compromising intensity of instruction. The special needs of young children with disabilities certainly challenge the boundaries of practitioner knowledge and organizational supports. This challenge should not be taken lightly. By definition, children with special educational needs have significantly greater difficulty with learning than the majority of children of the same age. Because of their disability, they are often unable to obtain the same benefits from regular education as their typically developing peers. Without appropriately intense instruction, children with SEN will not reach their potential in their current learning situation or in their lifelong accomplishments. As specified in the *Special Educational Needs Code of Practice* (DfES, 2001a), young children with SEN should be provided with interventions that are additional to or different from those provided as part of the setting's usual curriculum and strategies.

The challenge of early childhood personnel working in inclusive settings is to integrate the child-initiation aspects of quality early childhood education with specific intervention strategies for children with SEN. Left to their own initiative, many children with SEN would not make sufficient progress towards their individual goals and objectives, nor would they experience full inclusion in the various dimensions of the early childhood classroom. Thus early childhood personnel working in inclusive settings need to be both facilitators of child-initiated learning and intervenors for children with SEN in situations where more teacher direction is needed.

A related concern, however, is to focus almost exclusively on the accomplishment of individual goals and objectives and to rely too heavily on teacher-organized and teacher-directed activities. The result of this more direct approach tends to be isolated skill learning at the expense of child initiative and autonomy. The teacher-directed approach can also result in an exclusive versus inclusive experience for the child with SEN, even though the programme is organizationally designed to be a mainstream classroom.

Issues related to inclusion

Inclusion of young children with disabilities in classroom settings with typically developing peers is a relatively recent phenomenon, and research on the process and developmental outcomes is inconclusive (Odom, 2000). While research findings have generally supported the efficacy of full inclusion in terms of social and behavioural outcomes (Buysse and Bailey, 1993), it should be noted that a commitment to inclusion is often ideological and value-based, rather than grounded in a pedagogical rationale.

While many policy makers and administrators in school systems now identify inclusion as the first service alternative for young children with disabilities, there are still many unresolved issues to consider (Odom, 2000). One issue is the lack of uniform acceptance and/or understanding of what inclusion really means. For some, inclusion means the physical integration of children with special needs in the regular education classroom. True inclusion, however, includes instructional and social integration as well. These two dimensions of inclusion (i.e. instructional and social integration) are far more difficult to achieve than physical integration.

A related issue identified in the literature and often experienced at the community level is the differing understanding of how to provide specialized instruction in an inclusive setting. As Odom (2000) states, 'inclusion means different things to different people' (p. 21). For the child with special needs, his or her experience of service delivery also differs from programme to programme. In some cases, individualized services (or specialized instruction) is provided through a one-on-one approach; in other cases, such services are blended in with the activities and routines occurring in the classroom. Many would agree that progress is needed to refine the techniques used for specialized instruction in the inclusive classroom (Odom, 2000).

The social standing of young children with special needs in the inclusive classroom is of special concern. As research indicates, 'as a group, children with disabilities are at relatively higher risk for peer rejection than typically developing children' (Odom, 2000, p. 21). As a result, children with disabilities tend to be isolated in an early childhood classroom (Wilson, 2002). Young children with special educational needs generally do not engage in high levels of social interaction with typically developing children unless they are encouraged and supported in doing so (Odom, 2000; Wolery and Wilbers, 1994). Factors frequently associated with this lack of interaction include language and cognitive delays, poorly developed play skills, and behaviour disorders on the part of children with SEN. The greater the difference in the children, the less likely are interactions (Wolery and Wilbers, 1994). A special challenge, then, for early childhood educators is to achieve social integration between children with disabilities and their typically developing peers. As the levels of social interaction skills of these two groups generally differ to a significant extent, this challenge is particularly difficult to achieve. Ideas on how to address these social interaction concerns are presented in this book, especially in Chapters 5 and 11.

A related concern is implementing a play-based curriculum with children with widely varying levels of play skills. In a developmentally appropriate programme, child-initiated play is the primary context for learning. A child with poorly developed or 'primitive' play skills will thus be at risk for participating fully in a play-based curriculum. While most typically developing children play with a variety of toys and materials and learn to interact with others during play situations without anyone teaching them how to do so, young children with SEN often require the intervention of adults to show them how to play (Wolery and Wilbers, 1994).

Bruder (2000) calls attention to another concern relating to preschool inclusion – that of inclusion within the context of family routines and community activities. She says, 'If we are truly trying to facilitate the acceptance of children with disabilities into settings with their nondisabled peers, it would seem that our efforts should be in assisting families to orchestrate learning experiences in the everyday activities they value' (p. 228).

Guralnick (2000), in a recent review, identified other concerns with regard to four central goals of early childhood inclusion: (1) achieving universal access to inclusive programmes, (2) agreeing on and establishing feasible programmes, (3) having confidence that children's developmental and social outcomes are not compromised by participating in inclusive programmes, and (4) socially integrating children with one another in meaningful ways. Guralnick (2000) also recognizes the need 'to resolve many long-standing issues stemming from differences in values, philosophies, and practices' (p. 214).

Odom (2000), in sharing his research on 'what we know and where we go from here' regarding preschool inclusion, outlined some additional concerns. These concerns include: (1) how to assess progress made by individual children, as well as the more general effects of inclusive programmes; (2) the tendency to exclude children with severe disabilities from inclusive settings; (3) the quality of some childcare environments in which children with SEN are served; (4) the need to refine techniques used for specialized instruction in inclusive settings; (5) teachers' concern about their lack of knowledge about children with disabilities; and (6) policy barriers to inclusion, especially as these relate to programme standards, financial issues, and personnel and staffing issues.

Lewis (2000) also addresses the issue of quality in inclusive education.

He suggests that the focus on inclusion may overlook the need for quality and poses a very important question: 'How far is it tenable to assume that the education system as presently constituted provides a healthy environment for all, let alone the most vulnerable?' (p. 202). He thus urges us to remember the 'education' in inclusive education.

Obviously, there are many concerns related to preschool inclusion. The number and seriousness of the concerns, however, should not deter us from serving children with disabilities in inclusive settings. Research has shown us that children with disabilities perform as well in inclusive settings as in traditional special education settings and, in certain areas, perform even better (Odom, 2000, p. 20). As Odom (2000) notes, 'With political will, local leadership, willing parents, and committed teachers, most young children with disabilities can benefit from inclusive preschool settings' (p. 25).

Expanded role of the teacher

The traditional framework used to describe teacher roles and functions emphasized direct services to the child and family, usually in the context of the classroom. Today, we recognize the need for teachers to step beyond the classroom and to work with children and families in the context of the community. This move necessarily involves working in partnerships with other professionals and agencies serving children in natural environments.

Teachers working in an inclusive setting thus find that their role is considerably expanded. This role expansion applies to the regular education teacher as well as to the special educator (Guralnick, 2000). These changes are usually accompanied by special benefits and challenges. One challenge relates to the differing backgrounds and perceived roles of the teachers.

Historically, there are considerable differences in the professional preparation and practices of teachers who work primarily with young children with disabilities and those who serve typically developing children. Teachers from these differing backgrounds are often educated through different college or university programmes, tend to belong to separate professional organizations, and are familiar with different model programmes and bodies of research. Until recently, they have also worked in different types of settings – the special educators in separate and specialized programmes and the early childhood educators in public or private schools serving typically developing children. With these varied backgrounds and experiences, it is not surprising to see differing perspectives and assumptions about development and learning emerging and conflicting (Guralnick, 2000).

Recommended practices from both early childhood education and early childhood special education suggest that young children with and without disabilities should be served in the same (inclusive) programmes. Recommended practices also suggest that, to be consistent with the inclusion of young children with special needs in regular early childhood classrooms, the two-track professional development model (i.e. one track for special educators and one for early childhood educators) is not appropriate. Recommended practices thus call for a merger of the two disciplines in teacher-preparation programmes. This merger (already in place in some institutions) should retain the best of both disciplines and should go beyond the team-teaching or multidisciplinary approach (where an early childhood educator and early childhood special educator work side by side within the same classroom).

The recommended approach for including young children with disabilities in early childhood programmes is to work within a transdisciplinary model. Transdiscipline involves a crossing of disciplinary lines, a stretching of one's professional role and the development of additional competencies (beyond one's own discipline). For the early childhood educator, this means learning more about children with special needs and developing the skills to effectively modify the programme for them. For the early childhood special educator, this means learning more about human development during the early childhood years, becoming more familiar with the intricacies of developmentally appropriate practices, and learning how to work with a larger group of children with widely varying interests and abilities.

Team teaching, during all or part of the day, may occur within the transdisciplinary approach. When it does, the focus moves beyond working side by side to actually sharing roles and expertise. Transdisciplinary programming also requires skill in working with members of other disciplines (e.g. speech/language therapy, physical therapy) and parents. In recognition of the importance of a transdisciplinary team effort to early intervention, an entire section of this book is devoted to teaming with other disciplines and working in partnership with families (Part III).

Because many young children with disabilities need more individual assistance than their typically developing peers, inclusive programmes often make arrangements to have additional adults in the classrooms (e.g. paraprofessionals/teacher assistants, therapists, parents, and others who may serve as volunteers). The effectiveness of the paraprofessionals' and volunteers' contribution depends, in large part, on how well the teacher prepares for and develops a healthy working relationship with these individuals. It has been demonstrated that a healthy working relationship between teachers and therapists impacts on the relative benefits accrued through individual and group therapies in the classroom (Niemeyer *et al.*, 1999).

Maintaining integration and consistency of services is especially challenging when working with a variety of disciplines and agencies.

While the quality of services provided for a child with SEN can be greatly enhanced by the involvement of professionals from multiple disciplines and agencies, there is a danger that such services can also be quite splintered and unco-ordinated. This tends to be the case when professionals from different disciplines work from a multidisciplinary versus transdisciplinary model of interaction. In a multidisciplinary model, professionals from different disciplines serve the same child and family but do so without co-ordinating their efforts. The result, as experienced by the child and family, is a lack of integration and consistency. At times, conflicting messages and suggestions can actually result in confusion and added stress for all involved.

Feedback from regular classroom teachers regarding the inclusion of children with special educational needs indicates that they often feel unprepared and intimidated by the thought of their role in the process. They may defer to special educators as the experts in serving children with SEN and feel that they have little to offer. This way of thinking can serve as a formidable barrier to transdisciplinary teaming, which requires a back and forth' versus 'one-way' sharing of expertise.

Assessment issues

The term 'assessment' is sometimes used interchangeably with 'testing'. This usage is misleading, since assessment has a broader meaning than testing. Assessment – which may include, but is not equivalent to, testing – may be defined as the 'process of systematically gathering information about a child' (Wolery, 1994b, p. 71). To protect the child's and the family's basic rights, certain guidelines for assessment have been developed by the early childhood profession. One such guideline relates to the purpose of conducting an assessment and unequivocally states that unless the purpose is clear, assessment activities should not occur (Wolery, 1994b).

There are, of course, a number of reasons for assessing young children, including screening to identify possible developmental delays and disabilities, determining a specific diagnosis, determining eligibility for special services, planning intervention programmes, monitoring progress, and evaluating the effects of the early childhood services. Gathering information for one of these purposes may not be useful or appropriate for another purpose. For example, information gathered during screening may not be useful for planning the child's educational programme. Thus it is very important to clarify the reason(s) for assessment prior to initiating the assessment process.

Once the reason for assessment is clearly defined, the process for conducting an assessment must be determined. Recommended practices in the field indicate that this process should be as unintrusive as possible and should involve the family and child in a respectful and meaningful way. The assessment should be conducted in a place where the child and family feel comfortable. This may mean the child's home, a playgroup setting, or the facility of another community programme or agency (e.g. daycare/nursery school, health clinic).

Standardized tests are still being used for assessment, but this form of measurement is generally considered inappropriate for young children (Perrone, 1991). The use of portfolios for assessment is viewed as a more promising approach for measuring children's growth, development and achievement (Hanson and Gilkerson, 1999).

Parent involvement is another crucial component of recommended practices for assessing young children. Parental perspectives are especially important for children under the age of 5. Obtaining this parental perspective, while respecting their privacy and being sensitive to their feelings, is usually quite challenging for educators.

Ongoing monitoring and documenting the positive outcomes of individualized curricular accommodations represent other challenges relating to assessment. Ongoing monitoring addresses the following questions: To what extent is the child accomplishing his or her goals and objectives? To what extent is the child making developmental progress over time? Without ongoing monitoring, teachers may have difficulty deciding whether or not particular strategies are working, and may thus not be consistent in the use of such strategies. Without ongoing monitoring, teachers may also have difficulty informing parents and other members of the intervention team about child progress towards instructional goals and objectives.

Further issues and guidelines relating to assessment are presented in Chapter 9.

Working with families

Assisting families as they cope and adapt to the circumstances of having a child with a disability is another challenge faced by professionals working with young children with disabilities. Family education and support activities are critical components of early intervention programmes. A part of the challenge is recognizing and respecting the diversity of families in the types of parent education and involvement options available to them. Professionals need to work from the premise that 'each family has its own culture and a unique set of strengths, values, skills, expectations, and service needs' (Bailey, 1994, p. 28). Thus, just as the individualized needs of children with SEN require an individualized educational programme for them, so do the unique characteristics of families (including their priorities, values and resources) establish the need for a variety of parent education and involvement options. To best serve the needs of the families, these options must reflect an understanding and appreciation of the diversity that exists among families. Obviously, planning parent education and involvement programmes with diversity in mind is much more challenging than offering one plan which parents are expected to adopt and participate in. To the greatest possible extent, parents should have a voice in the development of family education and support activities, and their decisions about how to participate should be respected.

Times of transitioning the child from home to school and from one school setting to another tend to be especially difficult for families. Even families of typically developing children find that transitioning a child from home- to school-based learning is accompanied by a great deal of uncertainty and anxiety. All parents want their children to feel comfortable and competent when they enter school, yet there is no way to build in assurance that this will be the case. While this is true whether or not a child has a disability, the concerns are certainly magnified for children with special education needs. Common concerns expressed by parents of children with disabilities at times of transition from home to school relate to (1) medical fragility and/or special health conditions (e.g. seizures, asthma, immune deficiency); (2) peer acceptance and making friends; (3) participation in group activities (e.g. listening to stories, games in the playground); and (4) fear and distress in separating from parents. Addressing these concerns is one of the special challenges faced by professionals working with young children with disabilities.

The transition from home- to school-based learning places new expectations and demands on the child and family. Both child and family must become acquainted with new people in their lives and adjust to new schedules. Parents know there will be certain school-related behaviours that their child will be expected to adopt. They may be concerned about whether or not their child will follow directions, eat and toilet independently, and respond socially to other children. Parents may also be concerned about their child's safety. Will he or she be helped and supported on playground equipment? Will medication and adaptive equipment be used correctly? Will the other children play too roughly?

Parents, too, will be faced with new expectations as their child enters school. They will be expected to be informed of and involved in their child's educational programme. For some parents this can be intimidating – either because of the added time and energy investment this will entail, or because of their uncertainty or lack of confidence in how to relate to professionals.

The transitioning of a child with SEN from one educational setting to another can also generate a great deal of uncertainty and anxiety on the part of all involved – child, family, teachers and the rest of the intervention team. This uncertainty and anxiety can be minimized by viewing transition not as a single event, but rather as an ongoing process, beginning at least six months before a child leaves a programme (the 'sending' programme) and continuing throughout the child's adjustment to the new programme (the 'receiving' programme).

While most children experience some anxiety about moving on to a new classroom or school, reasons for such anxiety are usually greater for children with special educational needs. For typically developing children, emotional support, in the form of reassurance, is usually sufficient to ease the transition enough for them to move on with the likelihood of success in the new environment. Concern for children with SEN, however, 'must go beyond their initial emotional adjustment to the transition'(Atwater *et al.*, 1994, p. 168). This is due, in large part, to the fact that children with developmental delays often have considerable difficulty transferring what they have learned from familiar to unfamiliar settings. In dealing with new routines, different activities and unfamiliar people, children with SEN often fail to demonstrate competencies that they developed over time in their more familiar settings.

The consequences of transition difficulties for children with SEN should not be taken lightly. 'The child experiencing such difficulties is at a serious disadvantage for learning more complex skills, being a full participant in the activities of the new setting, and forming positive relationships with new teachers and peers' (Atwater *et al.*, 1994, p. 168). Children with SEN are also at increased risk of further delays, behaviour problems and future placement in more restrictive (i.e. separate special education classes) versus inclusive settings (Hanline, 1993).

Early childhood professionals, then, need not only to plan and implement a quality instructional programme, but also to ease the transition to their programme from the home setting and from their programme to the next educational placement. The special needs of children and families must be considered at each of these transitions. Unless these transitions are successful, the benefits of the programme to parents and children will be considerably limited. Some ideas on how to ease this transition are presented in Chapter 10.

Considering children's views

Whether or not they are recognized as such, children 'are important "stakeholders" in their own learning and education' (Wolfendale, 2000, p. 8). We may often think of young children as being too inexperienced and too cognitively immature to have valuable insights into what will be of benefit to them in their own learning and education. There is reason to challenge this assumption. According to Wolfendale's (2000) analysis, the rationale and justification for including children's views and consulting them regarding their own learning and education are threefold: on equal opportunities grounds, on educational grounds and on psychological grounds.

Regarding equal opportunities grounds, Wolfendale (2000) refers to Article 12 of the United Nations Convention on the Rights of the Child. Article 12, addressing free expression of opinion, indicates that children have a right to express an opinion in matters affecting them and that their opinions should be heard and given due weight. (See Chapter 7 for further discussion of this Convention.)

Regarding educational grounds, Wolfendale (2000) refers to what we know about how children learn – that is, children become more involved and engaged in activities which match how they think and what they value. Considering children's views is an important part of matching learning tasks to the learner.

Regarding psychological grounds, Wolfendale (2000) notes how 'direct, active involvement in learning increases learning rate and output' (p. 8). She also notes how cognitive involvement and social engagement with adults contribute to effective learning. Such involvement and engagement can be enhanced, she says, through dialogue based on children's views.

The *Special Educational Needs Code of Practice* (DfES, 2001a) also specifies that 'the views of the child should be sought and taken into account' (p. 7). A related SEN Toolkit (Section 4: Enabling Pupil Participation), states that 'all pupils need to be a part of these [decision-making] processes, to know they are listened to and that their views are valued' (DfES, 2001b, p. 2). This Toolkit also outlines several 'principles of pupil participation', including (1) the pupils' need for training and encouragement to help them become actively involved, and (2) the need for teachers and parents to learn how to involve the pupil. For pupils to participate in a meaningful way in the decision-making process, the Toolkit indicates that children need information that will enable them to work towards: (1) understanding the importance of information; (2) expressing their feelings; (3) participating in discussions; and (4) indicating their choices. The Toolkit indicates that adults need to (1) give information and support, (2) provide an appropriate environment, and (3) learn how to listen to the child.

But can young children express their views effectively? Several recent studies suggest that they can (Daycare Trust, 1999; Kitzinger and Kitzinger, 1990; Sherman, 1997; Uttig, 1998; Wolfendale, 1998). Wolfendale (1998) found that the parent and child working together could complete successfully a developmental profile yielding valuable information about young children's feelings and self-perceptions. The profile used was *All About Me* developed by Wolfendale (1998). Other work conducted by the National Society for the Prevention of Cruelty to Children (NSPCC, 1995) indicated that 5-year-old children can be insightful and perceptive about school-related issues, including the effectiveness of teachers, the usefulness of homework and problems associated with bullying. According to Wolfendale (2000), 'one of the main recommendations emerging from this consultation study is that schools should find a method of consulting pupils regularly' (p. 9).

Case study – Mary

Background information

Mary is the middle child in a family with three children. The other two children are boys and appear to be developing normally. Mary, however, has Down syndrome, and at the age of 6 is functioning more like her 4-year-old brother than her peers. Both of Mary's parents are teachers and were in their early thirties when she was born. All seemed to be going well throughout the pregnancy, so no special tests were done. Her disability at birth, then, came as a complete surprise. At the time of birth, Mary was blue and inactive. She did not cry very much and never learned to nurse.

During her preschool years, Mary seemed to enjoy being around other children and adults. She laughed easily and loved to hug people. Her language development was seriously delayed, with her first combination of words not appearing until she was about 3½ years old. Her motor development was also noticeably delayed. Mary took her first independent steps when she was nearly 2 years old.

When Mary entered her Reception year of school at the age of 4, she was still not toileting on her own. She also needed considerable help in dressing and eating. When Ms Forman first heard that Mary would be in her Reception year class, she objected strongly. Ms Forman had no previous experience of working with a child functioning so far below typically developing children and had many concerns. How would she make time to provide the kind of individual assistance Mary needed? How would the other children react to Mary, and what would the other parents say? Ms Forman also felt that she had neither the knowledge nor skill for meeting the intervention goals outlined on Mary's statement of special educational needs. After considerable discussion among members of the intervention team, it was decided that, in addition to consultation from a special education teacher and other specialists on the team, a teacher's assistant would also be assigned to the classroom to facilitate Mary's integration into the programme.

Three months after the beginning of the school year, the intervention team assembled again to review the status of Mary's placement and progress. At this meeting, Ms Forman was proud to report on Mary's accomplishments. Mary's language and self-help skills had improved considerably. She was well liked by her classmates and followed the classroom rules as ably as anyone. While Mary still required special assistance on many tasks, the teacher's assistant was excellent in working with her in a non-intrusive way. She also used the one-to-one time required for many self-help tasks, to work with Mary on individual goals in self-help, cognitive development and language. The specialists on the intervention team (i.e. the special education teacher, the physical and occupational therapists, and the communication specialist) made regular visits to the classroom. They often worked with Mary in small group settings, where she could interact with her classmates and learn a variety of skills by watching them. The specialists also provided pertinent information and demonstrated intervention strategies to Ms Forman, the teacher's assistant and Mary's parents, so that they could use these same strategies throughout the day. Mary loved school, and was always eager to show her parents and brothers what she had learned or accomplished at school each day.

Discussion

Ms Forman's initial concerns about having Mary in her classroom are understandable and probably similar to what many other teachers would feel in similar situations. Without ongoing assurance, information and support from members of the intervention team, Ms Forman's story after the first three months might have been entirely different. With such assistance and support, however, her feelings about working with a child with special educational needs changed considerably over a short period of time. In addition to feeling more open and confident about having children with SEN in her classroom, Ms Forman had also grown professionally by learning how to implement intervention strategies in developmentally appropriate ways. While Mary was clearly not performing at the same level as her classmates during her Reception year at school, there was no doubt that she was benefiting from the mainstream experience.

Part II

CHILD DEVELOPMENT ISSUES

How we view children and the ways in which they develop and learn influence, to a large extent, the types of educational programmes we provide for them. While there are varying perspectives on how young children go through the process of development and learning, the developmental perspective lays the philosophical groundwork for what is generally viewed as 'recommended practices' in the field of early childhood education and early childhood special education.

Part II begins with a description of the developmental perspective on human growth and development and presents a discussion of how this perspective relates to educational programming, both for children who are developing typically and children with atypical development. Major principles and patterns of growth and development are presented, as are concerns relating to the impact of different disabling conditions on the process of development and learning. Because disabling conditions impact not only on the individual child with the disability but on his or her family as well, Part II addresses some of the special concerns relating to parenting, parent–child interactions, and the maintenance of a healthy home environment when faced with the challenge of meeting the needs of a child with a disability.

Also presented is an outline of the different types of risk factors, the etiologies (or causes) of disabilities and different categories of disabling conditions. Finally, there is a discussion about how some disabilities, especially secondary handicaps, might be prevented. While most of the discussion in this section addresses complex issues relating to the nature and impact of disabling conditions, the implications for educational programming that are presented stress the importance of viewing the young child with a disability from a developmental rather than a deficit perspective. This means remembering that young children with special needs are children first – i.e. children who have many of the same characteristics and needs as typically developing children. They possess a set of complex skills or competencies, learn through active involvement with the environment, and need the opportunity and encouragement to explore and interact with their environment in positive ways.

3

TYPICAL AND EXCEPTIONAL EARLY DEVELOPMENT

Human development is a fascinating and complex phenomenon. The most remarkable changes that occur during this process do so between the time of human conception and the first few years of school. An understanding of these changes and the basic patterns in which they occur is a critical aspect of what it means to be an early childhood professional.

Without sufficient knowledge of developmental patterns for physical growth, as well as cognitive, language and social/emotional development, early childhood educators will be seriously hampered in making wise decisions on behalf of young children and their families. Knowledge of developmental patterns should guide decisions relating to such critical factors as: (1) screening and assessing young children to identify special educational needs; (2) selecting materials and activities that are appropriate for the developmental level of children while fostering maturation to the next levels; (3) selecting appropriate intervention objectives and strategies for young children with SEN, and (4) providing accurate and timely information and advice to parents.

A developmental perspective

Cultivating a thorough understanding of how human beings develop is a complex process and cannot be accomplished in a short period of time. Fortunately, there are many quality resources available relating to human development. While professionals should not regard these resources as substitutes for their own expertise, they can look to such resources to supplement a soundly established understanding of the way human beings develop. There follows a brief discussion of a developmental perspective on child growth and development, which – according to recommended practices in the field – is the perspective with the most promise for guiding wise decision making for young children and their families (Odom and McLean, 1996).

Parents of young children are often asked about the age of their child. Age is also the determining factor for participation in many educational and recreational programmes – for example a child must be at least 4 years old to participate in the Reception class and at least 5 to enter Key Stage 1 of the National Curriculum in the UK. While age is one aspect of child development, it is a critical error to equate development with age.

Development is far more complex than age. Age marks the passage of time – i.e. how much time has elapsed since the child's birth or, when talking about prenatal development, how much time has elapsed since conception. Development, however, occurs when the complexity of a child's behaviour increases (Allen and Marotz, 1989). For example, when a child's play behaviour moves from simply holding and manipulating toy dishes to pretending to cook and eat while using these toys, we can say that cognitive development has occurred. Similarly, when a child's balance and co-ordination improve to the point where he or she can kick a ball while running versus being able to kick a ball only from a stationary position, we can say that motor development has occurred.

Just as development is not the same as age, neither is it the same as maturation. Maturation refers to the universal sequence of biological changes that occur as one ages. Increased height represents one visible example of maturation. Maturation is closely related to development, in that maturation permits the development of psychological functions (Howard *et al.*, 1997). Certain psychological functions would never occur without sufficient maturation preceding it. The development of language is an example. The brain must first develop sufficiently before infants become capable of understanding and producing language. A child with severe brain damage may thus be prevented from ever developing a broad repertoire of language skills. While language stimulation plays a crucial role in the development of language, sufficient neurological maturation is also required. One without the other will not accomplish the task.

Misunderstandings about the maturation/stimulation relationship sometimes lead to inappropriate practices in intervention. It would be inappropriate, for example, to avoid working towards individual goals in the area most affected by the child's disability on the premise that he or she will never achieve sufficient neurological maturation to accomplish the desired goals anyway. If the goals are important to the child's successful functioning, alternative routes to accomplishing these goals should be identified. In the case of a child with severe brain damage who may be prevented from ever developing a broad repertoire of language skills, the goal of successful communication must still be pursued. Similarly, if the severity of a physical disability prohibits a child from ever writing his or her name, alternative methods of providing a personal signature should be explored.

Just as misunderstandings about the maturation/stimulation relationship might lead to inappropriate practices, a clear understanding of this connection can provide valuable guidance to educators working with both typically developing children and children with special educational needs. When working from a developmental perspective, professionals consider both maturation and stimulation to be critical factors in identifying appropriate educational objectives and strategies. Unless children are neurologically and/or physically ready for certain accomplishments, it is not appropriate to expect or teach related behaviours. Trying to teach a child to read before he or she can differentiate between similar but different symbols (e.g. the letters 'm' and 'n') is inappropriate. Elkind (1987) refers to attempts to teach young children skills before they are ready as 'miseducation', and suggests that this practice puts children at both psychological and physical risk.

Developmental milestones play a role in our understanding of the developmental perspective on human development. Developmental milestones represent major indexes of developmental accomplishments and are based on the average age at which children acquire certain skills or pass through certain stages. Developmental milestones have been identified across developmental areas (e.g. cognition, language, social skills) and are often used as guides for expectations in the different areas of development. For example, a typically developing child who has learned to pull himself up to a standing position while holding on to a piece of furniture may be expected to begin walking with support (i.e. either holding someone's hand or holding on to the furniture) in a relatively short period of time.

For children without disabilities, a listing of developmental milestones can thus be used in relation to expected ages at which they will develop certain skills. The norm (i.e. average age) for accomplishing the developmental milestone of independent sitting, for example, is six months. Some children – even those without disabilities – take longer to develop this skill, while others accomplish independent sitting before 6 months of age. Thus a 'range of normalcy' versus a simple average (i.e. the 'norm') should be used in relation to expectations. While the norm for independent sitting is 6 months, the range of normalcy is 4 to 8 months. The range of normalcy for developmental milestones should be clearly understood by all early childhood professionals and should be used as a guide in talking with parents about their child's development and appropriate expectations. An understanding of developmental milestones and the range of normalcy should also be used in helping to identify children who may not be developing at an expected rate. If developmental milestones do not occur within the range of normalcy, a child may be at risk of developmental delays. When this occurs, the child should be assessed to determine eligibility for special education services.

Brain research

Recent findings in the area of brain research offer interesting and potentially valuable insights into human development and the process of learning. While this research is greeted with enthusiasm, there are also related words of caution and controversy over how it may be applicable to educational practices. As the literature reports, we have seen in the 1990s an 'unprecedented explosion of information on how the brain works . . . and have learned more about the brain in the past 5 years than in the past 100 years' (Wolfe and Brandt, 1998, p. 8). Some suggest that the findings gained from this research can inform decisions about 'early childhood education, school readiness, child care, maternal and child health care, and family support' (Halford, 1998, p. 85). Others suggest that brain science, right now, 'has little to offer education practice or policy' (Bruer, 1998, p. 14).

A critical examination of some of the 'big ideas' revealed through brain science seems to suggest that educators might at least look at the findings and determine the extent to which educational practices are consistent with the research. This is not to say that brain science, at least at this point, should be dictating educational policy and practice.

John Bruer (1998) says that there are three 'big ideas' arising from brain science: '(1) Early in life, neural connections (synapses) form rapidly in the brain; (2) Critical periods occur in development; and (3) Enriched environments have a pronounced effect on brain development during the early years' (p. 14). Early childhood educators are likely to find something familiar in each of these ideas, as they are consistent with related research in human development and educational psychology. Bruer (1998), while indicating that we need not be critical of the ideas themselves, suggests the need for caution in how we interpret these ideas for educators and parents. Some of Bruer's concerns relating to the 'big ideas' emerging from brain research are presented in the following discussion.

Early synapse formation

A synapse is a connection through which nerve impulses travel from one neuron in the brain to another. Brain research indicates that human newborns have lower synaptic densities (number of synapses per unit volume of tissue) than adults. In the first few months following birth, however, synapses begin to form far in excess of the adult levels. By age 4, synaptic densities peak in all areas of the brain at levels 50 per cent above adult levels. As children reach puberty, a pruning process begins to eliminate synapses, reducing the densities to adult levels.

According to Bruer (1998), 'We have no reason to believe, as we often read, that the more synapses we have, the smarter we are. Nor do existing neuroscientific studies support the idea that the more learning experiences we have during childhood, the more synapses will be "saved" from pruning and the more intelligent our children will be' (p. 15). Bruer claims that there are more misunderstandings than valid interpretations of research relating to early synapse formation and cautions against jumping to the conclusion that there is a simple, direct relationship between synaptic densities and intelligence.

Critical periods in development

The theory behind the concept of critical periods indicates that if some motor, sensory and language skills are to develop normally, the child must have certain kinds of experience at specific times during early development. While this concept is often used to bolster support for some early educational practices, Bruer (1998) states that the neuroscientific research on critical periods 'is likely to have little relevance to formal education' (p. 16) and refers to the concept of 'critical periods' as 'windows of learning opportunity'. Wolfe and Brandt (1998) concur with Bruer, especially regarding terminology. They say, 'These stages once called "critical periods" are more accurately described as "sensitive periods" or "windows of opportunity"' (p. 12). In other words, while the early years are viewed as peak learning years, this does not mean that young children should be exposed to formal educational experiences (e.g. reading, maths) as a way of increasing their intelligence.

Neuroscientific research indicates that critical periods are quite complex and that different critical periods exist for different specific functions (Daw, 1995). For example, within the system for learning language the critical period for learning phonology (including learning to speak without an accent) ends in early childhood, but the critical period for learning a language's grammar does not end until about age 16 (Bruer, 1998). Neuroscientists also believe that there are three distinct phases within the critical period for each specific function of a sensory system: (1) a time of rapid change during which a function quickly matures; (2) a period of sensitivity to deprivation, and (3) a time of sufficient plasticity to compensate for deprivation and allow for the regaining of near-normal function if appropriate sensory experience occurs (Bruer, 1998).

According to Bruer (1998), critical periods 'contribute to the development of basic species wide abilities, like vision, hearing, or language' (p. 16). There are no reasons to think, he says, 'that there are critical periods for the acquisition of culturally and socially transmitted skills, like reading, mathematics, or music' (p. 17). It is for these reasons that 'critical periods say little about formal education' (p. 17).

The effects of enriched environments

According to Bruer (1998) and others (Nelson and Bloom, 1997), one of the new and exciting findings of brain science is that the brain can reorganize itself for learning throughout our lifetimes. Learning, he explains, is associated with exposure to complex environments; but, as Bruer cautions, 'we must be careful not to confuse *complex* with *enriched*' (p. 18). 'Enriched', in the popular and education literature, tends to be a value-laden term, in that 'enriched environments' are often described in relation to middle-class values. 'We should,' he says, 'be careful not to use neuroscience to provide biological pseudo-argument in favor of our culture and our political values and prejudices' (p. 18).

With the cautions offered by Bruer and others, are there any brain research findings that can be used to guide or support efforts in early intervention? A review of the literature suggests that there are several. McGeehan (2001) offers three such findings: '(1) emotion is the gatekeeper to learning; (2) intelligence is a function of experience; and (3) the brain stores most effectively what is meaningful from the learner's perspective' (p. 8).

Emotion: the gatekeeper to learning

Brain research indicates that learning is influenced strongly by emotion (LeDoux, 1996; Wolfe and Brandt, 1998). Positive emotions associated with an experience tend to support memory of that experience. Negative emotions (such as feelings of being threatened), on the other hand, tend to decrease the leaning potential of a situation or experience. Emotion, then, can be seen as a gatekeeper to learning (McGeehan, 2001).

McGeehan discusses the complex relationship between emotions and learning in terms of the body–brain partnership. She starts with a discussion on 'neurotransmitters' and 'informational substances'. The neurotransmitters, she says, are responsible for the synaptic leap between brain cells and represent one type of informational substance that carries out the process of learning. A second system of informational substance is represented by a variety of transmitters, peptides, hormones and protein ligands. These substances travel through intercellular pathways and reach receptors on the outer surfaces of cells throughout the body. Their role as they travel is to inform, regulate and synchronize. Peptides are the largest category of informational substances, and every peptide has receptors in the brain. The result is an ongoing 'conversation' between the body and the brain. The term 'bodybrain' is sometimes used in reference to 'the constant collaboration that takes place between mind and body' (McGeehan, 2001, p. 9). An understanding of this 'bodybrain' concept breaks down the traditional distinction between body and brain and provides some insights into the relationship between emotion and learning.

Robert Sylwester (1995), noted for his work on synthesizing and interpreting brain research, also addresses the connection between emotions and learning. Emotions, he says, 'drive attention which drives learning, memory, and just about everything else' (p. 72). Sylwester draws attention to two separate response systems in the brain: reflexive and reflective. When a possible threat is presented, our first defence tends to be reflexive. The threat may be physical, emotional, environmental, or attributed to academic confusion and frustration. An involuntary reflexive response to a threatening situation puts the brain in a survival mode. This response triggers an immediate adrenaline reaction – heart rhythm and blood pressure increase, stress hormones are released, and perspiration begins. This reflexive response can also activate primitive methods of dealing with stress – screaming, crying, hitting, hiding and so on (Kaufeldt, 1999). As such responses are not conducive to learning or supportive of the learning environment, it would be well for teachers to be aware of threatening or stressful conditions at school which may trigger an unwelcome reflexive response in some of the students. As outlined by Kaufeldt (1999), such conditions include fear of potential harm from a teacher or other students, embarrassment, put-downs, lack of time for reflection, unknown purpose or perceived irrelevance, inflexible schedule or agenda, competition and extrinsic rewards, and lack of personal meaning.

Kaufeldt (1999) also offers some strategies which students might use to help them move from a reflexive to a reflective response, allowing them to respond to stress with healthier coping strategies. These strategies, which can be taught, include time management, communication skills, conflict resolution, problem solving, self-reflection and anger management. In addition to teaching these coping strategies to students, teachers can also create an environment designed to reduce stress and tension in the classroom. They can do this by demonstrating and insisting on respectful and caring interactions, by using clear procedures to let students know what to do and what is expected of them, and by building a sense of community.

Early trauma and aggression

Recent advances in paediatric neuroscience have clearly established the fact that early traumatic experiences can alter development of a child's brain chemistry and anatomy in ways that inhibit concentration, inhibit learning, hinder attachment and bonding, and blunt empathy (Goss, 2001). These changes can predispose children to aggressive behaviour later in life. Traumatic experiences in the form of injury or abuse can be particularly damaging to children when it occurs before they have the language and cognitive ability to talk about the experience. Brain scans of abused/neglected children show abnormalities in those areas of the brain involved in the control of aggressive behaviour (Teicher, 2000).

Intelligence: a function of experience

Researchers agree that the brain changes physiologically as a result of experience. This means that the environment in which a brain operates determines to a large extent the functioning ability of that brain (Wolfe and Brandt, 1998). Home and classroom environments, then, should not be looked upon as neutral environments. They either contribute to learning and brain development or hinder such growth (Wolfe and Brandt, 1998). Complexity is one dimension of the environment associated with learning (Bruer, 1998; Nelson and Bloom, 1997). Complex environments also play a role in the physical development of the brain (McGeehan, 2001).

As previously discussed, it is important to distinguish complex environments from enriched environments (Bruer, 1998). Complex environments are characterized by rich sensory input and opportunities for firsthand experiences with real materials. Enriched environments, however, may focus on books, worksheets and other 'representational' versus 'real' materials. The connection between intelligence and experience supports the practice of focusing on rich sensory input and real materials during the early childhood years.

Personal meaning: the key to memory

Research indicates that the brain tends to pay attention to and remember what is relevant to daily life (McGeehan, 2001). Research also suggests that unless new information carries some emotional value and useful content, the brain will tend to efficiently ignore it. According to McGeehan, this research calls for 'a different approach to curriculum' (p. 11) – that is, a curriculum based on what is meaningful to the students. An obvious place to begin constructing this type of curriculum is to get to know the students well and, in the process, find out what is meaningful to them. Once we know our students well, we will be able to link new information and skills with what is important to them – that is, what they care about and what has relevant connections to their daily lives. The question 'So what?' might be used as a guide in developing curriculum – that is, what does this information, this activity, this experience have to do with the students and their priorities in life?

Normal developmental patterns

As indicated earlier, human development is a very complex phenomenon – certainly more complex than a listing of developmental milestones might suggest. Part of the complexity relates to the interaction between environment (i.e. stimulation) and maturation as experienced by the child. Through decades of observation and research, certain principles relating to normal developmental patterns have been identified. There follow six such principles with a brief discussion of each. An understanding of these principles can be crucial to making informed decisions about assessment procedures, instructional strategies and curricular materials, whether working with children with disabilities or with typically developing children.

Principle 1

Human beings at all levels of development possess a set of complex skills or competencies. All living organisms are competent in that they have the capacity to react to environmental stimuli. Infants, very young children and individuals with severe disabilities, however, are not always viewed as being competent. What they cannot do often overshadows what they can do. This perspective is not in the best interests of the child, and should certainly be avoided in intervention programmes.

While any one individual possesses competencies unique to his or her development, there are also certain competencies that are practically universal. These competencies include the ability to learn new behaviours, to solve problems and to adapt to changes in the environment (Howard *et al.*, 1997). Professionals working with young children with special educational needs would do well to identify the skills or competencies of the child, build on these skills to enhance the child's feelings of confidence and competence, and plan educational programmes that focus on competencies versus deficits. A competency-based approach to intervention recognizes and values the child's contributions to the learning process. As presented in Chapter 5, this competency-based approach is especially important in fostering the social and communication development of the child.

Principle 2

Human beings are active learners at all levels of development. Active learners construct their own knowledge versus passively receiving it from others; and human beings can be active learners at all levels of development. This principle underscores the importance of designing intervention strategies that recognize the involvement and contributions of the child to the instructional process. Teachers should thus be viewed as facilitators of learning versus instructors of knowledge. An important aspect of the teacher's role is to encourage and stimulate children to engage in exploratory and problem-solving activities.

In her essays on teaching and learning, Eleanor Duckworth (1987) talks about 'the having of wonderful ideas' as 'the essence of intellectual development' (p. 1), and indicates that the role of the teacher is to provide occasions for children to have such ideas. The 'wonderful ideas' that Duckworth refers to need not necessarily look wonderful to the outside world. She sees 'no difference in kind between wonderful ideas that many people have already had, and wonderful ideas that nobody has yet happened upon' (p. 14). The nature of the creative intellectual act remains the same. Duckworth does go on to say, however, that 'the more we help children to have their wonderful ideas and to feel good about themselves for having them, the more likely it is that they will some day happen upon wonderful ideas that no one else has happened upon before' (p. 14).

Principle 3

No area of functioning develops in isolation from other areas. We often refer to different developmental domains (e.g. social, physical, cognitive) as if they were separate areas of development. This reference, however, can be misleading and may contribute to inappropriate practices in intervention. Assessment and instructional strategies should be based on the understanding that 'independent areas and skills cannot be examined separately or in isolation; rather the whole of the child's development and the interrelatedness of developmental areas must be considered' (Hanson and Lynch, 1995, p. 6). Thus, if a child shows developmental delays in the area of social skills, other areas that should be carefully assessed include language and cognitive development. This recommendation is based on the fact that the child's social difficulties may be due primarily to deficits in the use of language (e.g. not knowing how to use language to express feelings and ideas).

Cognitive delays may also play a major role in how a child relates to others. For example, if adults and peers use vocabulary and sentence structure that the child does not understand, or they use representational materials in play and other instructional activities that the child cannot relate to, he or she may respond by withdrawing or 'acting out'. In either case the child may be labelled as having 'social problems', whereas the concerns with social development may be in response to language and/or cognitive deficits. Focusing on the development of language skills and/or considering the child's level of cognitive functioning in relation to expectations and learning activities may alleviate the child's social problems much more effectively than implementing a behavioural intervention plan.

Understanding that no area of functioning develops in isolation from other areas also lends support to the rationale for early intervention. By intervening early, the likelihood of secondary impairments developing in related areas is reduced. For example, children with language delays may become so frustrated in their attempts to communicate effectively that they may begin to use physical force to express their feelings of frustration and to get what they want and/or need. The pattern of using physical force may become such an established form of behaviour that, before long, these children are not only language delayed but 'behaviour disordered' as well. Behaviour disorder is an example of a secondary impairment that developed in response to an earlier existing disability. Early intervention focusing on the development of more effective communication skills could have prevented the development of this secondary impairment.

Principle 4

Skill development proceeds from unspecialized to specialized functioning. The pattern of human development has been likened to that of a tree (Lewis, 1984). The trunk of the tree – primarily with an undifferentiated functioning role – develops prior to the branches and leaves which perform more differentiated roles. Likewise, in human beings the pattern of skill development moves from unspecialized to specialized functioning. Thus for a young child, generalized skills (e.g. whole-hand grasping) develop prior to specialized skills (e.g. holding small items with thumb and forefinger).

Understanding that human development moves from unspecialized to specialized functioning is of considerable importance when working with children with disabilities (Hanson and Lynch, 1995). It can be particularly useful in determining appropriate goals and objectives for children with special educational needs and planning intervention strategies that focus on present and emerging stages of development. Without an understanding of this pattern of development, parents and professionals may base their intervention efforts on unrealistic expectations and involve the child in inappropriate instructional strategies. For example, milestones in language development include 'naming familiar objects' and 'describing objects'. An analysis of these two skills indicates that 'naming familiar objects' is less specialized than 'describing objects'. If a child has neither of these skills in his or her language repertoire, it would be unrealistic and inappropriate to make 'describing objects' a current instructional goal for the child. A realistic goal might be for the child to begin naming objects with which he or she is familiar.

Principle 5

Human development occurs in a predictable pattern. This principle of human development builds on the understanding presented in Principle 4 – i.e. skill development moves from unspecialized to specialized functioning. The predictable pattern or sequence of human development is applicable to children with and without disabilities. What varies is the individual timing of reaching certain developmental milestones. An understanding of this principle also has important implications for individual goal setting, as discussed with regard to Principle 4.

Principle 6

Human development represents an interactive process between an individual's status at any point in time and the environment in which the individual is immersed. Because the environment plays a crucial role in human development, the quality of the environment in which an individual is immersed can determine, in large part, the extent to which his or her potential is reached. 'Favorable conditions enable children to reach the high end of their potential, while unfavorable conditions can depress development toward the lower end of the range of a child's potential' (Howard *et al.*, 1997, p. 46). What are considered favourable or unfavourable environmental conditions, however, can vary in some instances from child to child. An environment rich in visual beauty or imagery may be favourable for many children. A child who is blind, however, may receive very little or no benefit from such an environment.

This principle, then, has considerable importance for serving young children with disabilities. As indicated already in Chapter 1, a disability may or may not be a handicap for individual children, depending upon the specific circumstances or demands of the environment. If the demands of the environment create problems for the children in their efforts to function and interact with that environment, then the disability becomes a handicap and gets in the way of allowing children to reach their potential. Professionals working with children with disabilities need to adapt the environment in ways that allow children with special educational needs to experience, explore and interact with the environment in positive ways. An enriched environment means nothing to a child who cannot interact effectively with it.

Atypical developmental patterns

A major difficulty in describing a young child who is developing atypically (i.e. in a way that is neither typical nor normal) begins with the problem of trying to define 'atypical'. The literature on atypical development includes children who range from those born prematurely to those with multiple and severe disorders. Thus children with atypical developmental patterns 'represent an extremely heterogeneous group, one from which clustering for the purposes of testing and analysis becomes difficult at best' (Hanson, 1996, p. 162). The most that testing and analysis generally offer is an indication that some children are not developing normally, rather than identifying how their developmental processes differ (Hanson, 1996).

By definition, children with special education needs fail to develop in concert with their typically developing peers. In one or more areas of development, children with SEN fail to accomplish developmental milestones within the range of normalcy. As indicated earlier, for many children with SEN, the sequence of skill development is the same as their typically developing peers; what differs is the age at which such skills are developed. At times, however, the nature of the child's disability prevents the child from ever accomplishing certain skills. An obvious example is a child who is profoundly deaf who will never be able to accomplish certain auditory discrimination skills. The important point to bear in mind, however, is that such a child can develop other sensory discrimination skills and accomplish many related cognitive and adaptive living goals through alternative routes.

Atypical developmental patterns are sometimes grouped into three general categories: delays, disorders and giftedness. Individual children may experience only one or a combination of these conditions. Many children with developmental delays and/or disorders are eligible for special education services for all or part of their academic careers. For some children with SEN, participation in an early intervention programme minimizes the impact of the delay and/or disorder, to the point where they can later function successfully in a regular education programme without any further special support services. While giftedness represents an atypical developmental pattern, it does not qualify children for special education services. The special needs of children who are gifted, however, should not be overlooked. There follows a brief discussion of the three general categories of atypical development (i.e. delays, disorders and giftedness).

Delays

Children with delays are those who experience delayed or slow progress in reaching developmental milestones in one or more areas of development, such as communication, cognition, adaptive behaviour (e.g. feeding, dressing, toileting), physical development, social and emotional development. The extent of delay is determined by comparing the child's actual performance level with his or her chronological age. For example, a child who is 50 months old (i.e. 4 years and 2 months) but receives an age-equivalent score of 40 months (i.e. 3 years and 4 months) in the area of communication is considered to have a 10-month delay in communication development.

In addition to using an age differential (e.g. the 10-month delay) to describe the extent of a child's delay, other quantitative descriptions sometimes used include (1) percentage of delay, and (2) standard deviations from the mean. For the child who is 50 months old but scores at 40 months on an age-equivalent measure of performance, the extent of delay would be 20 per cent.

Determining a standard deviation from the mean requires the use of an assessment instrument where standardized scores are obtained. A standardized score is one that has been transformed to fit a normal curve of development, with a mean (i.e. average) and standard deviation that remain the same across ages. In the overall population, most individuals score at or near the mean. As scores deviate from the mean (either greater than or less than), fewer instances of those scores will be observed. At a certain point, such deviations indicate atypical development.

The term 'standard deviation' is used to describe how far a score is from the mean (either above or below). As displayed in Figure 3.1, within the normal curve model, one standard deviation on either side of the mean encompasses approximately 34 per cent of individuals in a group. Two standard deviations on either side of the mean would encompass 48 per cent of individuals in a group. Thus for a child to score at one standard deviation below the mean would suggest that his or her performance was better than 16 per cent of the total population, while a score of two standard deviations below the mean would suggest that his or her performance was better than only 2 per cent of the total population. While standard deviations are sometimes used in the process of determining eligibility for special education services, the use of standardized assessment measures to obtain standardized scores is under a great deal of criticism, especially for young children (Appl, 2000; Fewell, 2000; NAEYC and NAECS/SDE, 1991; Raver, 1991). Reasons for this criticism and other issues related to screening and assessment are presented in Chapter 9.

How delays are quantified or referred to is certainly not as important as how to provide the most advantageous educational programme for children with developmental delays. Such programmes should be designed to minimize the extent of delay and to ward off the development of secondary handicaps.

Disorders

A 'disorder,' in terms of growth and development, refers to a condition that disrupts or changes the order of a child's developmental progress. A disorder differs from a delay in that a child with a developmental delay falls significantly behind developmental norms but still proceeds through the normal sequence of development. A child with a disorder, however, will not experience the same order of development in one or more developmental domains. Due to the disruption to normal development, a child with a disorder may require alternative routes for achieving certain

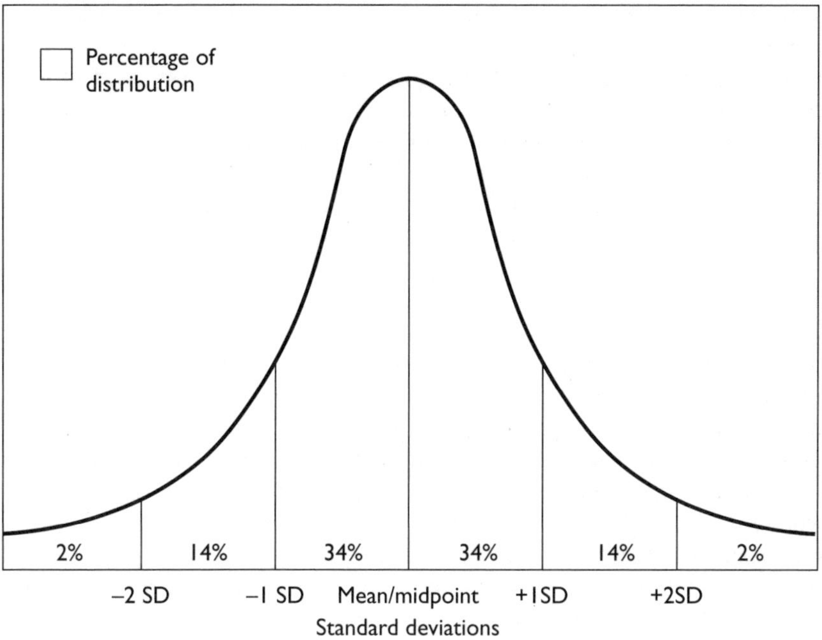

Figure 3.1 Normal curve

basic living skills. For example, a child with a serious motor impairment (i.e. disorder) may never be able to walk. He or she may still achieve independent mobility, however, by learning to use a motorized chair.

Disorders for which there is documented, descriptive information on child development include visual impairment, hearing impairment, motor impairment and Down syndrome. Most children with any of these disorders will also experience developmental delays in one or more areas of development. Educational programmes should consider both the disorder and the accompanying delay(s) in planning and implementing intervention strategies. While intervention programmes cannot remove the disorder itself, they can minimize the negative impact of the disorder on the child's development.

Gifted

Atypical development includes not only children with developmental delays or disorders who tend to fall below the norm in one or more areas of development, but also children who perform significantly above the norm or have the potential for such performance. While nearly every early education programme has children who are gifted, identifying such children is often difficult (Cook *et al.*, 1996). Characteristics to look for in identifying children who are potentially gifted include a large vocabulary, a high level of curiosity, a good memory, and an ability to concentrate intensely and for long periods of time. Such children also tend to learn rapidly, show a mature sense of humour, and enjoy the challenge of problem solving and abstract thinking (Cook *et al.*, 1996). While the needs of many young children who are gifted can be met through the enrichment of a quality regular early education environment, special encouragement from adults can add depth and breadth to their experiences.

Early recognition and nurturance of children's special talents and abilities may foster not only their cognitive and creative abilities, but their mental health as well. A substantial body of research indicates that 'the optimal years for child development in such areas as self-esteem and self-image, social competence, specific cognitive abilities, and achievement motivation are birth through 8 years' (Stile, 1996, p. 310). Without appropriate early intervention, young children who are gifted may be at increased risk of poor self-concepts, the development of behaviour problems and underachievement, or failure to perform in relation to their potential. Early intervention for young children who are gifted should include activities and materials that enhance creativity, promote higher cognitive processes, engage the child in problem solving and enquiry, and promote affective and social development (Cook *et al.*, 1996).

Origins of developmental disabilities

The origins or causes of developmental disabilities are varied and complex. For some children with disabilities, the origins are known; for others, unknown. At times, the origins relate to conditions and/or circumstances existing prior to or near the time of birth. At other times, the origin of a child's disability relates to conditions and/or circumstances experienced during early childhood or later years. Some disabilities that are present at birth are due to maternal and/or genetic conditions over which the parent has little or no control. Some disabilities, however, are caused by conditions within the physical or social environment experienced by the developing foetus or young child over which adults may have some control. Many of the disabilities caused by environmental conditions are preventable.

Maternal conditions

Certain health-related conditions of a pregnant mother can put a foetus at risk of developmental disabilities. These conditions include diabetes, hypertension, drug and alcohol addiction, heart disease and eating disorders. Of these conditions, alcohol addiction is perhaps the most damaging, in that it is the leading known cause of mental retardation and usually leads to lifelong disabilities (Howard *et al.*, 1997). While the negative effects of alcohol on the developing foetus have been known for a long time (Weiner and Morse, 1988), it was not until the 1970s that the term 'foetal alcohol syndrome' (FAS) was first used to describe a set of characteristics associated with this syndrome.

The three primary characteristics of FAS are growth deficiency, central nervous system dysfunction and abnormal facial features, including a short, upturned nose, thin lips, wide-set eyes and a flat midface (Burgess and Streissguth, 1992). Many young children with FAS also have serious behavioural problems. They tend to be hyperactive, impulsive, non-compliant, have language and communication difficulties (especially in pragmatics), and have problems with self-regulation, judgement and decision making (Burgess and Streissguth, 1992).

Dealing with the behavioural problems of children with FAS can be especially challenging in that the types of consequence that are usually effective with most children seem to have little effect on children with FAS. Parents and teachers who have tried the consistent use of such consequences as praise, smiles, reprimands, withdrawal of privileges and so on generally find that these strategies are ineffective with children with FAS. Children with FAS seem to miss the connection between their actions and the consequences that follow.

Age and certain genetic conditions (e.g. cystic fibrosis, PKU) of a pregnant woman can also place a foetus at risk. Mothers younger than 20 years and older than 40 years have an increased risk of a premature delivery and congenital abnormalities in their foetus. Intervention programmes that focus on educating women in these conditions and encouraging them to seek healthcare and counselling before becoming pregnant can significantly reduce the risk of having children with developmental disabilities.

Socio-economic conditions

A number of socio-economic factors also influence the relative health and developmental status of infants and young children. Young, single mothers with few support networks, for example, have a higher incidence of premature delivery and low birth weight infants than the general population (Report of Consensus Conferences, 1987). Poverty is another significant factor placing children at risk of developmental disabilities. Conditions of poverty make both direct and indirect attacks on children's development (Bowman, 1992). Since many low-income families lack the resources to ward off these attacks, children living in poverty are far more likely to experience developmental disabilities than children from other segments of the population. Even children from middle- or upper-class homes who experience serious perinatal stress are less likely to experience developmental disabilities than poor children who have not experienced such stress. Aylward (1990) found that 'by age 18, adolescents who lived in poverty were ten times more likely to have serious learning and behavioural problems than were those who had survived severe prenatal stress' (p. 3). Obviously, not all risk factors are equal in terms of probable impact. In fact, children living in poverty are considered to be the most at-risk population (Bellamy, 1998; Bowman, 1992).

Health-related problems make direct attacks on children living in poverty, and include such conditions as inadequate food, shelter and care. According to professional estimates, health problems (including low birth weight, lead poison, anaemia and hearing problems) may account for as much as 30 per cent of the variance between the cognitive development of poor and middle-class children (Bowman, 1992). Children with borderline nutritional levels, especially when compounded by poor health services, often experience chronic and acute viral and bacterial illnesses, which in turn foster irritability, distractibility and passivity. Children suffering from these conditions are less likely to engage in active exploration of the environment and are less receptive to environmental feedback. This situation represents an indirect but formidable attack on development and learning. Other indirect attacks include a sense of hopelessness, despair, and, at times, disorganized family functioning – all of which tend to be exacerbated by the conditions of poverty. In addition, living in a depressed community tends to make life dangerous and unpredictable, resulting in added stress for young children and their families (Bellamy, 1998; Bowman, 1992).

Environmental assaults

While 'within-family' problems can certainly put a young child at risk of developmental delay or disability, there are many other risk factors outside of the family which can be equally problematic. Such risk factors are more prevalent in low-income and racial minority communities (Blahna and Toch, 1993; Collin, 1993) and are usually outside the family's realm of control. Such risk factors include exposure to toxic pollutants in the air, water and food. Children living in low-income and racial minority communities experience higher than average exposure to such pollutants. A study carried out in the USA indicates that three out of every four toxic waste dumps that fail to comply with the Environmental Protection Agency regulations are in black or Hispanic neighbourhoods (Environmental Protection Agency, 1992). In response to this unequal distribution of environmental assault conditions, an environmental justice movement has been initiated. A major goal of this movement is to create public awareness of these unjust conditions and to stimulate action to rectify such conditions (Bullard, 1994; Chavis, 1992).

Most families living in low-income and environmentally degraded neighbourhoods do so not by choice, but because they lack the mobility to escape such areas (Rogue, 1993). Parents who live in these areas pay a high price for doing so – not in terms of financial costs to them, but in terms of increased health and learning problems for their children. Health problems linked to exposure to high levels of toxic wastes and other forms of environmental degradation include a higher incidence of deformed foetuses, cancer, respiratory illnesses, childhood leukemia and immune deficiency (Adeola, 1994). Children exposed to environmental hazards are also at greater risk of mental retardation and other forms of learning disabilities.

Social toxicity

James Garbarino (1997) uses the term 'social toxicity' in reference to the harmful social climate that is demoralizing families and communities throughout the world. The social environment of children today, he says, 'has become poisonous to their development – just as toxic substances in the environment threaten human well-being and survival' (pp. 13–14). Social conditions that Garbarino refers to as the 'social equivalents' to lead and smoke in the air, the PCBs in the water and pesticides in the food chain include violence, poverty, the disruption of family relationships, despair, depression, paranoia, nastiness and alienation. Such conditions mean that 'more and more children are in greater and greater trouble' (Garbarino, 1997, p. 13). The children who are most likely to be seriously harmed by these socially toxic conditions are those who have accumulated the most developmental risk factors.

Garbarino (1997) addresses the 'blaming-the-parent' issue in his discussions on social toxicity. He uses the example of a city plagued by cholera, where all parents face grave danger for their children. The ability to ward off this danger, however, varies in relation to the competencies and resources available to the parents. Some parents would have more success delivering drinkable water to their children than would other parents. Yet at times, even the more competent parents would fail. Garbarino asks, 'Would we blame them, or point the finger at the community's failed water purification system?' and notes that 'in a socially toxic environment, the same principle holds' (p. 15).

Impact of a disability

Disabilities affect not only individuals with special needs, but others who interact with them as well. Major impacts are felt by other people both in the home and school environment.

Impact in the home

A headline in a community newspaper read as follows: 'Parents give up child with genetic disorder' (*The Blade*, 1997). The child referred to is Kyle, a 6-year-old boy suffering from Fragile X syndrome, a common form of hereditary mental retardation. According to the article, Kyle's parents gave temporary custody of their son to the county children services agency, because they found that Kyle's genetic disorder made it impossible to control his temper. While the action taken by Kyle's parents represents a more extreme response to dealing with a child with a disability than that taken by most parents, frustration and feelings of not knowing what to do are not unusual for parents of children with behaviour disorders and other types of special needs.

From the moment a disability is manifested and/or identified, parenting does become more complex and difficult. Yet it would be incorrect to assume, just because Kyle's parents found it impossible to deal with his special needs, that all or most parents of children with disabilities are somehow unable to cope.

Research on families of children with disabilities conducted prior to the 1990s suggested that such families had an increased risk of family dysfunction. Parent education and involvement programmes were then developed with this assumption in mind. Family needs assessments, for example, were often designed to identify the families' weaknesses. It was also not unusual for early interventionists to assume that families were having trouble coping and that, because of this, it would be better to keep the child in a full-day versus half-day programme. The reasoning was that, due to the way the families were 'handling the situation', time with the parents was not in the best interests of the child.

Recent research, however, focuses less on 'the pathology of deficiency' and more on strengths and resources available to families of children with disabilities. Findings from this research suggest that the psychosocial functioning of families of children with disabilities is more similar to that of families of children without disabilities than it is different from them (Howard *et al.*, 1997). This line of research is based on the premise that all families experience needs and stressors, but that they also have unique ways of coping with stress in their lives. Some families require the assistance of outside agencies to deal with this stress and meet some of their needs; others do not. Having a child with a disability, however, is not considered to be the determining factor in whether or not the family needs special assistance for coping with the challenges of daily living. In fact, as many parents have indicated, one of the things they want interventionists to keep in mind is that having a child with a disability does not make them 'special, unusual, dysfunctional, or in any way homogeneous' (Howard *et al.*, 1997, p. 318).

It is true that, in addition to the basic needs of all families (e.g. financial stability, adequate housing, safe neighbourhoods, food and clothing, healthcare), certain stressors may be more prominent in families of children with disabilities. While such stressors do not make the families deficient, weak or dysfunctional, they may call for a greater amount of family 'hardiness' (Failla and Jones, 1991). Howard *et al.* (1997) define hardiness in relation to the following three dimensions:

1 a sense of control or the ability to influence events rather than being controlled by them;
2 a commitment to becoming actively involved in events and viewing them as meaningful;
3 recognition of life changes as opportunities for growth and development, and not as a burden.

Life is different, not dysfunctional, when a family has a child with a disability. One area of difference often experienced early in the child's life relates to parent–child interaction. The first minutes and hours of life are crucial to the bonding process. A risk or disabling condition that prevents the parents from interacting with their newborn child can get in the way of such bonding. In response to this concern, nurseries and neonatal intensive care units are now allowing parents more opportunities to hold, touch and observe their newborn children.

A possible adverse response to this research, however, could be an increase in parental anxiety and negative emotions already associated with the prospects of parenting a child with special needs (Hanson, 1996). A healthier response, in terms of parent–child interaction, would focus on a wide range of individual variation in meeting a child's psychological requirements.

This does not mean that early attachments are not important. Early attachments are linked to the child's social/emotional development and the formation of subsequent relationships (Ainsworth, 1973; Bowlby, 1982). Parents and interventionists need to appreciate this importance and focus on enhancing parent–child interactions. Infants born at risk often demonstrate behavioural difficulties that make engagement in social interactions especially challenging. Awareness of these difficulties can help adults become better observers and interpreters of the child's interactional cues and more effective in establishing a mutually rewarding relationship.

The behavioural difficulties often experienced by infants born at risk or disabled tend to be in the areas of responsivity, irritability, motor, feeding and visual responses. These difficulties tend to exert a powerful negative influence on the dynamics of parent–infant interactions. The infant's physical characteristics can also play a role in the way parents relate to their child. Muscle tone, posture and medical fragility, for example, can affect the way the mother handles and positions the child. Even as the child grows older, his or her disability may continue to influence parents to be anxious and overly protective. They may find themselves restricting their child's independence and explorations.

Young children with disabilities are often less active and responsive than their typically developing peers. They also tend to provide fewer or different interactional cues, making them less competent interactive partners. In adjusting to these interactional differences, parents of children with disabilities tend to be more directive (i.e. use more commands) and less interactive than may typically occur with non-disabled children (Hanson, 1996).

It is not only the presence of a handicapping condition that should be considered when analysing parent–child interactions. Other characteristics of young children that affect the parent–child interactional process include sex, birth order, temperament and age. In working with parents, interventionists should thus consider the dynamics of the whole situation versus being specifically focused on the handicapping condition. Interventionists are probably most helpful to parents when they support them in their role (versus 'taking over' for them) and provide assistance to them in reading, understanding and responding to their child's cues.

Impact on the school environment

Young children with disabilities require individualized educational experiences to promote attainment of their unique potential. Individualized experiences, however, need not be provided in a separate classroom or school setting. Most young children with special educational needs can be served in the regular classroom as long as special supports are provided as needed. Such supports may include adaptive equipment, a teaching assistant and the involvement of specialists (e.g. special educator, speech/language pathologist, occupational and/or physical therapists).

Having a child with SEN in the classroom places additional responsibilities on the teacher and special challenges for all involved, including intervention specialists, administrators, support staff and even peers. Individual adaptations often have to be made in the areas of curriculum, materials, space, instruction and expectation. In addition to issues of accessibility which need to be addressed, other areas of concern include social acceptance, health and safety, the increased need for one-to-one assistance, individualized educational goals and objectives, and ongoing assessment. The following case study illustrates how these added responsibilities and challenges might impact on an educational programme.

Case study – Michael

Background information

Michael, aged 7, lives in a small apartment of an older building in the 'slum' section of a city with his mother and twin siblings who are just a year younger than Michael. Michael has cerebral palsy, and has considerable difficulty with mobility and balance. He wears a leg brace and uses a walker to enhance his mobility skills. At school, he also uses special adaptive equipment for positioning and balance while seated. Michael does well at school, his favourite subjects being reading and science. He also enjoys computers and has been communicating with a pen pal in Australia through e-mail. Michael and his pen pal like to share information about the natural environment in their respective countries and about special environmental concerns in their local communities. In addition to being identified as a student with special educational needs due to his physical disability, Michael has also been identified as being gifted.

The intervention team working with Michael recognized his special talents and interests during his Reception year of school. They decided at the time to introduce him to computers and to use his interest in science and the environment to motivate him to learn computer skills. Michael caught on quickly and was soon reading and writing at a level far beyond that of his classmates.

Discussion

Michael was environmentally at risk for special education needs even before he was born. His mother was young, single and living in poverty. The cerebral palsy, evident soon after birth, placed him in the established risk category as well. But Michael's exceptionalities also included giftedness. To help Michael achieve his potential, the intervention team looked at all aspects of his situation. They knew that, due to his cerebral palsy, Michael would have motor difficulties. Not wanting this to interfere with reaching his potential, the early intervention team made sure that Michael had the appropriate adaptive equipment to provide the necessary support while working at the computer and using other instructional materials. Computer-assisted instruction allowed Michael to pursue his special areas of interest in considerable depth for his age. While motor control problems prevented him from doing well at 'paperwork' assignments, an enlarged keyboard made it possible for him to type his work on the computer. Thus both curricular and physical adaptations were used in the classroom to meet Michael's special needs in the areas of motor development and giftedness.

4

CONCERNS RELATED TO COGNITION, COMMUNICATION AND EMERGENT LITERACY

Cognitive delays

Cognitive development involves progressive changes in children's perceptions, knowledge, understanding, reasoning and judgement. Another important aspect of cognitive development – which is sometimes overlooked – is the application of cognitive competencies to daily life experiences. Such application enables the individual to become gradually more independent in dealing with a broad range of environmental demands and challenges (Dunst *et al.*, 1996). Efforts to promote cognitive development, then, should focus not only on the acquisition of knowledge and understanding, but applying such knowledge and understanding to daily living situations as well.

While listings of cognitive competencies needed for meeting the challenges of daily life experiences vary across theoretical models, 'cognitive abilities considered hallmarks of the first 6 years of development . . . include but are not limited to, perception, memory, comprehension, symbolic representation, problem solving, purposeful planning, decision making, discrimination, and idea/intention generation' (Dunst *et al.*, 1996, p. 161). Observations of children's play behaviours indicate that the cognitive competencies of young children with disabilities and the way such competencies develop are more alike than different compared to those of typically developing children. What differs is the rate of development. Findings from these observations suggest that efforts to promote the cognitive competencies of young children with disabilities 'need not differ much from practices used with typically developing children' (Dunst *et al.*, 1996, p. 164).

The process through which young children learn (especially throughout the first six years of life) is tied closely to their interactions with people and objects in their environment. Rather than learning primarily in terms of perceptual attributes (e.g. colour, size, shape), young children learn through the actions they perform or are engaged in. Such actions include manipulating, exploring and practising.

The role of play

Play activities offer many opportunities for manipulating, exploring and practising, and are thus highly recommended as avenues for fostering the cognitive competencies of young children (Dunst *et al.*, 1996). While the value of play to the social and emotional development of young children has long been recognized, an understanding of its role in cognitive development has been growing steadily, especially since the cognitive theories of Piaget and Vygotsky came into prominence in the late 1960s (Johnson *et al.*, 1987). While at play – especially when engaged in 'make-believe' or 'pretend' play – children frequently use one thing to stand for something else or they adopt the role of another person. According to Vygotsky, such use of 'representations' or symbols fosters the development of abstract thought.

While at play, children often practise newly acquired mental as well as physical skills. Mental skills involved in play may include discrimination, problem solving and decision making. According to Piaget, engaging in play behaviours can not only provide practice for such skills, but lead to consolidation of skills as well. Due to the high merits afforded to play for young children, some educators are now beginning to plan their entire programme around play activities, with extended periods of time allotted to 'free play'. For them, a word of caution is in order. Not all forms of free play contribute to cognitive and/or social development. In fact, 'there is little evidence linking gross motor play or non-social forms of dramatic play with growth in intellectual or social skills' (Johnson *et al.*, 1987, p. 18). Characteristics of play that seem to contribute to development include: (1) adult and peer involvement (Johnson *et al.*, 1987); (2) activities that reflect or slightly stretch the child's current social or cognitive abilities (Johnson *et al.*, 1987), and (3) activities that are initiated by the child (Dunst *et al.*, 1996).

Recommended practices

Recommended practices for cognitive-based intervention are consistent with the research into the value of play and the characteristics of play most conducive to development. There follows a presentation of several of these recommended practices, along with a brief discussion of each.

- 'Intervention activities should be planned and implemented so that they complement and encourage child-initiated play and interactions with people and objects' (Dunst *et al.*, 1996, p. 178). As previously discussed, children are active participants in the learning process. They acquire cognitive skills through the construction of their own knowledge rather than as passive recipients of what is handed to them. Planning educational programmes around child-initiated play reflects an understanding of children as active learners and competent beings. When given meaningful choices, the activities that children self-initiate usually reflect their current interests and level of competence. As research indicates, children tend to participate more actively and intensely in child-directed versus adult-directed activities and 'are more likely to attend to and retain information that relates directly to their interests and that is within their range of competence' (Dunst *et al.*, 1996, p. 178).

Many teachers find it challenging to use play and child-initiated activities as a primary context for accomplishing individual child goals. They find that children do not always initiate activities related to their intervention targets (i.e. individualized objectives). Rather than giving up on child-initiated activities and working from a different approach, Dunst *et al.* (1996) suggest identifying intervention targets that are consistent with the child's interests and current levels of competence. 'Intervention targets that build on what children already do and how they behave in various settings will naturally lead to intervention procedures and strategies that lead to activities that are competence enhancing' (Dunst *et al.*, 1996, p. 179).

While intervention for cognitive development should be based on child-initiated activities, the environment in which this intervention takes place should be arranged so as to elicit the desired behaviours (i.e. focusing on the targeted goals for the child). Research findings indicate that both physical and organizational characteristics of the environment influence the nature of children's activities in the early childhood classroom, but that the 'interventive' impact of environmental determinants is often neglected by early childhood teachers (Dunst *et al.*, 1996). Because of the importance of the environment to the curriculum, a more detailed discussion about the 'environment as curriculum' is presented in the first section of Chapter 11.

- 'Responsive teaching methods are the instructional strategies of choice when promoting cognitive competence' (Dunst *et al.*, 1996, p. 180). The term 'responsive teaching' describes an instructional approach that uses social responsiveness (e.g. smiles, praise, hugs and other forms of positive attention) as a reinforcer to maintain or evoke further desired behaviours from the child. Positive social reinforcers tend to exert powerful influences on the acquisition of early cognitive competencies for both typically developing children and children with special educational needs.

Elements of responsive teaching include: (1) identifying and attending to materials and circumstances which elicit and maintain a child's engagement with objects and people; (2) arranging the physical and social environments in ways that invite and reinforce child-initiated activities; (3) using contingent social responsiveness to support and encourage elaboration of targeted behaviours; and (4) capitalizing on 'teachable moments' that arise naturally in unstructured or semi-structured situations.

Speech/language difficulties

Without effective communication skills, young children are at considerable risk of serious social and academic difficulties, as well as emotional and behavioural problems. Children with speech/language disabilities should be identified as early as possible and receive appropriate intervention services while they are still quite young, as 'it is unlikely that individuals are apt to fulfil their potential unless efforts to maximize their communication skills are taken' (Goldstein *et al.*, 1996, p. 197).

There was a time when intervention services for children with speech/language disabilities focused primarily on the speech aspects of communication. In fact, the primary interventionists in the field were referred to as 'speech therapists'. This orientation stresses expressive language (giving messages) without paying due regard to receptive language (receiving messages). It also focuses on the form (structure) of language at the expense of function (use). Today, the intervention focus is much broader. Instead of focusing on just speech – or speech and language – the emphasis is on communication. Speech and language are viewed as tools for communication rather than as ends in themselves, and communication is understood to encompass both oral and non-oral modes of expression.

A similar shift of focus has occurred in the study of children's development of communication. Until about twenty years ago, the focus of study was on the form and structure of language. Today, the emphasis is on the purposes of children's communicative behaviour within meaningful social contexts (Cook *et al.*, 1996). A context is considered to be meaningful only if both a communication partner and a reason to communicate are in place. For this reason, speech therapy focusing on isolated skills development apart from the child's natural environment (e.g. classroom or home setting) is rarely considered to be appropriate for young children.

Speech/language concerns can take many different forms and relate to both the expressive and receptive domains of language. Concerns in speech and language are usually assessed in relation to certain subskills of language. These subskills include pragmatics, semantics, syntax, morphology and phonology. Knowing which subskills are involved in the breakdown of successful communication can provide valuable insights into the types of intervention strategy that may be most effective for an individual child. Many children with speech/language disabilities have deficits in more than one of these subskills.

Pragmatics

Pragmatics refer to rules and conventions that govern how language is used for communication in different situations. Pragmatics encompass both verbal and nonverbal aspects of communication, as well as the expressive and receptive domains of language (Cook *et al.*, 1996). Receptively, while children with deficits in the area of pragmatics may understand the meaning of individual words that are spoken, they may still 'miss the message' intended by the speaker. For example, if a teacher announces that it would be nice to have all the parents attend an open house at school, a child with pragmatic language difficulties may not understand that the teacher is suggesting that students invite or urge their parents to come to the open house. Unless the teacher specifically says, 'Vickie, ask your mother to come to the open house', Vickie may not know that this would be an appropriate response to what the teacher just said.

In addition to 'missing something' in reading other people's messages, children with pragmatic language skills may have trouble with expressive language as well. Here follow some examples of how pragmatic language deficits in the expressive domain might be manifested: (1) not knowing how to initiate, maintain or terminate conversations; (2) not knowing how to introduce new topics for conversation; (3) having difficulty adjusting communicative style to the speaking context, and (4) failing to consider the emotional impact of certain types of messages. Children with pragmatic deficits may fail to adjust the volume of their voice to different settings (e.g. libraries, hospitals), may make remarks that hurt the feelings of others (e.g. telling a classmate or an acquaintance 'You're too fat' or 'I don't like you'), and interject statements and questions completely unrelated to the topic of conversation.

When assessing young children for possible pragmatic language deficits, expectations for their age must be taken into consideration. A summary of the developmental stages of pragmatic language skills is presented in Table 4.1 and may be used to help identify children with pragmatic language difficulties.

A tool for assessing the pragmatic language development of young children is presented in Figure 4.1. This checklist of pragmatic language skills includes a rating scale which could be helpful for establishing a baseline (i.e. where the child performs prior to intervention) of an individual child's performance. This scale could also be used for periodic re-evaluation.

Table 4.1 Developmental sequence of pragmatic language skills

Age	*Communicative functions*	*Conversational competence*
0–5 mos.	Uses crying and cooing to express pleasure and pain	Responds to talking by looking at speaker Makes vocal sounds when played with
6–11 mos.	Begins using first words	Responds to mother's communicative acts by smiling and maintaining eye contact Plays games like 'peek-a-boo' and 'pat-a-cake' Responds with appropriate gestures to some words (e.g. waves when hears 'bye-bye') Responds when addressed (e.g. coos or gurgles in response to his or her name)
12–23 mos.	Uses voice and gestures to obtain a desired object Follows two or three consecutive commands Begins using simple sentences to give information or manipulate the listener (e.g., 'Me go.')	Looks at mother or father when asked 'Where is Mommy?' or 'Where is Daddy?' Uses and imitates more words instead of using gestures Refers to self by name
24–35 mos.	Understands some complex sentences Asks for help when needed	Understands and uses a vocabulary of about 20 words Uses at least three words in sequence (e.g. 'Me want cookie')
36–47 mos.	Asks questions Uses directive speech (e.g. commands, requests, threats)	Talks about experiences from recent past
4–6 yrs.	Gives useful information	Begins to be less egocentric and more social in conversations
7–8 yrs.	Understands purpose for doing something when given an oral explanation	Recognizes the close relationship between making friends and being accepted by adults and peers and having the ability to communicate effectively with others Identifies various emotions and implied meanings expressed through nonverbal communications By being courteous and attentive begins to respect the right of others to give their opinions

Child ______________________ Birthdate ______________________

Person completing form ______________________ Relationship to child ______________________

Date ______________________

Key 1 Needs no improvement 2 Acceptable 3 Needs improvement 4 Critical need for improvement 5 Non-existent

RECEPTIVE AREA

1. *Attending behaviour*

Makes eye contact	1 2 3 4 5
Maintains attention to speaker	1 2 3 4 5

2. *Auditory listening skills*

Attends to sounds	1 2 3 4 5
Responds to sounds	1 2 3 4 5
Localizes source of sounds	1 2 3 4 5
Listens actively to sounds	1 2 3 4 5
Attends to significant auditory information in presence of background noises (*selective attention*)	1 2 3 4 5
Maintains attention over a period of time (*sustained attention*)	1 2 3 4 5

3. *Comprehension of meaning*

'Reads' typical nonverbal cues (e.g. frowns, gestures)	1 2 3 4 5
Carries out requests or commands	1 2 3 4 5
Understands much of what is said to him or her (i.e. relates spoken language to what it represents)	1 2 3 4 5
Understands verbal hints (*implied messages*)	1 2 3 4 5
Understands questions	1 2 3 4 5
Interprets environmental sounds	1 2 3 4 5

EXPRESSIVE AREA

1. *Communicative functions*

Imitates sounds	1 2 3 4 5
Requests assistance	1 2 3 4 5
Requests information (i.e. asks appropriate questions)	1 2 3 4 5
Uses directive speech (e.g. commands, threats)	1 2 3 4 5
Expresses desires	1 2 3 4 5
Uses the names of objects, events, etc.	1 2 3 4 5
Formulates questions	1 2 3 4 5
Offers assistance	1 2 3 4 5
Disagrees verbally or argues	1 2 3 4 5
Justifies own actions (i.e. gives reasons)	1 2 3 4 5
Recognizes problems and offers solutions	1 2 3 4 5
Makes self understood (i.e. is able to get a point across)	1 2 3 4 5

continued

2. *Conversational competence*					
Uses good voice habits (i.e. neither too loud nor too soft)	1	2	3	4	5
Answers questions	1	2	3	4	5
Talks about experiences	1	2	3	4	5
Varies speech according to setting and other speakers	1	2	3	4	5
Acknowledges what another speaker has said	1	2	3	4	5
Demonstrates appropriate turn-taking behaviour	1	2	3	4	5
Initiates conversational topics	1	2	3	4	5
Makes conversational transitions in an appropriate manner	1	2	3	4	5
Participates willingly in social conversations	1	2	3	4	5
Makes suggestions and shares ideas	1	2	3	4	5
Provides sufficient (but not too much) information when answering questions	1	2	3	4	5
Communicates about self	1	2	3	4	5
Communicates about things outside self (i.e., describes objects)	1	2	3	4	5
Communicates about concrete experiences	1	2	3	4	5
Communicates abstract ideas	1	2	3	4	5
Describes an object or explains how something works	1	2	3	4	5
Tells a simple story in proper sequence	1	2	3	4	5
3. *Social interactive skills*					
Expresses feelings in socially acceptable ways	1	2	3	4	5
Honours established social conventions	1	2	3	4	5
Adapts a message to the social context	1	2	3	4	5
Initiates contact	1	2	3	4	5
Responds to contact	1	2	3	4	5
Engages in interactive play	1	2	3	4	5

Figure 4.1 Checklist of pragmatic skills

Semantics

Semantics refers to the meaning of words. Young children generally learn word meanings through direct experience with objects or events relating to what the words stand for. For example, children learn to associate the word 'book' with the actual object it represents when they have books read to them and available to them for their inspection. Children may have a great deal of difficulty, however, associating the word 'desert' with the type of geographical region it stands for if they have never been to a desert. Failure to understand the meaning of words may thus be related directly to the child's lack of experience. Adults can enhance a child's development in semantics by pairing vocabulary with actual objects and experiences. For example, when talking about a basket, adults can make a variety of baskets available for children's exploration. Adults can also assist young children in the area of semantics by using the names of objects and events when talking to the children versus using unspecific terminology. For example, saying 'Put the book on the table' is more instructive than saying 'Put this over there'.

At times, a child's problems in the area of semantics does not become evident until he or she is challenged to understand the meaning of words in combinations, such as 'more juice?' or 'yellow book'. To help a child understand words in combination, adults should continue pairing actual objects with words and avoid speaking too rapidly.

Sometimes, a child's difficulty with semantics is revealed as much in his or her expressive language as it is in receptive language. If children tend to use 'indefinite descriptors' such as 'that thing' or 'this one', instead of using the names of things (book, cup, chair), they may have semantic language problems.

Syntax

Syntax refers to rules determining correct word order in sentences. Certain patterns of words form the structure for statements, while other patterns form the structure for questions and commands. For example, in making a statement we might say, 'Jon is working at the computer'. In asking a question, the word order is different and might be 'Is Jon working at the computer?' For a command, the word order might be 'Jon, work at the computer'. Obviously, for children to give and receive messages effectively, they must be able to express and interpret a variety of sentence structures.

Morphology

Morphology refers to rules for changing the form of individual words, such as changing a word from singular to plural or using a different verb tense. While there may be other reasons why children have difficulty with morphology, a hearing loss would certainly contribute to the problem. Even a mild to moderate hearing loss can cause a child to miss the ending sounds on words such as 's' or 'es' to form plurals, or the 'ed' and 'ing' used with different verb tenses.

Phonology

Phonology refers to the sound systems of speech and language and involves not only individual speech sounds (i.e. phonemes), but the pitch and rhythm of language as well. There are forty-four phonemes in the English language, and most children learn to produce all of them by the time they are 4 years old. Articulation errors in the production of certain consonants (especially 'l', 'r', 's', 'j' and 'z') and many consonant blends (e.g. 'sh', 'ch', 'th'), however, are still within the range of normalcy for 4-year-olds and should not be cause for alarm.

Recommended practices

Interventions to promote communication skills usually focus on enhancing the ability of children with special needs in one or more of the following areas: (1) to receive information from others; (2) to share information with others; (3) to use language to mediate their actions and cognition, and (4) to control their environment (Odom and McLean, 1996). To be consistent with this focus, assessment for communication concerns should consider the comprehension and production of content, form and social functions of the child's performance. Recommended practices also suggest that the child's communicative performance be assessed in a variety of situations (e.g. home, classroom, playground) and 'with a variety of communicative partners represented in the child's everyday life, including peers without disabilities' (Odom and McLean, 1996, p. 394).

In working with young children to enhance their communication skills, adults should recognize and respond positively to the child's communicative attempts and build on the child's interests, requests and comments. Speech/language therapy for young children should usually be done within the child's natural environment (i.e. classroom or home setting) and should include typically developing peers as well as familiar adults (Odom and McLean, 1996). In addition, the environment should be arranged 'to enable and accommodate children's unique receptive and expressive modes of communicating' which may include properly functioning assistive devices such as hearing aids, glasses, communication boards and so on (Odom and McClean, 1996, p. 396).

Emergent literacy concerns

Dictionaries sometimes define literacy as the ability to read and write, and discussions about the topic often suggest that people fall into one of two categories: those who are literate and those who are illiterate, or unable to read. Issues related to literacy, however, are not so clearly defined. Perhaps a good starting point for discussing some of these issues is with the understanding that illiteracy, as a distinct state, does not really exist. It is more accurate to think of the literacy development of any individual as being on a continuum of increasing competence, with no one being at the zero point. From the moment of birth – or perhaps even sooner – children begin the process of 'reading' their surroundings and learning the intricacies of language. This is a part of literacy development which certainly precedes reading instruction.

Literacy is a process (rather than an endpoint) and involves four areas of learning: listening, language, writing and reading (Wardle, 2000). Young children need experience in all of these areas in order to develop the competencies associated with literacy. We can thus describe 'becoming literate' as a dynamic process, through which literacy-related competencies grow and change. Literacy, then, is much broader than reading; and ways of achieving literacy-related competencies go beyond 'methods of instruction'. Literacy development can, in fact, be supported in a wide range of settings and activities, some of which involve no print at all.

There are many unacknowledged ways of learning to read and write. Some of these fall into the category of 'folk practices'; that is, long-established practices associated with what many parents and children often do at home, such as reading a book together (Wilson, 2000a). In addition to reading to children, other 'folk practices' which foster literacy include playing with different sounds (e.g. cooing, rhyming words, animal sounds) and conversing about a topic of mutual interest.

Referring to such 'folk practices' as ways to foster literacy may suggest that literacy occurs spontaneously. This premise, however, would be misleading. Literacy does not occur in a vacuum. Literacy skills emerge within a community of literacy. As the focus of a community is on people versus materials, commercial or 'teaching' materials (such as worksheets, basal readers and skill-building programmes) have little to do with emergent literacy. Human interactions such as sharing a picture book, telling a story and talking about experiences are central to emergent literacy.

The term 'emergent literacy' refers to the reading- and writing-related behaviours that proceed and develop into conventional literacy. Children who are still in the process of learning what reading and writing are all about are sometimes referred to as 'emergent readers'. At this stage, they are also in the process of learning how to read and write.

As children learn to read, they also grow in phonemic awareness – namely the insight that spoken words are composed of somewhat separable sounds. Not only is phonemic awareness one of the prerequisite skills to becoming a proficient reader, it has also been identified as one of the best predictors of early reading and writing (Graves *et al.*, 2001; Robinson *et al.*, 2000). There is, in fact, a substantial body of research supporting the link between phonological processing difficulties and the development of reading skills. 'These studies emphasised the important role of deficits in phonological awareness at the preschool stage for predicting reading problems' (Most *et al.*, 2000, p. 89).

Phonemic awareness is not the same as phonics – that is, it is not knowledge about which letters represent particular sounds. Phonemic awareness is an insight about speech itself. It is an awareness of the sounds of language. Phonemic awareness thus requires attention to the sounds that are contained within words. While phonemic awareness is not necessary for speaking or for listening, it is vital to reading. Phonemic awareness includes 'the ability to treat speech as an object by analyzing or manipulating its units rather than to focus on the meaning' (Most *et al.*, 2000, p. 90). With phonemic awareness an individual must be able to shift attention away from the content, or meaning, to the form of speech.

Phonemic awareness has not always been well understood. The term itself first appeared in 1966 in the doctoral dissertation of Marie Clay. Since then, phonemic (or phonological) awareness has been recognized as 'one of the most important concepts to arise out of the past 20 years of research in reading' (Robinson *et al.*, 2000, p. 50).

According to the literature, phonemic awareness does not develop spontaneously or naturally (Graves *et al.*, 2001; Robinson *et al.*, 2000). It is fostered, however, by many of the 'pre-reading' activities typically found in many homes and early childhood classrooms. These activities include telling stories, sharing picture books, singing songs and playing with rhymes. Through frequent participation in such activities, most children (estimated at more than 80 per cent) will achieve phonemic awareness by the middle of first grade.

Some children, however, will not pick up on the concept as fast as others. For them, intervention should be initiated. The extent of intervention, however, should be based on the individual child. 'How much attention to phoneme awareness is necessary depends on the child' (Robinson *et al.*, 2000, p. 52). Fortunately, for children who need a little more help, findings from research studies suggest 'phonemic awareness can be taught successfully' (Robinson *et al.*, 2000, p. 76). Recent studies of phonemic awareness training have investigated the relative merits of different approaches to such training. The primary approaches are (1) oral language training, (2) interaction with print, and (3) a combination of oral language training and interaction with print. These studies suggest 'that programmes that encourage high levels of student engagement and interaction with print (for example, through read-alouds, shared reading, and invented spelling) yield as much growth in phonemic awareness abilities as programs that offer only a focus on oral language teaching' (Robinson *et al.*, 2000, p. 76). The overall recommendation drawn from this research is to combine interaction with print and paying explicit attention to sound structure in spoken words.

While it is important for teachers and administrators to understand the nature and significance of phonemic awareness to reading success, they should take care not to misuse or over-generalize the related research findings. These findings do not support such practices as dedicating specific amounts of instructional time to phonemic awareness training for all children or requiring the use of a particular training programme for all children (Robinson *et al.*, 2000). The following suggestions for developing a rich literacy programme for young children are offered by Robinson and colleagues (2000). These guidelines are designed to foster both phonemic awareness and success in learning to read.

- provide a print-rich environment;
- engage students as both readers and writers;
- provide language activities that focus on both the form and content of spoken and written language;
- provide opportunities for students to practise reading and writing for real reasons in a variety of contexts.

It would be a mistake to consider early reading difficulties an isolated area of concern. Children with early reading difficulties are at risk of developing long-term learning disabilities and school maladjustment. Children who fail to develop phonemic awareness by the middle of the first grade have a slim chance of becoming successful readers, especially under current instructional plans (Robinson *et al.*, 2000). Low levels of social acceptance, peer rejection and problems with making friends are also related to early reading difficulties (Most *et al.*, 2000).

Related conditions

Down syndrome

Chromosomal disorders are a common cause of disabilities, with Down syndrome representing the most recognizable and commonly known of such disorders. Down syndrome is a non-inherited chromosomal abnormality and is usually (in 95 per cent of cases) associated with an extra chromosome. Developmental and educational outcomes for children with Down syndrome vary widely, from only mild to very severe implications for development and learning.

Children with Down syndrome are usually recognized by certain physical features evident in infancy. Such features include a small head with a flattened back, extra skin at the inner corner of the eyes making them appear to be slanted, low muscle tone, a single crease across the palm and soles of the feet, a flat nose bridge, and short, wide hands with an inward curve of the little finger. In addition, a high palate and a small oral cavity often lead to tongue protrusion and/or drooling. Medical conditions also tend to accompany this disability, to the point where in the early part of the century, the life expectancy of children with Down syndrome was only 9–12 years. Today, unless there are significant associated health problems, the life expectancy of individuals with Down syndrome is greater than 50 years (Hanson and Lynch, 1995).

Children with Down syndrome tend to function closest to their peers during the first two years of life. As they grow a little older and are faced with the demands of language and higher order cognitive skills, the discrepancy between the performance of children with Down syndrome and their typically developing peers usually widens (Batshaw and Perret, 1992). Even with this increasing gap, serving children with Down syndrome in mainstream programmes is usually quite beneficial to them. 'Playing and learning alongside typically developing peers often provides the motivation that children with Down Syndrome need to increase motor and communication skills, as well as opportunities to practice social interactions that form the foundation for later relationships' (Hanson and Lynch, 1995, p. 22).

In addition to providing a stimulating environment designed to enhance development across developmental domains, intervention for children with Down syndrome should also include a close monitoring of their hearing and vision. Well over 50 per cent of children with Down syndrome have vision and hearing impairments. The hearing impairments are often related to middle ear disease, which is more common in children with Down syndrome than in the general population. Thus to prevent or minimize the development of secondary handicaps, the vision and hearing of children with Down syndrome should be routinely assessed. It is also critically important that an interdisciplinary team of professionals work closely together in planning and implementing an intervention programme for young children with Down syndrome. Physical and occupational therapists should be involved, as should communication specialists.

Traumatic brain injury

Traumatic brain injury is a disabling condition that occurs after birth; that is, it is an acquired injury to the brain. Head injuries may be caused by physical assault (abuse) or accidental trauma to the head such as a car accident or a serious fall. Data from 1998 (Howard *et al.*, 2001) indicate that child abuse is the cause of 90 per cent of cases of traumatic brain injury (TBI). Traumatic brain injury results in total or partial functional disability or psychosocial impairment (or both) and adversely affects a child's educational performance. Impairments are often expressed in one or more of the following areas: cognition; language; memory; attention; reasoning; abstract thinking; judgement; problem solving; sensory; perceptual; and motor abilities; psychosocial behaviour; information processing; and speech.

The severity and manifestation of brain injury depends on the extent and location of damage and ranges from mild to severe. The chances of decreasing the symptoms of brain injury are greater for infants and preschoolers than for older children, as their brains are still growing at a rapid rate. At any age, however, early (i.e. as soon after the injury as possible) and ongoing intervention offers the best hope for improvement. Children with afflicted TBI (abuse) are more likely to experience long-term deficits than children who suffer accidental TBI. This may be due to the concomitant environmental factors associated with child abuse (Howard *et al.*, 2001).

Case study – James

Background information

Seven-year-old James is in a Year 2 class at Dorr Primary School. James has had frequent bouts of otitis media (middle ear infection) during his early childhood years, with accompanying hearing loss. While the medical condition seems to be under control, related social and academic concerns make him eligible for special education services. In the area of speech/language development, James seems to be functioning one to two years behind his peers.

James is fascinated by living things, especially animals. He spends a considerable amount of time watching the birds clustering around the bird feeder and the fish swimming in the aquarium. His favourite books are about dolphins, birds, dogs and insects; and play outdoors for James usually involves digging in the ground or poking around among leaves and grass. The intervention team identified several strategies relating to his unique interests to foster James' communication competencies. These strategies were also designed to foster emergent literacy skills.

The first strategy was to focus on materials and circumstances which tended to engage James' attention. Ms Smith, the Year 2 teacher, noted James' interest in living things and decided to join him in some of his explorations. She found a large chart depicting the various songbirds that frequented the bird feeder. She talked with James about the different birds he had already seen at the feeder and 'wondered out loud' which birds are there most often. She suggested 'keeping track' of the different birds seen at the feeder over the next three days. With James, she constructed a simple chart with pictures to record the information. Ms Smith helped James to write his name on the chart, attached it to a clipboard and hung it near the observation window.

James showed great interest in this project and eagerly recorded information about the different birds he saw. After the third day of observation and recording, Ms Smith suggested that James might like to 'write' a report about his project. She offered to do the writing if he would tell her what to write. James liked the idea, but suggested they write a book instead of a report. Ms Smith agreed readily and the two began the process.

Discussion

In this scenario, Ms Smith identified what James was interested in and then provided materials and devised related activities to extend his understanding about the topic (i.e. birds). In addition to providing information and new understanding, Ms Smith also introduced James to different ways of thinking about the topic. Instead of simply learning the names of birds, Ms Smith encouraged closer observation and data collection skills. She did this not by showing and telling, but by engaging James in an interesting and meaningful activity. By working with him, Ms Smith was able to elicit and maintain his engagement over time.

Another strategy suggested by the intervention team was to arrange the physical and social environments in ways that would invite and reinforce self-initiated activities. Again, Ms Smith used James' interest in living things to implement this strategy. In the process of writing the *Book of Birds* with James, Ms Smith brought in several library books about birds. James spent time examining these books and then suggested that their book should include some pictures. Ms Smith and James looked at the library books and noticed that some pictures were photographs and others were drawings of birds. James said that he would like to have both photographs and drawings in their book, so Ms Smith looked for ways to facilitate this.

In addition to bringing in a camera and helping James get 'some good shots' of the birds, she also introduced bird-related materials to the art centre, including some feathers. She made a rubbing of a feather and suggested that it might be used to decorate some of the pages in the book. James agreed and decided to make some rubbings of his own. He also dipped a feather in some paint and discovered that the feather worked like a paintbrush. James was excited about his discovery and called Ms Smith over to the table to share it with her. Ms Smith, in turn, suggested that James should also show some of the other children what he had discovered. James was very proud to do so. Here, James was motivated to communicate, since he felt he had something important to share.

The physical environment, in this instance, was arranged to include new materials relating to the bird project, while the social environment (especially Ms Smith's availability and support) reinforced James' own initiatives. In the process, James was exposed to various forms of representation and discovered interesting properties about such materials as books, feathers and paints. He also gained confidence and competence in purposeful planning, decision making and social interaction.

In addition to implementing the strategies suggested by the intervention team, Ms Smith was able to capitalize on 'teachable moments' in the classroom to foster James' competence and confidence in using speech and language to interact with others. One such moment occurred a short while after the *Book of Birds* was complete and shared with the rest of the class. This incident involved one of the other children, Lynette, who recalled that several weeks previously a local author visited the classroom and that the children had the opportunity to interview her. Lynette suggested that they interview James about his book. Concerned that a 'whole class' interview might be intimidating to James and that he may not handle it well, Ms Smith suggested that the interview be conducted as a news report, with Lynette serving as the interviewer. The children loved the idea! Ms Smith used this opportunity to introduce the class to different types of interview done on radio and television and involved them in interviewing each other with pretend microphones. Ms Smith thus used a 'teachable moment' (i.e. the moment Lynette suggested interviewing James) to plan a class activity that would involve the whole group while focusing on several of James' targeted intervention goals, including using speech and language to relate personal experiences.

5

SOCIAL, EMOTIONAL AND BEHAVIOURAL CONCERNS

Social interaction concerns

Humans are social beings. Even as newborns, they have the neurological system to selectively attend to the social responses of people around them and to engage in behaviours that illicit social responses from others (McEvoy and Odom, 1996). Initially, the behaviours in infants that generate social responses are not consciously purposeful – i.e. infants do not engage in such behaviours as crying and fussing for the purpose of getting a social response. They cry or fuss because they are uncomfortable, hungry or feeling distressed. Such behaviours, however, do tend to elicit social responses from others, usually in the form of positive attention, food and/or other sources of comfort.

Infants gradually perceive the connection between their signals of distress and the accompanying social responses. They then begin to use such behaviours in a purposeful way (e.g. they cry to 'tell' adults that they are uncomfortable or hungry). Attentive adults understand the infants' messages and respond by tending to their needs. Over time, infants learn that social behaviour is structured around certain predictable patterns. This predictability tends to foster feelings of security and attachment and thus the emotional development of young children.

The predictable pattern of social behaviour also provides incentives for infants and young children to engage in further social interactions. They have learned that participation in this pattern can prove beneficial to them. This predictability also provides incentives for adults to engage in further social interactions with the child. Adults feel good about being able to read or interpret the infant's messages and successful in providing appropriate responses. For example, adults hear the infant's cry, interpret the cry as hunger, provide food for the infant, and then see that he or she is comforted by the food. The adult is rewarded by being able to comfort the child, and the child is rewarded by having his or her needs met.

While in the twentieth century social learning theory placed the emphasis on the caregiver's contributions to the social development of the child, more recent understandings about the reciprocal nature of social interactions indicate that the child's contributions also play a major role (Rothbart, 1996). Our understanding of the child's contributions has been influenced by a number of factors, including the following:

- Piaget's study of cognitive development indicates that children individually construct their own understanding of the physical and social world from their experiences with it.
- The work of psychoanalytically oriented investigators (e.g. Spitz, 1965) have called attention to the impact of infant biology on social and emotional development.
- Studies on attachment indicate that the infant's contributions play a major role in the nature of the caregiver–infant attachment, and that as the child's maturational status changes, so does the nature of the child's relationship with the caregiver (Ainsworth *et al.*, 1972, 1978).
- Studies in infancy research indicate that even young infants possess a set of complex skills or competencies (Howard *et al.*, 1997).

As children grow a little older (but still during their preschool years), interactions with peers become an important part of the child's social development (Kemple and Hartle, 1997). The confidence and competence with which young children engage in social interactions with peers seem to be related positively to the robustness of their social competence and secure attachment relationships acquired earlier with their caregivers. A similar relationship seems to exist between early social competence and more advanced development in cognitive and communication skills (Odom, 2000). It should not be surprising, then, that the early childhood literature stresses repeatedly the importance of social competence to the overall development of the child (McEvoy and Odom, 1996).

While most typically developing children learn to interact confidently and competently with adults and peers without any special intervention or instruction, the same is not true for many children with disabilities. Because of the critical nature of social competence to overall development, early intervention programmes often make the promotion of social development an essential aspect of their programme (Guralnick, 1994; Odom *et al.*, 1999).

As stated above, the social development of young children proceeds in a transactional manner, with both the caregiver and the child playing critical roles. Characteristics and/or behaviours of both the caregiver and the child will thus influence the nature of the transactions (i.e. social interactions) that occur between them. If one side of the social transaction is ineffective or unresponsive, the other side will certainly be negatively affected. If the caregiver is absent, unable to interpret the child's cries or unresponsive, the child's incentive and opportunities for learning to be socially competent and emotionally secure will be diminished. While maternal responsivity to infants' behaviour appears across cultures and seems to be a universal principle of early child development, some research indicates that socio-economic and demographic variables (e.g. maternal education level) influence the degree to which maternal responsivity occurs (McEvoy and Odom, 1996). Low levels of responsivity (e.g. not recognizing and/or responding to the infant's social cues) can lead to delayed development of social and emotional competencies in the infant and young child. A high level of responsivity, on the other hand, encourages infants and young children to engage in positive social interaction with caregivers (Lussier *et al.*, 1994) and leads to healthy attachment relationships in the first year of life (van Ijzendoorn *et al.*, 1995). Secure attachment relationships, in turn, foster the development of many social behaviours and the formation of healthy peer relationships (Lyons-Ruth *et al.*, 1993).

The competencies and behaviours of children also influence the nature of the social interactions that occur between adult and child. If children are unable to receive or interpret adults' responses, they cannot provide the expected feedback or rewards that serve as incentives for the adults to provide the consistency or predictability of response. Children with disabilities are often unable to provide the same kind of positive social feedback to their caregivers and other adults – or even to their peers – as can children without disabilities. A child who is deaf, for example, cannot hear the mother's comforting voice as she prepares a bottle in response to the infant's cry. This child may then cry longer and be more difficult to calm than a child who is not deaf. Similarly, a child who is blind cannot see the teacher's smile and outstretched arms, and may thus be less responsive to invitations to let go of the mother's hand and join the group of children around the science table. This reluctance may be viewed as a problem in social and/or emotional development. The underlying problem, however, relates directly to the child's disability – i.e. not being able to see.

In addition to sensory impairments, other factors within the child that can hinder social and emotional development include medical problems, physical disabilities and mental retardation. Young children with medical problems are often irritable, tend to tire easily and have irregular sleep patterns. In trying to deal with their child's medical problems and related concerns, parents may feel stressed and frustrated. They may also have difficulty reading their child's social cues and have a tendency to withdraw or become passive in interacting with their child.

Medical problems can also negatively affect children's social interactions at school. Children with medical problems may miss school frequently and may not feel as comfortable as their classmates about the daily routine, the proper use of materials and so on. Due to absences, it may also take children with medical problems longer to get to know their classmates and to make friends. In addition, medical problems may cause children to tire easily and thus be less inclined to join the other children in group activities.

A similar pattern of diminished interaction may occur with children who have a physical disability or mental retardation. In either case, children's response to adults' attempts to engage them in social interaction may be delayed and less gratifying. Parents and teachers may then withdraw from children with special needs and be less inclined to expend the time and energy required to engage them in social interaction.

Children with disabilities often face similar problems in peer relationships. During early childhood, peer interactions occur primarily through the vehicle of play. Children with disabilities, however, tend to engage in more solitary and less social play than do their non-disabled peers (Odom *et al.*, 1999). Children with disabilities, who often engage in less competent interactions with their peers, also tend to receive lower peer-rating scores than do children who are more socially competent (Odom *et al.*, 1999). As a result, children with disabilities tend to be less involved in interactions with peers than children without disabilities. This situation puts the children with disabilities in a special bind. As social skills are learned primarily through social interactions, fewer interactions result in fewer opportunities for learning the very behaviours which young children need to become more socially competent. Fostering the social competence of young children with disabilities, then, should be one of the major goals of early intervention programmes (Odom *et al.*, 1999).

Social competence, in this context, may be defined as the 'ability of young children to successfully and appropriately select and carry out their interpersonal goals' (Guralnick, 1990, p. 4). According to Guralnick (1990), social competence is drawn from skills in various development domains. These, he says, must be organized over time. 'Gains in cognitive, motor, and language development are important correlates of improved social competence' (Guralnick, 1990, p. 5).

Social interaction and inclusion[1]

The social competence of young children with disabilities is related closely to how well they do in an inclusive educational setting. Before discussing this concept, a distinction needs to be made between the terms 'integration' and 'inclusion'. While these terms are often used interchangeably, there is

1 An earlier version of this section was published in *Early Childhood News* (March/April 2002). It is used here with permission and referenced.

a great deal of difference between the two. 'Integration' usually refers to the placement of children with disabilities in the regular education classroom. 'Inclusion', on the other hand, means taking in as part of the whole so that each child is included in *all* aspects of the programme. In the context of meeting the needs of young children with disabilities, integration alone is empty and shallow. Integration without inclusion leads to physical proximity without social affinity. It develops situations where children are physically integrated but socially isolated. Inclusion in the social dimension of a programme is of special concern, as children who are not socially included miss out on many valuable opportunities for growth.

For some children with special educational needs, simple inclusion in a programme with socially competent peers may be sufficient intervention for supporting positive peer interactions. Many children with disabilities, however, require more intense intervention with carefully planned and supported opportunities to interact with peers.

Social isolation

There are a number of factors affecting the extent to which young children will interact with each other. One factor has to do with the social competence of the children involved. While many typically developing children enjoy social competence without any special instruction, young children with special needs often do not. Children with special needs are thus at greater risk of social rejection and isolation (Odom, 2000). It follows, then, that two children in the same classroom – one with a disability, one without a disability – may have vastly different experiences (Odom, 2000). In the social realm, the child with special needs is more likely to experience isolation, while the child without special needs can anticipate rewarding relationships.

Some manifestations of social isolation are blatantly obvious. Consider the experiences of young children on a field trip to a local park. The children bounded off the bus and raced towards the visitors' centre. The children were laughing and talking excitedly to each other and with the adults who accompanied them. After most of the other children were already in the building, one child with braces on her legs got off the bus with a teacher's assistant. While the assistant led the girl to some nearby picnic tables, her gaze followed the last of her classmates entering the visitors' centre. The little girl and her assistant waited in the picnic area for at least twenty minutes before the group joined them to eat lunch. The child with special needs was seated with her aide throughout lunch, although physical assistance for eating was never required. She was also accompanied back to the bus while her classmates were still eating or milling about in the picnic area. During this entire period there were no social interactions between the child with special needs and the rest of the children – nor did the child with special needs ever get to see the maps, the pictures and the other people in the visitors' centre.

Meyer (2001) shares a similar story about Jessica, a young girl in a wheelchair. In this instance, a photograph was taken on a field trip to a park. A close look at the picture shows Jessica in the front row. She is sitting in her wheelchair, with her teacher aide next to her. The aide is the only adult in the picture of the children. As Meyer describes the situation, 'Jessica did not need "supportive picture taking". She did not need to have anybody there with her, she was quite capable of smiling for the picture along with everyone else' (p. 26).

Membership and relationships

Odom (2000) states that 'if children with disabilities are to reap the benefits of participation in classes with typically developing children, they must be socially integrated into the inclusive program' (p. 24). While Odom also indicates that there is not yet a well-established criterion for determining the degree to which children are socially integrated, it seems obvious that, for Jessica and the other child discussed above, success has not yet been achieved. Successful inclusion extends beyond membership; it must also involve positive relationships.

Meyer (2001) discusses six different types of social relationships which, she says, apply to all children. The six types, or 'Frames of Friendship', are: (1) Best Friend, (2) Regular Friend, (3) Just Another Child, (4) I'll Help, (5) Inclusion Child, (6) Ghost or Guest. It is appropriate for all of us to experience these six Frames of Friendship in different circumstances and with different people. Problems arise when a child's social experiences all fall within certain frames and do not include positive social relationships and friendships with peers (Meyer, 2001). For children with special needs, being 'Just Another Child', 'a Regular Friend' or a 'Best Friend' are the Frames of Friendship they are less likely to experience. These children's experiences are often restricted to being a 'Ghost or Guest', an 'Inclusion Child' or in an 'I'll Help' relationship (where the child with special needs is always the one receiving the help).

The child with special needs becomes a 'Ghost' when everyone in the room goes about their business as if the child with a disability does not exist. Other children might even be told not to stare at the child with a disability or to ask questions about his or her condition or special equipment. The child becomes a 'Guest' when he or she is placed in the regular classroom on a trial basis. If the 'insiders' can decide to solve the problem by excluding the 'outsider', the child with special needs was never more than a guest in the classroom. Just as caring families never consider 'disowning' or 'getting rid' of a child when there is a problem, so truly inclusive classrooms operate from the premise that all the children belong.

Concerns associated with the 'Inclusion Child' status include seeing and relating to the child with special needs as being so different as to require special treatment, even from his or her peers. This special treatment sometimes takes the form of over-protection, exemptions from rules or 'babying' the child with special needs. Meyer (2001) shares the example of a young school-age child using 'baby talk' and trying to talk 'like a teacher' to the classmate with severe disabilities. She observed that, 'on some occasions, it almost looked as if the nondisabled child was playing with a pet' (p. 18). This is certainly not a desirable social experience for either child.

The 'I'll Help' status appears in the social lives of many children who are always being helped by peers, but are not expected to help anyone else in return. There are some fairly common practices in integrated classrooms that tend to foster the 'I'll Help' frame of friendship. One such practice involves posting a list of 'helpers' including who will push Tommy's wheelchair or who will hold Jenni's hand as the class walks to the music room. 'If children continually describe those interactions as "working with" and "helping" the child with disabilities, what would otherwise be normalized helping situations turn into a hierarchical social status among children' (Meyer, 2001, p. 18). Obviously, an emphasis on this Frame of Friendship is not a desirable outcome of an 'integrated experience'.

Play and social development

To help a child with special needs to experience the joy of being 'Just Another Child', a 'Regular Friend' or 'a Best Friend', the role of play needs to be considered, as children tend to develop friendships through play activities. Interactive play also serves as an important context in which children acquire both social skills such as turn taking, sharing and co-operation, and social knowledge including the ability to understand other people's thoughts, perceptions and emotions.

Interactive play, sometimes referred to as 'social play', differs from other types of play (i.e. object, symbolic and motor play), in that its major focus is on play with others versus playing alone. Original scales, focusing on the developmental progression of social play, outlined four different social levels: solitary, parallel, associative and co-operative (Parten, 1932). These original scales have been extensively critiqued and enhanced over the years (Johnson *et al.*, 1987). Later scales, developed by Carollee Howes (1980), is perhaps the most useful enhancement of the developmental progression of social play for assessment and intervention purposes. Howes' system (see Figure 5.1) analyses social play, particularly parallel play, in a more fine-tuned manner than Parten's original formulation. The different categories represent increases in the complexity of interaction between play partners and could be useful for assessment and intervention purposes.

Level	*Category*	*Description*
Level 1	Parallel play	Children are engaged in similar activities without paying any attention to one another.
Level 2	Mutual regard	Children are engaged in similar activities with awareness of and some attention to each other. They engage in no verbalization or other social bids.
Level 3	Simple social	Children are engaged in similar activities along with social bids such as talking, smiling, and offering toys.
Level 4	Complementary	Children are collaborating in the same activity with mutual awareness but no social bids.
Level 5	Complementary	Children are collaborating in the same reciprocal activity with social bids.

Figure 5.1 Howes' categories of social play

The category or level of play in which a child is engaged most of the time gives some indication of the types of social skills he or she has developed and the types of goals appropriate for an individualized social intervention plan. The category of play in which a child is engaged at any particular time, however, might not be an accurate reflection of the child's level of social competence. In addition to child factors such as the child's skill level, motivation and interest, environmental factors also influence the level of social play behaviour. Who are the play partners? What play materials are available? What events have preceded this play period? Such questions are relevant to determining appropriate intervention strategies.

Emotional competence

Social situations are rarely devoid of emotion, and emotional competence plays an important role in establishing and maintaining satisfying peer relationships (Garner and Estep, 2001). This seems to be especially so at the early childhood level, where peer interactions are often characterized by high levels of positive and negative emotion. Children who are knowledgeable about emotions and who can control the expression of emotion are more likely to negotiate complex interpersonal exchanges with their peers.

Research indicates that children who are adept at understanding expressive and situational cues of emotion are better liked by peers than other children (Garner and Estep, 2001). While social-emotional development was, at times, viewed as a single developmental domain, emotional competence is now being recognized as a domain of development that is separate from (yet related to) social competence (Garner and Estep, 2001). Emotionally competent children know how to vary their behaviour to correspond with their play partner's thoughts and feelings. They are also less likely to be involved in angry disputes with peers and to use constructive strategies in response to potentially conflicting situations.

Research on emotional competence suggests that there are different types or aspects of this area of development. Garner and Estep's research (2001) focused on four types of emotional competence: situation knowledge, explanations of emotions, positivity of emotional expression, and emotional intensity. The first two (situation knowledge and explanations of emotions) represent children's knowledge of emotions – that is, an awareness of one's own and others' emotions. Skills related to knowledge of emotions include (1) inferring the thoughts and feelings of others, (2) justifying own behaviour to peers, and (3) expressing sensitivity to the emotions of others. Children who are deficient in emotional knowledge tend to misinterpret social and emotional cues which, in turn, interferes with their ability to initiate and maintain positive social interactions with peers. Children high in emotional knowledge, on the other hand, experience a greater number of positive peer interactions than do other children (Garner and Estep, 2001).

The other two types of emotional competence (positivity of emotional expression and emotional intensity) focus on children's expressivity. These two types relate to how emotions (both positive and negative) are expressed. Emotionally competent children are able to modulate emotional expressions and behaviour (Garner and Estep, 2001). Situation knowledge relates to children's understanding of contextual clues used to infer the cause of an emotional display. Situation knowledge also relates to children's decisions about how to respond to emotionally charged situations. Children who are knowledgeable about emotions tend to have fewer negative exchanges with peers, and, when disagreements do occur, they seem better able to use reasoned argument to resolve the conflict than children with deficits in emotional understanding (Garner and Estep, 2001).

Explanations of emotions relate to children's ability to talk about the causes and consequences of others' emotions. Such emotional discourse skills are often used to negotiate conflicts and misunderstandings. Children's talk about emotions also provides a constructive way to convey their own feelings and to elicit feedback about those feelings. Research has found, for example, that children's explanations of emotions were related positively to their expressions of sadness and fear in the peer environment (Denham, 2001).

Positivity of emotional expression deals with emotion management skills. Children use their emotion management skills to initiate and maintain peer interactions, to offer comfort and to minimize negative interactions. Related research indicates that children who have difficulty managing the expression of emotion are less likely to respond appropriately during highly charged negative interactions with peers (Garner and Estep, 2001).

Healthy emotional development has been identified as a key factor in facilitating the ability to learn (Roffey and O'Reirdan, 2001). Different aspects of emotional development include the feelings children have, how they express their emotion, how they understand what they feel, their control of impulses, and their awareness and understanding of others' emotions.

To guide young children appropriately in dealing with their emotions, it is necessary to be aware of what the expectations are at different stages of development. Roffey and O'Reirdan (2001) developed a list of skills and abilities that can be expected of most 5-year-old children who are developing at an optimum rate. In terms of emotional understanding and behaviour, the skills and abilities identified include:

- enthusiastic and motivated to learn
- experiences a wide range of feelings, but not necessarily able to identify them clearly
- aware of feelings and able to relate these to wants
- has a range of varied, complex and flexible ways of expressing emotions
- uses language for emotional control and expression
- increasing emotional control but is not able to hide feelings completely
- uses play to work out emotional issues
- growing sensitivity to the feelings of others
- cares about pets and younger children
- comforts distressed peers
- identifies what is right and wrong in relation to family and cultural values
- tests behavioural boundaries from time to time.

Children who are slow to develop emotional competencies are at risk from a host of negative developmental outcomes, including disruptive behaviour, impaired social functioning and poor school performance (Roffey and O'Reirdan, 2001; Shields *et al.*, 2001). Children who are unable to monitor and modulate their emotional arousal usually find it very difficult (or impossible) to maintain an optimal level of engagement with the school context (Shields *et al.*, 2001). They tend to have trouble adjusting to classroom structure, complying with rules and limits, and negotiating co-operative relationships with their peers.

There are a number of research studies supporting a positive correlation between young children's emotional competence and their success in school. Garner and Estep's research (2001), for example, suggests that children who are knowledgeable about emotions and able to control the expression of emotions in the classroom may perform better on cognitive tasks than other children. Other research studies found that preschoolers' emotion regulation at the start of the school year was associated with school adjustment at year's end, whereas early emotional liability/negativity predicted poorer outcomes (Shields et al, 2001). Such research supports school-based interventions focusing on children's emotional development.

Preventive interventions recognize that teachers can play a key role in fostering children's emotional competence (Denham, 2001). Examples of specific interventions include coaching students on emotion recognition, coping, situation knowledge and perspective-taking skills (Shields *et al.*, 2001). While these more didactic interventions have proven effective, studies examining teachers' naturally occurring influences indicate that preschoolers' secure emotional attachments to their teachers also influence children's display of emotions in school. Preschool children who develop secure attachments to their teachers are less likely to engage in unregulated anger and behaviour problems. They are also more likely to exhibit positive emotions in the school setting (Shields *et al.*, 2001). A warm, close relationship between student and teacher, then, may play an important role in young children's emerging emotional competence.

Research findings indicate that emotion regulation and emotion understanding play an important role in children's classroom adjustment. According to Shields and colleagues (2001), however, 'In the majority of preschool contexts . . . emotion socialization does not have an easily defined place in the curriculum, and emotional issues are likely to receive sustained attention from school personnel only during crisis situations' (p. 90). For a more preventive approach, they suggest that teachers act as 'emotion coaches' and models in even routine situations during an average school day. They suggest that teachers use everyday situations in the classroom to help children identify emotions and develop effective coping skills. There are many naturally occurring opportunities for children to learn how to deal with the frustration of mastering a new academic skill, how to negotiate the complex behaviours involved in sharing and co-operative interactions with peers, and how to manage angry feelings when limits are placed on their behaviour. Teachers are also exhorted to consider seriously the importance of establishing strong relationships with young children as a vehicle for fostering emotional competence.

Behavioural concerns

Teachers working with young children generally expect a range of skills and developmental levels in their classroom. Their tolerance, however, for differences in behaviour tends to be more narrowly defined than differences in other areas of development. In fact, for many teachers, behaviour problems represent the most challenging aspect of working with young children, especially those with special needs. Thus it is not surprising to find that management of problem behaviour has been described as a significant issue in early intervention (Stephenson *et al.*, 2000, p. 232).

Understanding the source of behaviour problems is a starting point for dealing effectively with such behaviours in the classroom. Behaviours do not occur in a vacuum, nor does behaviour represent an isolated area of development. Behaviours are motivated by conditions within and around the child. Thus the admonition, 'You had no reason to do that' is far from accurate. To help children with behaviour problems, an understanding of the reasons behind the behaviours is essential.

The first thing to note about behaviour problems is that the definition of such varies widely. What one teacher labels as a behaviour problem may be viewed differently by another teacher. The following is an example. One teacher, Ms Miller, is reading a story during group time. Four-year-old Aaron gets up, walks over to the puzzle centre and dumps the puzzle pieces on the floor. The classroom assistant takes Aaron's hand and tries to lead him back to the group. Aaron yells, 'No', and throws himself on to the floor. The teacher and her assistant label Aaron's group time behaviour as 'unacceptable'. An entry in the 'daily observation notes' reads as follows: *Aaron was disruptive during group story time. He left the group, dumped puzzle pieces on the floor, and then refused to rejoin the group.* Later, in completing a behaviour checklist, Ms Miller rated Aaron as being distractible and disobedient.

A second teacher, Mrs Landon, responds differently to a similar situation. She notices Annie leave the group and move over to the manipulative area. The classroom assistant, instead of working to get Annie back into the group, sits in Annie's place in the circle and puts her hand lightly on the child next to her who has seemed distracted by Annie's movements. The following notations were made in the daily log: *Annie stayed with the group during story time for about 4 minutes. She then worked with a 3-piece puzzle (successfully!) for about 4 more minutes. She spent the rest of group time (about 5 minutes) sitting in the manipulative area with a 'rabbit' puppet on her lap. She sat quietly watching the group and apparently listening to the story.* Later, in completing a developmental checklist, Mrs Landon rated Annie as being able to attend to a story for short periods of time and being able to complete a three-piece puzzle on her own.

Similar behaviours – different interpretations. This is not unusual. While studies indicate that there is considerable agreement about what constitutes 'behaviours of concern' in the early years of school, there may be widely varying interpretations of such behaviours. What is generally accepted, however, is the concern that 'problem behaviour of older students and adults is likely to have had its roots in difficult behaviour at a young age, and that problem behaviour is associated with poor academic achievement, poor interpersonal skills, and increased risk of mental health problems' (Stephenson *et al.*, 2000, p. 225). Behaviours of concern, then, cannot be ignored.

Some studies indicate that distractibility and disrupting the activities of others tend to be the most troublesome behaviours for early childhood teachers. Physical aggression and bullying are also of considerable concern (Stephenson *et al.*, 2000). Other behaviours of concern include making excessive demands for the teacher's attention (e.g. does not work independently), failing to stay on task for a reasonable time, not following established class rules, expressing anger inappropriately, not getting along with other children, ignoring the feelings of others, telling lies and misusing materials. The motivations for, and causes of, such behaviours are quite varied but all relate to what is going on within and around the child. These motivations and causes of behaviour warrant special attention.

Motivations and causes

As mentioned above, children's behaviour is closely tied to development in other domains. Emotions, social skills, cognitive abilities and even language skills play a role in how children behave. Emotions help children sort out what is appropriate or inappropriate behaviour. Guilt and empathy are two of the most influential emotion-based regulators of behaviour (Kostelnik *et al.*, 1999). A sense of guilt tells children to refrain from acting in hurtful or unacceptable ways, while empathy prompts them to engage in positive behaviours towards others. There are certainly other emotions as well which can lead to acceptable or unacceptable behaviours. Such emotions as frustration, anger and fear can be the root cause of aggression; while love and trust may motivate helping and even self-sacrificing behaviours.

Some behaviour problems are clearly related to social interaction deficits. The behaviours of concern have to do with how to relate to others. With young children, this often takes the form of not knowing how to play with other children, or not having the play skills to be a successful play partner. Skills needed to be a successful play partner include knowing how to initiate play, how to join a group at play, how to make suggestions about the play situation, how to take suggestions, and how to deal with unpleasant social situations (e.g. disagreements, interruptions, shortage of materials). If children lack these skills, they may be rejected as play partners and thus miss out on many of the rich opportunities for further growth.

A child's ability to reason about what is 'right and wrong' and to understand the perspective of other people also influence behaviour. The moral reasoning of young children is immature, and their ability to understand what other people think, feel and know is limited. The cognitive ability of young children, then, should be taken into consideration as their behaviours are critiqued in reference to what is 'good and bad'. By stating expectations clearly and providing reasons for those expectations, adults can foster the development of moral reasoning in young children.

Some children's behaviour problems are related closely to deficits in language. If children lack the language skills to communicate their feelings, needs and wants, they may resort to physical expressions – some of which may be socially inappropriate and/or hurtful to others. In such cases, intervention should focus on the underlying cause of the unacceptable behaviour (i.e. language deficits) rather than just on the behaviour itself.

Thriving in group environments

To thrive as active learners in a group environment, children need a sense of how to behave in that environment. Skills related to success include knowing how to express needs and wants constructively, responding with compassion to others, being polite, taking care of materials, acting safely, engaging constructively in learning activities, attending to instruction, distinguishing between acceptable and unacceptable classroom behaviour, helping others, and being co-operative (Kostelnik *et al.*, 1999). Obviously, these are skills which children need to learn over time, and not all children learn them as easily as others. Just as variability in other areas of development are recognized, so individual differences in developing constructive behaviours should also be expected.

Children are not born with a sense of acceptable and unacceptable behaviour; nor do they have the understanding or skills to regulate their behaviour according to the expectations of others. Adult guidance is crucial in helping children learn how to interact with others and manage their own behaviours. Behaviours of concern (as outlined above) call for adult intervention. Such intervention, however, should not focus on 'correcting' the child. The focus should be on teaching the child 'appropriate alternative strategies they can eventually apply on their own' (Kostelnik *et al.*, 1999, p. 204). Through such strategies, children develop self-discipline.

Self-discipline, as defined in the literature, 'is the voluntary, internal regulation of behavior' (Marion, 1995, p. 26) and is the ultimate goal of behaviour intervention. Self-discipline 'involves acting in socially acceptable ways based on reasoning, concern for others, and an understanding of acceptable and unacceptable behavior' (Kostelnik *et al.*, 1999, p. 204). The process of developing self-discipline involves a gradual shift from being controlled by others to being able to control one's own behaviour. Components of self-discipline, as outlined by Kostelnik and colleagues

(1999), include: (1) initiating positive social acts (e.g. inviting another child to join a play situation); (2) making and carrying out social plans (e.g. developing a turn-taking plan for use of a wagon in the playground); (3) resisting temptation (e.g. helping to put toys away when tempted to move over to the snack table at 'clean-up' time; (4) inhibiting negative impulses (e.g. asking another child for a toy instead of just taking it when the other child is not looking); (5) delaying gratification (e.g. waiting for other children to finish their stories before talking about their own experiences or ideas).

Related conditions

Children with special education needs tend to experience greater difficulty than others in developing self-discipline. This is especially true for children with attention deficit hyperactivity disorder (ADHD), children with autism, and children with Tourette syndrome. The following is a discussion of these conditions.

Attention deficit disorder/attention deficit hyperactivity disorder

One of the most commonly diagnosed disorders in children is attention deficit hyperactivity disorder (ADHD) (Andrews, 1999). Estimates vary considerably as to the prevalence of ADHD – from 3 to 5 per cent by some estimates; all the way up to 10 to 15 per cent by other estimates. While there is some controversy and disagreement as to the utility and meaning of the terms attention deficit disorder (ADD) and attention deficit hyperactivity disorder (ADHD), the descriptions of behaviours associated with these conditions have been recognized for over fifty years. Such descriptions include aggressive, defiant, resistant to discipline, little self-control (or impulsivity), inattention (or poor attention span), and overly active (or hyperactivity).

With ADD, the primary concern is inattention, which is manifest when children fail to attend and concentrate on the activity or task at hand. Young children with ADD often move quickly from one activity to another and, when asked, often cannot explain what they should be doing or attending to. Children with ADD seem to be distracted easily by what is going on around them (e.g. other children playing, people talking, movement in the hallway, sounds from the next room).

Children with ADHD also exhibit inattention but demonstrate impulsivity and hyperactivity as well. Children who act with impulsivity seem to be unaware that their actions have consequences. They respond to situations quickly and with apparently little thought as to the appropriateness or results of their actions. Thus they tend to interrupt others in conversation and in work or play activities, have trouble waiting their turn, and seem to base decisions on emotion or impulse versus reflection or thought.

Hyperactivity is the primary symptom associated with ADHD. It is also the most widely known and easiest to recognize of the characteristics associated with this disorder. Children who are hyperactive tend to move about constantly, making noise and fidgeting. As such, they are often referred to as being disruptive in the classroom. Not surprisingly, secondary characteristics associated with ADHD include poor school performance, learning disabilities and poor problem-solving skills. Additional characteristics include delays in speech and language development, slightly more difficulties in sensory and motor skills and poor self-concept.

ADD/ADHD starts generally during the early childhood period (Andrews, 1999) and continues throughout one's life (Barkley, 1990). Stimulant medication therapy is the primary treatment for this disorder. The two most common medications are Cylert and Ritalin. While both drugs have proven to be quite effective in dealing with the symptoms of ADD/ADHD (Barkley, 1990), there are some concerns relating to the side-effects, including weight loss, insomnia, headaches, dizziness, reduced speech, irritability, sadness and nightmares.

Behavioural interventions (e.g. reward systems, behavioural contracting and self-management techniques) have also produced some positive outcomes for young children with ADD/ADHD, especially when used by parents in the home (Barkley, 1990). As students grow older, behavioural interventions – alone or in combination with medication – have also been effective in the school setting (Abramowitz *et al.*, 1992; Andrews, 1999).

It is important to keep in mind that most young children tend to be active, impulsive and easily distracted. This is normal and should be viewed as such by adults working with young children. Early childhood educators, then, should adapt the environment and introduce activities that match the way young children function, rather than trying to mould the behaviour of the students into patterns that are not natural to their developmental level. Behaviours associated with ADHD are often more noticeable in highly structured classrooms where sustained attention and more directed activities are the norm (Andrews, 1999). In an open-classroom arrangement – more typical of early childhood programmes – symptoms of ADHD may be overlooked.

While symptoms can be exacerbated or ameliorated by environmental factors, children with attention deficit disorders cannot be expected to behave in the same way as children without this disability. Thus teachers would do well to prepare the environment with the special needs of children with ADD and ADHD in mind and be willing to accept a higher level of activity than what is normally preferred.

> When the question of ADHD exists for a young child in an early childhood program, practitioners must evaluate whether or not the learning environment for the particular child is developmentally appropriate. Children may appear overly active when sustained attention is expected in activities that are not age or developmentally appropriate, or activities that are too long.
>
> (Andrews, 1999, p. 116)

There follow some specific classroom adaptations that may be helpful in working with children with ADD and ADHD:

- Monitor carefully the amount of visual and auditory stimulation present in the room. Because many children with ADD/ADHD have difficulty filtering out extraneous sights and sounds, teachers should take care to limit the noise level and visual stimuli surrounding these children (Cook *et al.*, 1996).
- Provide a 'quiet place' where children can retreat and have some time away from the larger group.
- Provide ample equipment and materials to minimize the need for waiting and/or sharing desired objects and activities.
- Space work areas (e.g. tables, learning centres) far enough apart so that children working in one area are less likely to disturb children working in an adjacent area.
- Make directions extremely clear and easy to follow. For example, instead of telling a child to clean up the art materials, give step-by-step directions, such as 'Put your finished work in your folder, and then throw the scrap paper in the waste basket.'
- Analyse tasks and present them in small, sequential steps.
- Use the child's name often when working with a group to help focus his or her attention on the task at hand.
- Maintain a calm voice and calm behaviour, as anxiety tends to heighten the child's level of activity.
- Provide clearly defined work spaces (e.g. carpet squares or pieces of tape on the floor) and definite locations for individual belongings.
- Keep materials in the classroom well organized. Storing learning materials and other supplies in clearly marked, sturdy containers helps adults and children find and return materials in an orderly way. Storage containers used by the children can be marked with both words and pictures to help them see easily where items belong.
- Establish and maintain a regular routine. Children with ADD/ADHD tend to thrive in a predictable environment. While children should have choices throughout the day, their choices should fit within the structure of the daily routine.
- Provide frequent, immediate and specific feedback for both desired and undesired behaviours.

- Use preferred activities for appropriate behaviour and removal of such reinforcers for inappropriate behaviour.
- Work closely with parents in developing interventions.

Autism

Autism is a complex syndrome with no known cause. Since the disorder was first identified in the 1930s, however, there have been numerous theories about its cause, some bringing great pain to parents. At one time, it was theorized that rejection or lack of emotional attachment by caregivers was the primary cause of autism. Today we know that there is absolutely no support for this theory. Recent studies in neurophysiology suggest that autism is related to atypical structure and/or neural transmission processes of the brain, although the nature and causes of these differences are still not well understood (Klein *et al.*, 2001). It has also been suggested that autism is the expression of multiple etiologies, and that there really is no such thing as 'autism'. What we refer to as autism may be many different brain disorders with similar characteristics or expressions (Howard *et al.*, 2001).

Autism represents one of the pervasive developmental disorders. Common to all these disorders is the poor and/or atypical development of social skills. To be diagnosed with autism, a child must exhibit significant delay in social communication and symbolic skills prior to the age of 3. In addition, he or she must demonstrate each of the following: (1) significant delay or inappropriate use of language; (2) failure to develop normal social relationships and interactions; and (3) obsessive or ritualistic, repetitive behaviours (such as spinning objects and insisting on exact repetitions of sequences of nonfunctional behaviour). Autism, then, may be viewed as a spectrum of disorders with significant concerns in the areas of social interaction, communication and behaviour.

Many children with autism also demonstrate neurological hyper-responsitivity – that is, they seem to have extremely acute sensory abilities, especially in the areas of hearing and touch (Klein *et al.*, 2001). Their hypersensitivity to certain sensations can be quite troublesome to them. For example, while many children may be able to block out the sound of traffic outside the classroom, a child with autism may find this noise not only distracting but also irritating. They may even find the sounds within the classroom painful or overwhelming. Their hypersensitivity may also take the form of tactile defensiveness, demonstrated by efforts to avoid body contact with different textures and being touched by others. At the same time, children with autism often engage in self-stimulatory behaviours, such as twirling, rocking or hand flapping.

The most defining characteristic of young children with autism, however, is a pervasive failure of the development of social communication.

Most children with autism avoid making direct eye contact, preferring instead to use their peripheral vision. This behaviour is often interpreted as not paying attention (Klein *et al.*, 2001). It may also be interpreted as not being interested in other people.

Children with autism generally avoid social interaction. They may walk away when approached and avoid joint reference (that is, shared attention, directed by an adult or peer, to an object or event). The absence of language, or the use of nonfunctional language, is also a characteristic of autism. Children with autism may engage in echolalia (repetition of the same phrase or sentence over and over again) and make unusual sounds (e.g. squealing). Because the social interactive behaviours of people with autism are puzzling and the condition generally not understood, they have sometimes been labelled as deaf, retarded, disturbed and/or insane (Williams, 1992). The condition has also been described as childhood psychosis, childhood schizophrenia and atypical personality disorder.

Helping children with autism is difficult and frustrating. The first step in providing appropriate intervention is a careful multi-factored assessment to rule out other potential causes of autistic-like behaviour. Such potential causes could include other syndromes (such as Rett, foetal alcohol and Tourette), hearing impairments and mental retardation. Of course, a child can be autistic and have other developmental concerns as well. In fact, about 75 per cent of people with autism have some degree of mental retardation, and about 40 per cent of people with autism fall into the severely retarded range (Howard *et al.*, 2001).

About two-thirds of children with autism are identified in infancy when such behaviours as indifference to or avoidance of social interaction, disinterest in toys, irritability and stiffness, abnormal patterns of eye gaze with caregivers, failure to acquire the social smile during infancy and aberrant sleep patterns are noted. The other third of children with autism are usually identified around the age of 12 to 18 months when failure to develop language and social skills is noted. The language of young children with autism is often nonverbal, delayed, echolalic or lacking in pragmatics (Kohler *et al.*, 2001).

Boys are three to four times more likely to have autism than girls. Research indicates that having one child with autism increases the risk of autism for other children in the family. Some researchers have also found that close relatives of children with autism often exhibit milder and nonpathological characteristics consistent with autism, including lack of emotional responsiveness and limited or atypical social communication skills. Other researchers have failed to replicate these findings. (Howard *et al.*, 2001).

Autism is considered to be one of the most demanding of developmental disabilities for families (Howard *et al.*, 2001). It is a lifelong condition and is usually accompanied by some very challenging behaviours. While the most severe behavioural disturbances associated with autism tend to occur during the early childhood years (ages 2 to 5), adolescence and young adulthood are often very difficult years as well (Howard *et al.*, 2001).

Early and intensive intervention has proven to be effective in managing some of the behaviour problems and remediating some of the pervasive social skill deficits of children with autism (Brown and Kalbli, 1997; Kohler *et al.*, 2001; Strain and Danko, 1995). Key ingredients of these intervention efforts have been outlined by Strain and Danko (1995) and include '(a) regular and planned access to typical peers, (b) multiple-setting opportunities to practice emerging social skills, and (c) intensive data collection in order to make midcourse corrections to existing intervention plans' (p. 2). Additional suggestions for intervention for young children with autism include the following:

- Provide intervention services within the context of a mainstream or inclusive setting and encourage children with autism to participate in the same activities as their typical peers at whatever their ability level.
- Use narration to reinforce appropriate social behaviours. When using narration, adults state out loud what they see the child attempting to do during explorations. The narration is used to provide support as well as information related to the child's actions. Narration might be used, for example, to help the child to become more aware of cause and effect and to promote the opportunity for increased social interaction. Such narration may be perceived by the child as a form of approval and validity (Brown and Kalbli, 1997).
- Teach classmates in the inclusive setting to make persistent social overtures towards the child with autism and relate to him or her as a friend. Specific overtures might include: (1) attracting the friend's attention by tapping him or her on the shoulder and calling his or her name; (2) inviting the friend to play by handing him or her a toy; (3) suggesting play ideas to a friend; (4) offering the friend assistance or asking for it; (5) making encouraging comments to the friend by saying that he or she is doing a nice job.
- Train parents to prompt siblings and/or the child with autism to interact socially. Parents can provide prompts by suggesting, directing or asking for such social interactions.
- Train siblings to serve as intervention agents in the home. Their role as interventionists should focus, in large part, on engaging in persistent social overtures towards their sibling with autism. Such overtures as presented above for classmates in the school-based setting are recommended.
- Identify and work towards specific versus general intervention goals. 'For all practical purposes, teaching young children with autism remains a behaviour-by-behaviour undertaking' (Strain *et al.*, 1995,

p. 108). 'Accepting a toy from a friend when offered' is an example of a specific behaviour, while 'socially responding to other children during play' is a more general description of a targeted behaviour.

- Recognize nonviable attempts at social interaction as meaningful communicative attempts. For example, if a child with autism moves into an area where one or more other children are playing, interpret this behaviour as an attempt at establishing social interaction. Trying to get the child to then also verbalize his or her intentions will likely lead to withdrawal or escape from the situation. Brown and Kalbli (1997) therefore suggest that teachers and teacher's assistants observe carefully and document antecedent behaviours that may be linked to a child's decision to flee or stay.
- Critically examine the actions demonstrated by a child with autism and the social interaction potential that the situations may offer. Brown and Kalbli (1997), who have studied the potential for such 'reflection', suggest using the following sets of questions relating to (1) self-initiated play, (2) social interaction potential, and (3) environmental variables.

Self-initiated play

1 Does the child attempt to pick up an object or toy?
2 Does the child attempt to manipulate an object or toy?
3 Does the child have gross motor skills that would allow him/her to play with an object or toy successfully?

Social interaction potential

1 Is the child staring at another peer or group of peers for more than three seconds?
2 Can the child play independently with a peer or a group?
3 Can the child tune out external distractions when making an attempt to enter into a group?
4 Can the child tune out external distractions when playing with a peer or group of peers for an extended time period?

Environmental variables

1 Does the child prefer to play in a particular area?
2 Does the child prefer to play with a particular toy or object?
3 Do certain sounds cause the child to leave an area?
4 Are certain sounds relaxing to the child?

Tourette syndrome

Tourette syndrome is another perplexing and sometimes devastating disability. Until 1972, the condition was considered to be quite rare, with only fifty known recorded cases at that time. Today, the syndrome is identified in as many as one out of 200 children (Howard *et al.*, 2001). The most noticeable characteristic of children with this disorder is the expression of tics, which may take the form of purposeless and irregular body movements (e.g. eye blinking, kicking, licking, spitting, squatting) and /or vocalizations (e.g. barking, grunting, humming, snorting). Such tics generally appear around the age of 5, but may be noticed earlier or later in some children. For some children, tics occur rarely, and usually when they are tired or tense. For the more severely affected, tics may occur 100 times per minute (Howard *et al.*, 2001). Tic patterns may vary over one's lifetime, and periods of remission allow some individuals to be symptom free for different lengths of time.

The most challenging characteristic of Tourette syndrome is a disinhibition of aggression, often taking the form of kicking, hitting, and throwing or smashing objects. Approximately 50 per cent of children with Tourette syndrome also have learning disabilities, and many experience some form of attention deficit. Obsessive compulsive behaviour is also observed in 55 to 74 per cent of cases of Tourette syndrome and tends to take the form of needing to complete tasks to perfection or perform certain rituals (Howard *et al.*, 2001). It is not surprising to find that children with Tourette syndrome are particularly vulnerable to psychological distress, including frustration, low self-esteem and serious anxiety related to social encounters (Howard *et al.*, 2001). Approximately one-third of all children with Tourette syndrome also have coprolalia, the involuntary use of vulgar or obscene language and/or gestures. This behaviour is not purposeful, nor is it rooted in a psychological disorder – it is a part of the syndrome.

The first step in intervention for individuals with Tourette syndrome focuses on understanding the condition. It is important for parents and other family members, school personnel and peers to understand that tics are out of the control of the individual with Tourette syndrome. This understanding may help reduce the stigma of tics and lead to better management of activities and conditions which tend to exacerbate the frequency and intensity of behaviours associated with tics. Tics are more evident when individuals with Tourette syndrome experience stress, anxiety, fatigue and excitement. Physical and emotional relaxation, on the other hand, tends to minimize the expression of tics and other symptoms associated with Tourette syndrome.

Medication is sometimes used to help control tics and/or the attentional deficits associated with Tourette syndrome. As there are some potentially serious side-effects to the medication used, this form of intervention should be limited to situations where the symptoms of Tourette syndrome are so intense that they compromise a child's development. Behavioural self-management strategies have been used as an alternative treatment producing some successful results. The complexity of this approach, however, makes it less appropriate at preschool level. The emphasis of treatment for young children should focus more on promoting understanding, minimizing stress and encouraging relaxation.

Case study – Ronnie

Background information

Ronnie was diagnosed soon after birth as having foetal alcohol syndrome (FAS) and cerebral palsy. His mother, Cheryl, who was 17 at the time, had consumed alcohol several times a week during her pregnancy. Cheryl was unmarried, had dropped out of school and had no permanent living arrangements. She was not interested in keeping her baby. Ronnie's father Larry, however, felt that the baby should not be given up for adoption. As Larry was not able to care for the child, Ronnie was placed in a foster home upon his discharge from the hospital. Ronnie was still living in this same foster home when he entered his first year (Reception year) of school.

Ronnie was small for his age, unable to walk independently or sit unsupported, and seemed to be functioning cognitively about two years behind his peers. Ronnie also had some behaviour problems. He would often strike out at the other children when they were 'too close' to him and would throw around his toys and other materials when he was angry or frustrated.

Mrs Housman, the Reception year teacher, had been the school district's 'Teacher of the Year' two years previously. Her award was based on her creative use of literature and the arts in working with young children. While she had had children with SEN in her class before, none were as behaviourally challenged as Ronnie. Ronnie's inattentiveness and distractibility were major obstacles to his participation in many of the group activities that Mrs Housman had always found quite successful, even with children with varying abilities.

The first challenge faced by the school at the time of Ronnie's enrolment was physical accessibility. A wheelchair-accessible bus had to be rerouted to provide transportation for Ronnie to and from school. A ramp had to be installed at one of the school entrances, and the learning centres in the classroom were rearranged to accommodate Ronnie's wheelchair. Several pieces of adaptive equipment were ordered, including a corner chair and safety swing, to provide support for Ronnie during both indoor and outdoor activities.

One of the most frustrating situations for Mrs Housman was having to deal with Ronnie's emotional outbursts during the day. Not only did these outbursts disrupt group activities, they were also distressing for the other children. Some children were fearful and cried when Ronnie screamed at them or hit them. Most of the children avoided being near him. Mrs Housman also found it difficult to attend to Ronnie's many physical needs. Ronnie needed special assistance during lunchtimes and snacks, as attempts to eat on his own always resulted in spills, and he sometimes threw food and eating utensils around. Ronnie needed one-to-one assistance when going to the bathroom, when being transferred to or from his wheelchair or other seating arrangements, when putting on a sweater or coat, or when engaged in almost any other self-help task. Mrs Housman tried to balance large group activities with individual assistance. When leading a group activity in which Ronnie seldom participated, Mrs Housman would tell Ronnie that he would have to wait for assistance until she was ready to help him. Ronnie usually responded by screaming, throwing things if he could, and tearing at his clothes.

Discussion

While physical adaptations were made to accommodate Ronnie's special needs, sufficient social and instructional adaptations were not provided. In addition, Mrs Housman approached the challenge more as a one-person task versus turning to others for support and assistance. While the physical therapist, occupational therapist and speech/language specialist each worked with Ronnie for forty minutes every week, they did so in isolation from each other and in a therapy setting away from the regular classroom. A considerable amount of time each session was devoted to trying to get Ronnie to attend to the planned activities. After three months into the school year, Ronnie was showing very little progress towards his physical and occupational goals and no improvement in his use of language, social interaction skills and ability to attend to tasks. The other children still avoided Ronnie; his outbursts continued on a frequent basis, and he showed little interest in group activities of any kind. Mrs Housman and Ronnie's foster-mother began talking about moving Ronnie to a more restrictive classroom – i.e. a classroom serving only children with special behavioural problems. They felt that since Ronnie was not participating in group activities or interacting with the other children anyway, he would benefit just as much from a setting serving only children with SEN.

Intervention for Ronnie tended to focus more on isolated therapy goals than on behavioural and social concerns needed for success in the classroom. A more positive outcome might have been achieved if members of the intervention team had worked together to guide and support Ronnie within the context of the classroom activities.

This support in the classroom might have provided the one-to-one attention Ronnie needed to participate successfully in various activities. Recognizing that full participation in some of the group activities was not realistic at this point, partial participation could have been the goal towards which the team worked. In addition, peers in the classroom could have been coached on how to approach Ronnie as a potential friend. Instead of being either too close and upsetting Ronnie or avoiding him altogether, peers might have been coached to wave to him during a game, offer him a biscuit at snack-time, and say hullo to him when he arrived.

While costly, the physical adaptations for a child with SEN are often the easiest types of adaptation to make. Social and instructional adaptations can be more complex and require more planning and team involvement. Without the social and instructional adaptations, however, the physical adaptations that are made may serve little purpose in achieving a successful mainstreaming experience.

6

CONCERNS RELATED TO SENSORY AND PHYSICAL DEVELOPMENT

Sensory, physical and neurological concerns represent a variety of areas that place a child at risk for special educational needs. Conditions relating to these concerns are often present at, or soon after, birth. Such conditions include significant infection and genetic syndromes (e.g. Down syndrome).

Presented in this chapter are discussions relating to some of the more common sensory, physical and neurological concerns, including vision problems, hearing problems, orthopaedic impairments and other health-related problems. The two areas of sensory impairments – i.e. vision and hearing – are presented first. While vision and hearing impairments are considered to be 'low incident' handicapping conditions for the general population, they are common findings among young children with SEN (Howard *et al.*, 1997).

Hearing problems

Types of hearing problem

A significant number of young children experience some degree of hearing problem. These problems may be temporary or permanent, but either way are likely to cause learning difficulties. Temporary hearing losses are often caused by otitis media (middle ear disease), which is believed to affect over 75 per cent of children within the first two years of life (Northern and Downs, 1984). Permanent hearing losses are usually sensori-neural (i.e. resulting from damage to the cochlea or auditory nerve) and vary from mild to profound. Children with a severe hearing loss usually experience major communication problems. They often experience other significant academic and social problems as well.

The two major types of hearing loss are conductive and sensori-neural. With a conductive hearing loss there is a disruption of the mechanical conduction of sound as it is transferred through the outer ear to the middle ear. Most causes of conductive hearing loss (which in most instances is otitis media) can be treated through medical intervention. To avoid developmental and learning problems, however, educational intervention is also warranted in many cases. A comprehensive model for addressing the developmental and educational concerns relating to otitis media has been developed by Johnson (1981) and seems to offer some promise of positive long-term benefits (Mandell and Johnson, 1985). While serious sensori-neural loss is related to genetic inheritance in approximately 70 to 80 per cent of cases, noise pollution can also lead to sensori-neural loss. There are some indications that even the ambient noise in incubators – if not closely monitored – can cause some hearing loss in premature infants (Howard *et al.*, 1997).

Impact on development

Due to the strong, positive relationship between hearing and language development, early detection of hearing loss is critical. Such detection, however, does not occur on a regular basis. Even though the critical period for language development is during the first three years of life, as many as 50 per cent of infants with hearing impairments are not identified until much later (Howard *et al.*, 1997). By then, serious language and learning problems may already exist.

Indicators of a hearing loss in young children include failing to react to loud noises, difficulty in localizing the source of sound and delayed acquisition of language milestones. Hearing losses are sometimes misdiagnosed as cognitive delays, since children with hearing losses fail to respond to language stimuli (e.g. questions, commands, greetings) and to use age-appropriate expressive language (e.g. naming and/or describing things, providing information). When tested on nonviable measures, however, children with hearing losses generally score within the normal range of intelligence.

Intervention strategies

Decisions about medical and educational interventions should be based on a number of different factors including etiology, location, severity of damage and time of onset of the hearing loss. The educational intervention for young children with hearing impairments should focus on both the use of residual hearing and on language development. In many cases, an augmentative communication system should be introduced early. An augmentative communication system augments, or adds to, a traditional or mainstream communication system (e.g. the English language). Sign language and the use of communication boards are examples of augmentative communication systems often used with individuals who are hearing impaired. Sign language, which uses hand gestures to communicate, is used widely by individuals who are deaf. It is very important that children with hearing losses who are introduced to sign language also learn to make use of residual hearing, lip-reading and oral speech to communicate. The method of combining manual signs with oral means of communication is referred to as 'total communication' and is the method used most frequently when introducing children to an augmentative communication system.

Communication boards are visual devices using pictures or symbols to represent communicative ideas. Communication boards can be elaborate and expensive electronic devices or simple, home-made constructions. Some teachers and parents make communication boards by using a flat piece of cardboard and a set of pictures representing simple items, places and activities familiar to the child. Once the pictures are attached to the board, the child simply points to individual pictures to tell others what he or she needs or wants. Thus by pointing to a picture of a bathroom, a child can inform the teacher that he or she needs to use the bathroom. Similarly, by pointing to a picture of a TV, a child can ask his or her parents if he or she can watch a TV programme.

In addition to the use of an augmentative communication system, auditory assistive devices can also be used to enhance the development and learning of a child with a hearing loss. Hearing aids and sound field amplification systems represent two different types of auditory assistive devices. Both hearing aids and sound field systems amplify sound but do not replace natural hearing.

Hearing aids amplify sound for the individual person wearing the aid. Most hearing aids have the disadvantage of amplifying all environmental sounds, including distracting or interfering noises. Hearing aids also tend to distort sounds. Thus for young children still learning the intricacies of spoken language, the sounds amplified through their hearing aids may include the dog barking, the fan humming and the mother talking. In this case, a child may have great difficulty attending to the sound of the mother's voice. Even when the child does attend and can discriminate between relevant and irrelevant sounds, he or she may still not hear the mother correctly, due to sound distortions. If the mother says 'now' the child may hear only the 'ow' sound and not understand the intent of her message. The child may thus choose to ignore the fact that the mother is speaking to him or her. When adults are unaware of the child's hearing difficulties (even after amplification), they may mistakenly read this response (or non-response) as misbehaviour. This, of course, will be frustrating for both the child and the adults working with that child.

Sound distortions, which often accompany the use of hearing aids, may lead to speech and language problems as well. If children cannot hear a word correctly, they have no consistent model on which to base the pronunciation of words. In addition, children with hearing problems often have difficulty learning the rules of language, including sentence structure, the use of pronouns, plurals and so on.

Sound field amplification systems differ from hearing aids in that they amplify sound throughout a designated space, such as a classroom, rather than to just one specific individual. When sound field amplification is used in the classroom, the teacher wears a small wireless microphone which can be switched on and off as needed. Two or more speakers are placed strategically in the classroom. When the microphone is on, the teacher's voice is amplified throughout the room. The extent of amplification is usually about ten decibels, which is just enough to help the students attend to the teacher's voice while disregarding irrelevant environmental sounds (e.g. students coughing, carts moving in the hall, nearby traffic noise).

One of the major disadvantages to the use of sound field amplification in the classroom is that only the speaker's voice is amplified. While this may be fine for instruction at higher grade levels, for instruction with young children this raises some concerns. Since much learning occurs through interactions with other students, amplifying only the teacher's voice provides limited assistance for a child with a hearing impairment.

Research related to the classroom use of sound field amplification is limited. However, the studies that have been done provide support for its use as an instructional tool (Linton, 1995). Research findings suggest that the use of sound field amplification can (1) improve the academic performance of children with learning disabilities in mainstream settings (Ray *et al.*, 1986); (2) improve the test-taking skills of students, including students with minimal hearing loss (Burgener, 1980); (3) reduce the number of children referred for special education services (Osborn *et al.*, 1992); (4) have a positive effect on students' behaviour (Linton, 1995), and (5) reduce teacher stress in the classroom (Linton, 1995; Wilson, 1988). As articulated by Wilson (1988) and Linton (1995), a major caution in using sound field amplification with young children relates to the appropriate use of this technology. Young children need to be engaged in active, hands-on experiences and not be expected just to sit and listen. The teacher's voice should thus not dominate the classroom throughout the day. If sound field amplification is used with young children, teachers should be clearly aware of when to use it (e.g. during a large group activity) and when it is not appropriate to do so (e.g. when children are working alone or in small groups).

Classroom/school adaptations

Serving children with hearing impairments in the regular classroom does require some special accommodations. In addition to the possible use of amplification systems (i.e. hearing aids and/or sound field amplification), other recommendations presented in the *Special Educational Needs Code of Practice* (DfES, 2001a, 7: 62, p. 88) include:

- flexible teaching arrangements
- appropriate seating and acoustic conditioning
- access to alternative or augmented forms of communication
- regular and frequent access to specialist support.

Vision Problems

Types of vision problem

Vision problems take many forms, with widely varying implications for a child's development and academic performance. Such problems range from relatively minor and remediable conditions to total blindness. The time of onset also varies and plays a major role in the child's ability to adapt socially and psychologically, as well as to achieve academic success.

Vision problems can be related to visual acuity and/or peripheral field of vision. Visual acuity refers to the distance at which a person can discriminate an object in relation to the distance at which a person with average visual acuity (20/20) can discriminate the same object. An individual with 20/90 visual acuity, for example, would be able to see accurately up to only 20 feet (6 metres) what a person with average visual acuity could see as far away as 90 feet (27 metres). A person is considered legally blind if his or her visual acuity is 20/200 or less in the best eye with correction. A person is also considered legally blind if his or her peripheral field of vision is 20 degrees or less, even though visual acuity may be normal.

Legal blindness is a relatively low incidence disability, occurring approximately only once per thousand people. Blindness, however, is not the only vision problem causing a child to have special educational needs. Low vision (where visual acuity is 20/70 or less in the best eye with correction) can also be a significant factor negatively affecting a child's development and learning. In fact, approximately 30 to 70 per cent of children with severe visual loss experience special educational needs (Kirchner, 1988).

The incidence of both visual impairment and blindness seems to be rising (Kirchner, 1988). This may be due in part to the increased survival rate of premature and low birth weight infants and to the increased numbers of children living in poverty. Many cases of blindness and serious visual impairment – especially in instances where the condition seems to be related to poor environmental conditions – are considered preventable. In fact, as many as two out of three cases might be prevented through control of infection and malnutrition (Howard *et al.*, 1997).

Although assessing actual visual acuity in infants is very difficult, there are indications that newborns do not have 20/20 vision. In fact, the average visual acuity of newborns is estimated to be about 20/200. Acuity improves gradually but probably does not reach 20/20 until about the age of 5. The term 'developmental visual impairment' is sometimes used to refer to the vision status of children under the age of 5 (Howard *et al.*, 1997).

Impact on development

Children who are visually impaired often experience delays in other areas of development as well. Delays in cognitive development are common. This is due in part to the fact that children with visual impairments cannot rely on their sense of vision to give them reliable information about their world. Without such information, it is difficult for children to construct knowledge about the world in which they live.

Another factor negatively affecting the cognitive development of children with visual disabilities is the fact that by not seeing what is available for exploration and manipulation, they are not adequately motivated to become engaged with the world outside themselves. Thus they miss out on not only the information available through the medium of vision, but information from other channels of learning as well. For example, if a child with a visual impairment cannot see the funnel and cup in the sandbox or what other children are doing with them, he or she may not be motivated to explore the potential of these materials.

Normal vision is thus a significant factor in encouraging or motivating a child to explore his or her world. In addition, seeing the world around them fosters the development of visual memory in young children and enables them to feel safe in exploring their world (Howard *et al.*, 1997). Children with visual impairments do not have the opportunity to develop this visual memory and may thus feel unsafe or insecure in relating to new materials, new places and new circumstances. The reluctance often observed in children with visual impairments suggests that this may be true.

In addition to the negative impact on cognitive development, visual impairments tend to imperil other areas of development as well, especially language and social development. Eye contact, so critical for social and language interactions, is often absent or present only minimally for children with visual impairments. Also absent is the ability to see mouth movements involved in producing speech. Thus young children who are blind or visually impaired often experience speech delays and/or disorders. Because children with visual impairments have difficulty seeing the nonviable aspects of communication, they also experience difficulties associated with both the expressive and receptive aspects of effective conversation. These speech, language and social interaction difficulties can lead to self-orientation and/or social isolation, which are typical characteristics of children with visual impairments (Hoon, 1991).

Motor difficulties are also common in children who are blind or visually impaired. These difficulties are usually evidenced in both gross motor and fine motor development. Gross motor skills involve the movement and control of large muscle groups, and affect such activities as walking, kicking and jumping. Fine motor skills involve the movement and control of small muscle groups to perform such actions as grasping and manipulating a variety of materials. Children who are visually impaired are usually hampered in such fine motor activities as working switches, folding paper and fastening buttons. Since normal mobility is impeded for children who are blind or visually impaired, they sometimes develop hypotonic muscle tone (i.e. low muscle tone leading to excessive versus controlled joint movements), stereotypical behaviours (e.g. rocking), and postural abnormalities (e.g. leaning to one side when standing and/or walking, or tilting the head).

Intervention strategies

Early intervention for children who are blind or visually impaired should focus primarily on helping them make the best use of their residual vision (i.e. the visual ability remaining to an individual with a visual loss) (Howard *et al.*, 1997). Related instructional strategies should teach children with visual impairments to pay attention to relevant visual stimuli as they seek new information (Morse, 1991). Children with visual impairments must also learn to apply previously gained information to new situations. For example, if a child with a visual impairment discovers that some doorways mark a change in elevation (i.e. a step up or a step down) or type of floor covering (e.g. from carpeting to tiles), he or she should learn to take this into consideration when walking through unfamiliar doorways.

One of the ways adults can help children with visual impairments to use their residual vision is to limit the amount of assistance they provide. Generally, assistance should be provided only in situations where safety and/or success call for intervention (Howard *et al.*, 1997). If assistance is provided when the child would be able to figure things out on his or her own, a form of 'learned helplessness' may hinder the child from exploring his or her environment and moving about independently.

Special instruction in orientation and mobility skills can also help children with visual impairments to make use of their residual vision and increase their ability to explore and move about independently. Orientation involves an awareness of space and the environment, especially in terms of one's own body position in space. Through orientation training, children are taught to take advantage of their other senses (i.e. touch, hearing, smell) to replace sight in learning about their environment and their body's position in that environment. For example, by becoming more aware of the breeze across the face and the sound of the wind in the trees, a child with a visual impairment may deduce that he or she is near an open window.

By pairing orientation with mobility training, children are taught to move about their environment with confidence, independence and a sense of purpose. For example, a child who is blind can learn to move from the classroom to the cafeteria independently by orienting him- or herself in the right direction (e.g. turn left when leaving the classroom) and then using his or her hand against the wall to 'follow the path' to the cafeteria (e.g. perhaps going past two more doorways before entering the cafeteria). In addition to using one's hand and other body parts, other types of aids that can be used to increase mobility for children with visual impairments include canes, 'walking ropes' and large push toys.

Walking ropes consist of one or two ropes running horizontally that serve as tactile guides for individuals moving from one place to another. While a walking rope could be used along the wall to help a child find his or her way to the cafeteria, it would have the disadvantage of 'broken space' when crossing open doorways. In addition, the walking rope may provide more assistance than the child really needs. If the child can learn to use his or her hand along the wall, the walking rope should not be installed.

In fact, the use of walking ropes has been criticized as an example of 'overmodification' of the environment. The presence of walking ropes 'may interfere with the children's awareness of normal environmental features, which can provide generalizable clues for orientation to the environment and independent mobility' (Lang and Deitz, 1990, p. 4). However, for some children, the wall alone may not provide enough assurance that they are on the right path. Masking tape along the wall could serve as a modified and less intrusive guide. Out of doors, however, walking ropes may be necessary to help children with visual impairments feel safe and 'oriented' to their surroundings.

Large push toys, such as sturdy toy grocery carts, can be used to provide support while walking. Using a push toy when moving from one place to another can help a child feel protected from falls and bumps. The use of a push toy instead of a cane or walker for this purpose is less intrusive, in that, when used appropriately, it does not make the child with a visual impairment appear different from the other children.

To prevent or minimize the development of secondary disabilities, intervention should also focus on fostering motor, language and social skills. A variety of enriching experiences with activities, materials and interactions that involve residual vision as well as the other senses (i.e. auditory, kinaesthetic, tactile and olfactory) should be provided. At all times, the goal should be to increase the child's confidence and competence in interacting with his or her physical and social environment.

Classroom/school adaptations

Adaptations in the classroom and other areas of the school will certainly have to be made for children with visual impairments to enable them to be active learners in a fully inclusive way. Classroom teachers working with children who are blind or visually impaired will usually have access to a qualified teacher of the visually impaired and/or a mobility officer qualified to work with visually impaired children. Such specialists can be of considerable assistance and should become an integral part of the transdisciplinary team serving the child who is visually impaired.

In addition to the use of mobility devices (such as the examples provided above), other adaptations and suggestions that may be helpful for children with visual impairments include the following.

- When moving through unfamiliar or crowded areas, pair the child who is blind with a sighted guide (either an adult or peer).
- Use handrails, lighting and contrast application, uncluttered pathways, and more tactile and auditory stimuli to help the child orient to his or her surroundings.
- Provide modified eating utensils to prevent or minimize spillage.
- Provide appropriate information technology, such as voice synthesizers linked to computers.
- Allow the child more time to accomplish certain tasks.
- Define classroom areas (e.g. block area, book area), work space (e.g. portion of a table top), and personal space (e.g. 'cubby-hole', locker) with easily identified cues, as needed. Such cues might include brightly coloured tape, carpet squares, concrete objects and 'work trays'.
- Provide additional tactile, auditory and olfactory cues to materials, activities and communicative exchanges, as needed. For example, in addition to putting your finger over your mouth to ask for quiet, use an auditory signal as well. One way to adapt materials is to add texture cues to games or toys, such as a sandpaper square glued next to the start button for a music box.
- Place objects at the child's level and encourage him or her to examine them tactually. The other children in the class could be involved in a similar activity by asking them to feel and describe items in a 'feelie' bag.

Cerebral palsy

Cerebral palsy (CP) occurs in about 1.5 to 2.7 per 1000 live births, making it one of the most common disabilities in our society (Howard *et al.*, 1997). CP results from brain injury sustained during the early stages of development, and affects muscle tone, movement reflexes and posture. The nature and extent of disability resulting from CP differs considerably from one individual to another. CP can affect one or both sides of the body and can result in high muscle tone (hypertonia), low muscle tone (hypotonia) or spasticity (the tendency to have sudden, involuntary contractions of the muscles).

Conditions related to high muscle tone, or hypertonia, include shortened muscles and ligaments, with eventual restrictions on joint movement. Over time, this can lead to joint dislocation, deformities of the spine and contractures (Bigge, 1991). Low muscle tone, or hypotonia, is usually characterized by weakness, 'floppiness', poor posture and hypermobile joints. Children with low muscle tone sometimes need external support for positioning and mobility and are usually delayed in motor skill development. Spasticity is characterized by a tightening of the muscles and a resistance to movement. Spastic movement has been described as a 'jack-knife' response, where joints first express hyper-resistance to extension or flexion up to a certain threshold, then a sudden release of resistance.

CP is not a progressive disease in that the damage to the brain does not get worse over time. Related physical deformities, however, can get progressively worse, especially if appropriate intervention is not provided early in life. Children with CP are usually diagnosed as having a severe, moderate or mild disability based on the severity of involvement. Thus 'a diagnosis of cerebral palsy is almost meaningless unless it is also paired with a description of the degree . . . to which a child is affected motorically' (Howard *et al.*, 1997, p. 158). With a diagnosis of severe CP, the child will usually experience total dependence in meeting physical needs, is likely to have poor head control, and will often be prevented from achieving academic and age-appropriate motor skills. With moderate CP, the child will usually achieve some independence in meeting physical needs, will have functional head control, and will probably experience some perceptual and/or sensory integrative deficits. Such deficits often interfere with achieving academic and age-appropriate motor skills. With mild CP, the child will probably achieve independence in meeting physical needs and, with therapy intervention, have the potential for improving the quality of motor and/or perceptual skills. Without effective intervention, however, regression in motor and perceptual skills may occur.

Most children with CP experience some difficulty with self-help skills. Feeding difficulty is an especially common and troublesome problem. Estimates are that approximately 50 per cent of children with CP experience feeding problems and 48 per cent have growth retardation

(Thommessen *et al.*, 1991). Some of the problems related to feeding include poor swallowing and chewing, poor self-feeding skills and long, tiresome feeding sessions. Due to the feeding difficulties, it is not unusual for children with CP to be on restricted diets, consisting in large part of puréed or powdered foods. Such diets are often unappealing and offer little incentive for expending energy for self-feeding and/or co-operation in assisted feeding: 'Subsequently, children's energy intake and nutritional status are frequently compromised' (Howard *et al.*, 1997, p. 159), often leading to problems with growth patterns and developmental progress.

Because CP is caused by damage to the brain, some people believe (mistakenly) that CP inevitably involves mental retardation as well. This is not true. While children with CP are more likely to experience some cognitive deficits and/or delayed development in sensorimotor behaviours than children without CP (Cioni *et al.*, 1993), it is important to understand that not all children with CP have intellectual deficits. It is also important to consider that the motoric limits to exploring and interacting with the environment experienced by children with CP may be as much a factor in the delayed development in sensorimotor behaviours as mental retardation resulting from brain damage. A crucial consideration in intervention for children with CP, then, is finding ways to facilitate their interaction with the environment, so as to enhance their opportunities for cognitive development and other types of learning.

Another important consideration when working with children with CP is appropriate handling and positioning. High muscle tone and spasticity can make certain activities, such as dressing, very difficult. Appropriate handling for children with high muscle tone may involve strategies to relax the child's muscles, including gentle stroking, soft lighting, music and a soothing voice. Appropriate handling for a child with low muscle tone usually involves strategies to support the child during an activity. In feeding, for example, proper head positioning and support may make a notable difference as to how well the child eats and how he or she feels about the experience.

Other important considerations in working with children with CP include:

- working closely with occupational and physical therapists as members of the intervention team;
- positioning the child for maximum safety, support, and inclusion in the instructional and social dimensions of the programme;
- arranging co-operative learning activities with opportunities for all children to make contributions to the learning tasks;
- alerting all teachers and adults in the school to the child's support and positioning difficulties and making them aware of basic measures they should take to overcome or circumvent the difficulties;

- seeking the views of and involving the child's parents at each stage of the educational programme;
- exploring the possible use of, and, where practicable, secured access for the child to appropriate technology, including computer-assisted instruction, and providing training in the use of that technology for the child, his or her parents and staff, so that the child is able to use that technology across the curriculum in school and, where appropriate, at home;
- adapting toys and other instructional materials to enhance independent use. Adaptations to materials (e.g. pencils, crayons, puzzle pieces, feeding utensils) are often used to help stabilize the materials and to assist in grasping and controlling them;
- adapting the physical environment and using adaptive equipment in the classroom and other areas of the school (e.g. bathroom, playground) to encourage and support exploration, involvement, independence and inclusion on the part of the child with CP. Such adaptations may call for the installation of handrails and ramps, wider than usual passageways and work areas both inside and outside of the classroom, support straps and/or 'bolsters' on indoor and outdoor gross motor toys and equipment, and the use of therapeutic equipment, such as corner chairs and standing boards;
- keeping adaptations as non-intrusive as possible so that the child with a disability is not seen as 'more different' than the other children. For example, adaptive seating should be used only when necessary and should be arranged so as not to put the child with a disability at an unequal height with the other children. In addition, because wheelchairs and wheelchair trays tend to isolate individual children from the group, such adaptive equipment should be used on a limited basis. For children who need additional support for balance and/or safety, adaptations should be devised so as to enable them to use floor space or table tops alongside their peers.

Developmental co-ordination disorder (DCD)

Some children experience a type of movement difficulty characterized by a lack of motor co-ordination. At one time – and still in popular language use today – such children are often referred to as being 'clumsy'. Clumsiness is usually associated with bumping into things and other people, falling down easily (often due to tripping), spilling substances, dropping objects, and having difficulty with such skills as throwing and catching a ball. Other terms have also been used in reference to children with significant movement skill difficulties, including 'congenital maladroitness' (Ford, 1966), 'developmental dyspraxia' (Portwood, 1996), 'specific developmental disorder of motor function' (World Health

Organization, 1992), 'movement difficulties' (Sugden and Keogh, 1990) and 'Developmental co-ordination disorder' (American Psychiatric Association, 1994). As Stafford (2000) notes, the term 'movement difficulties' appears to be the most compatible with the terminology employed currently in the education system in Britain. The term favoured by leading researchers in the area, however, seems to be 'developmental co-ordination disorder' (DCD) (Stafford, 2000).

Developmental co-ordination disorder is described by the American Psychiatric Association (APA) as follows:

> The essential feature of this disorder is a marked impairment in the development of motor co-ordination that is not explainable by Mental Retardation and that is not due to a known psychological disorder.
>
> (APA, 1987, p. 48)

Evident from this description is the understanding that the DCD diagnosis is restricted to children who exhibit movement difficulties but do not have attendant physical or mental disorders. The APA also makes it clear that the diagnosis of DCD is given only if the impairment adversely affects academic performance or success in daily living activities.

Stafford (2000) recently raised some issues concerning DCD and the curriculum for primary children in Britain. As Stafford notes, the curriculum at the primary level calls for more active involvement on the part of students today than it did for students in the past; and the demands of active learning may pose some special problems for children with DCD. He sites current practices from the maths section of the National Curriculum as examples: manipulating coins, constructing with 'unifix' cubes and working with a variety of interlocking shapes. The result? 'A child with manual dexterity problems spends a vast amount of time trying to fix cubes together, arranging them correctly and picking them up from the floor when they fall off the desk and neglects the learning of mathematical principles' (p. 83).

Other issues raised by Stafford (2000) include: (1) the decreased amount of time devoted to physical education at the primary level; (2) the inadequate training of teachers to address movement skill development; and (3) the lack of early assessment and ongoing monitoring of children's movement skills. According to Stafford (2000), 'The more active primary school curriculum may mean that some children's "inefficient motor performance" leads them to have more negative experiences in more school subjects' (p. 84).

Case study – Tara

Background information

Tara's parents realized that she was not hearing properly when she was 6 months old. Tara was not responding differentially to sounds (e.g. looking up when the doorbell rang or turning towards someone when her name was called), nor was she playing with the sound of her own voice (e.g. babbling, cooing). Audiological testing indicated that she had a moderate to profound hearing loss.

Through home-based early intervention services, Tara and her parents were introduced to signing (i.e. the use of sign language) before her second birthday. Tara also started wearing hearing aids by the age of two. The response to both the signing and the amplification (i.e. hearing aids) was very positive. Amplification benefits, however, seemed to be limited to discriminating high-volume environmental sounds versus aiding in understanding speech.

At age 4½ years, Tara participated in a mainstream Reception class and coped quite well with making friends, playing co-operatively with others, making choices, and showing initiative in play activities. She communicated with her parents primarily through signing, and with her teachers and friends through a combination of gestures, signs and utterances. Support was provided by a special education teacher and Tara's mother, who each spent one afternoon a week in the classroom to help the teacher and the other children learn some signing and other ways to communicate effectively with Tara. A speech/language therapist also provided consultation and assistance on a regular basis.

After the Reception year, Tara was enrolled in a mainstream Year I class. A major concern at this time related to a more academically focused curriculum, with a heavier emphasis on language and literacy than that to which Tara was exposed in the Reception year. The Year 1 classroom teacher was not skilled in signing and was quite concerned about meeting Tara's special educational needs.

An intervention team meeting was held prior to the first week of school. Attending the meeting were Tara's parents, the classroom teacher, the special education resource teacher, the speech/language therapist and the Reception year classroom teacher. During the meeting, all shared ideas on what environmental and curricular modifications would be most helpful to Tara. Decisions were made to introduce Tara (and her parents) to computers and picture communication boards (i.e. visual devices using pictures or symbols to represent communicative ideas). It was also decided that the speech/language therapist would work with Tara's classroom teacher and classmates to teach them about what it means to be hearing impaired and to help them learn some basic signs. Both the speech/language therapist and the special education resource teacher would work with Tara (along with the classroom teacher) to develop beginning reading and writing skills and would encourage her to begin using these skills to enhance her communication abilities.

Discussion during the meeting also focused on how to assure full integration for Tara (i.e. in the instructional and social aspects of the programme as well as the physical). Questions were raised about how Tara might participate meaningfully in music and drama as well as in classroom discussions and co-operative small group learning activities. Because of her warm and outgoing personality, there was little concern about Tara being able to make friends. All agreed, however, that this would have to be monitored carefully, with observations about such concerns as to whether or not Tara was being invited to classmates' birthday parties and if other children were reaching out to her during both indoor and outdoor play activities.

Discussion

In spite of the challenges that faced Tara and the intervention team as she entered Year 1, there were a number of factors enhancing Tara's chances for success. There was, first of all, an understanding that full inclusion means more than physical integration. For Tara to do well in the regular classroom, she would need understanding, acceptance and ways to communicate effectively. She would also need to learn what the other children were learning (e.g. reading, writing, maths, science), even though alternative methods would have to be introduced. These alternative methods included sign language, the use of a communication board individualized to Tara's situation, and computer-assisted instruction. The use of these alternative methods to help Tara benefit from the regular curriculum represents a merging of developmentally appropriate practices with exceptionality appropriate practices. Such a merging would certainly enhance Tara's chances of doing well during her Year 1 experience.

Part III

FOCUS ON THE TEAM

Meeting the needs of young children with disabilities requires a community versus single discipline effort. It requires comprehensive and co-ordinated services that are possible only through an attitude and practice of teaming at both the interdisciplinary and interagency level.

Some of the special challenges that need to be addressed by the intervention team include appropriate assessment of young children, individualized programming in inclusive early years classrooms, co-ordination of services, monitoring child progress and programme evaluation. Some of these challenges are addressed in Part III, along with some discussion as to what constitutes an effective team and different models from which teams may operate. First, however, there is a brief discussion of children's rights and the need for a community to work together as a team to protect those rights. At all levels of teaming, parents are considered equal partners in the process of planning, implementing and evaluating services for their young children.

7

THE ECOLOGICAL FRAMEWORK

The needs of young children with disabilities are complex and multifaceted. Meeting these needs requires the support and involvement of a community of people. Parents cannot do it alone; neither can teachers or doctors or therapists. A variety of disciplines and agencies must come together to form a co-operative team if the best interests of children are to be protected. This chapter, focusing on children as part of a community, includes a discussion of children's rights within the community and the formation of teams to protect those rights.

Children's rights

All children require special attention. Whether or not they are disabled or handicapped, they are certainly vulnerable. An understanding of this vulnerability and the need for special attention was first brought to the public's awareness in 1946 with the founding of UNICEF (United Nations International Children's Emergency Fund) after the Second World War, when there was a concern that children would not be adequately protected in the war relief effort. At the time, the concept that children required special attention was considered revolutionary (UNICEF, 1997).

At the end of the post-war reconstruction period, UNICEF's initial relief mandate was enlarged to include the survival and development of children. Recently, this mandate has changed dramatically once again. 'The idea that children have special needs has given way to the conviction that children have rights, the same full spectrum of rights as adults: civil and political, social, cultural and economic' (UNICEF, 1997, p. 9).

The conviction that children have rights was formalized as the 'Convention on the Rights of the Child' and adopted by the United Nations General Assembly on 2 September 1990. The adoption of this Convention by countries across the world suggests that 'a global consensus about the meaning of childhood is emerging' (Garbarino, 1997, p. 15). Childhood, as proclaimed in this document, 'is a protected niche in the social environment, a special time and place in the human life cycle, having a special claim on the community' (Garbarino, 1997, p. 15). The Convention clearly icates that children have a right to be cared for, and that, while parents sually want to provide such care, they are not always able to do so without some support and assistance. In such cases, as outlined in the United Nations (UN) Convention, 'society should pick up the tab' (Garbarino, 1997, p. 15).

To date, all the UN countries apart from Somalia and the USA had ratified the Convention, making it the most widely ratified human rights treaty in history. Ratifying the Convention obligates a country to undertake all appropriate measures to assist parents and other responsible parties in fulfilling their obligation to children, as described in the Convention.

The rights of children outlined in the Convention are comprehensive and include: (1) the right to survive and develop to their full potential; (2) the right to the highest attainable standard of healthcare; (3) the right to express views and receive information; (4) the right to express an opinion in matters affecting the child; and (5) the right to protection from all forms of sexual exploitation and sexual abuse. These rights also include the right to play (Article 31) and 'the right of a physically or mentally disabled child to special care and assistance that will enable him or her to enjoy a full and decent life in conditions that ensure dignity and promote self-reliance' (Article 23). While the Convention recognizes that not every country has the resources necessary to ensure all economic, social and cultural rights immediately, it does commit all countries involved to make those rights a priority and to ensure that those rights are implemented to the maximum extent of available resources.

A Committee on the Rights of the Child has been established to monitor the process of implementing the Convention. Governments are required to report to the Committee within two years of ratification and every five years thereafter, outlining the steps taken towards protecting the rights of children. In addition to submitting their official reports, some countries have chosen to submit alternative reports as well as a way of adding depth, detail and perspective. The UK Agenda for Children, produced by the Children's Rights Development Unit, represents one such alternative report. Inspired by the Convention's directive to let the views of children be heard and make the Convention provisions widely known to adults and children alike, this report includes the input of children. There follow several examples of children's voices expressed in this report (UNICEF, 1997, p. 10):

- 'We need more bridges over the road so we can get to the park' (8-year-old from Bristol).
- 'Parents shouldn't have the right to hit children. It just makes children grow up to be violent' (13-year-old from Lincolnshire).
- 'Kids can't play where I live; needles everywhere, stolen cars, no one cares' (14-year-old from Manchester).

The process of implementing the Convention is still in its infancy, but this international treaty has already started to make an impact. All around the world, lawyers, police officials, judges, teachers and caregivers are being trained in the principles and application of the Convention. Individual countries have initiated important changes, such as the demobilization of child soldiers in Sierra Leone. While such changes are reason to celebrate, much remains to be done. More than 12.5 million children under the age of 5 in developing countries die each year, 9 million of them from causes for which inexpensive solutions and measures such as immunization and antibiotics have been routinely applied in the industrialized world for fifty years (UNICEF, 1997). As discussed in Chapter 3, there are many other social and environmental conditions that put young children at risk. These conditions are often associated with complex and difficult situations that can be remedied only through a concerted team approach in communities across the world.

Ecological model for education and development

Children and families do not live in isolation; they live within a larger unit called a community. There are various levels of community affecting young children. These range from the community of the child's own family, to the local and state community, and finally to the global community extending across different countries of the world. The rights of young children need to be addressed and protected within each level of community.

Historically, intervention services for young children with disabilities focused primarily on the child with special needs, without much consideration as to the communities to which he or she belonged. Early intervention professionals spent most of their time assessing young children and planning instructional activities to enhance their development. While this child-focused approach will always be a part of early intervention, recent understandings add a broader perspective to the factors that influence children's growth and development. Understandings based on the influence of one's community and systems theory have contributed significantly to this broader perspective.

According to the systems theory perspective, individuals, families, organizations and agencies are viewed not as separate units, but as components of an 'organized whole'. This 'whole' comprises interrelated and interdependent components. If one component experiences change, the whole system changes. If one component is weak or in trouble, the whole system is weak and in trouble. If a child has a disability, his or her entire family is affected, and the 'whole system' (i.e. the community) needs to be involved in providing the support and resources necessary for maximizing the child's growth and development.

An understanding of systems theory has led to the development of an ecological model for education and development. According to this model, a child's ecological environment is 'a nested arrangement of structures' (Bronfenbrenner, 1979), where each level is contained within the next level. Bronfenbrenner identified four levels of the environment: microsystem, mesosystem, exosystem and macrosystem.

The *microsystem* is the setting in which the child spends most of his or her time and usually includes the child's home, the homes of other relatives and friends, and childcare centres or family daycare homes. For some children with special needs, the hospital or other institutional settings may also be included in their microsystem. The *mesosystem* consists of relationships among the microsystem components of which the child is a part of at a particular point in his or her life. For a young child with special needs, the mesosystem often includes relationships between parent and teacher(s), therapist(s) and physician(s), as well as professional-to-professional relationships. The *exosystem* consists of such societal structures as public and private service agencies, advocacy groups and churches. The *macrosystem* consists of the cultural and legislative contexts in which the three other levels of the child's ecological environment operate. Such contexts include societal attitudes and values, court rulings, and governmental and agency regulations.

From a systems theory perspective, it would be of minimal use to plan intervention strategies without consideration of the dynamics at each level of the child's ecological environment (i.e. microsystem, mesosystem, exosystem and macrosystem). Likewise, from a systems theory perspective, co-ordination of efforts within and across the different levels of the ecological structure represents a more effective intervention strategy than working in isolation from each other.

Interdisciplinary/interagency teaming

Comprehensive services for young children with special needs are provided by a team of professionals representing a variety of disciplines (e.g. education, speech/language therapy, physical therapy) and agencies (e.g. education, health, social service). Interdisciplinary teaming (i.e. teaming across disciplines) occurs at two different but overlapping levels. The first level involves parents and professionals directly concerned with planning, implementing and evaluating a child's programme. This level will be referred to as 'collaborative teaming'. The second level involves multiple agencies working together to provide co-ordinated and comprehensive services for young children with special needs and their families. This level will be referred to as 'community collaboration'. These two levels are interconnected and interdependent, in that success in achieving targeted goals at one level depends on collaboration and successful teaming at the other level.

Collaborative teaming

Collaborative teaming involves professionals from varying disciplines and parents agreeing to work together to achieve common goals. A primary purpose of collaborative teaming is the co-ordination and interpretation of information from various disciplines and parents and/or other caregivers. A second purpose is to be mutually accountable for planning, implementing and monitoring of strategies to achieve desired goals. Collaborative teaming, when done effectively, represents a more efficient and ecologically valid service delivery model than individuals working alone (Howard *et al.*, 2001; Klein *et al.*, 2001).

Professionals involved in collaborative teaming for young children with special educational needs often include medical personnel, physical and occupational therapists, speech/language therapists, educators and educational psychologists. While each of these professionals has a special part to play in providing necessary services to young children with SEN, some overlap exists in the mission and roles of the various disciplines. In addition, the effectiveness of services from any one discipline is usually enhanced when professionals from different disciplines co-ordinate their efforts and work towards common goals. Since an understanding of discipline-specific roles is often a first step towards successful collaboration, a brief description of various disciplines often involved in direct services to young children with SEN is presented in Box 7.1.

Collaborative consultation is often an important part of collaborative teaming. Collaborative consultation represents one type of joint activity that has been used successfully to foster collaboration among staff from various disciplines. Consultation entails the giving and receiving of information between two or more people for the purpose of (1) resolving a need, issue or problem; (2) improving the understanding that one or both individuals have of the issue at hand; and (3) improving the ability of the individuals involved to respond effectively to similar problems in the future (Bruder, 1994).

Collaborative consultation is often used to provide both direct and indirect services to a child with special educational needs. Direct services are provided when the consultant works directly with the child. This may be to assess the child and/or to provide instruction in a particular area of concern (e.g. speech/language, self-help skills, reading). Indirect services are provided when the consultant works with the teacher and/or parents versus directly with the child. Indirect consultation services are designed to enhance the knowledge and improve the skills of the direct service providers (i.e. teachers and parents) in relation to addressing the child's special needs. For example, an occupational therapist provides indirect services when he or she consults with a teacher on how to position a child at the computer in a way that will provide maximum support for the child with balance and co-ordination problems. In this example, the

Box 7.1 Discipline-specific roles

Discipline and major role(s)

Medical personnel
- Diagnose and treat medical illnesses
- Promote optimal health and well-being

Occupational therapy
- Assess and monitor development and functional performance in relation to purposeful activities (e.g. play and self-help skills)
- Develop and implement interventions to enhance functional performance in purposeful activities

Physical therapy
- Assess motor development needs of the child
- Develop and implement interventions to enhance performance in motor-related activities
- Assess need for adaptive equipment and secure such equipment as necessary

Speech/language pathologist
- Assess language and communicative competence of the child
- Develop and implement interventions to enhance speech, language and communicative competence

Educator/teacher
- Plan and implement appropriate social, emotional, academic and behavioural interventions in consultation with the rest of the intervention team
- Monitor child progress
- Share information with the parents and involve them in the educational programme
- Work with the therapists on the team to incorporate therapy activities within the context of daily activities

School psychologist
- Assess psychological/behavioural characteristics of children
- Assist in planning appropriate social, emotional, academic and behavioural interventions

occupational therapist is providing indirect service to the child by instructing the teacher on appropriate adaptations.

Indirect consultation can be effective in meeting the needs of children with SEN. In fact, consulting models of indirect service delivery in special education have proven to be as effective as direct services provided in therapeutic settings (Bruder, 1994). In addition, teachers who worked with consultants demonstrated positive changes in their instructional techniques for working with children with SEN (Bruder, 1994).

Community collaboration

Services for young children with disabilities and their families must be organized in a coherent and co-ordinated manner if they are to be effective in safeguarding the rights and meeting the special needs of the children involved. Sometimes, this co-ordination can be quite difficult, due to the fact that one family may be receiving services from multiple agencies. The Department for Education and Skills (DfES), in recognizing this need, devotes an entire section on 'Working in partnership with other agencies' in the *Special Education Needs Code of Practice* (DfES, 2001a).

The co-operation required among different agencies serving young children and their families must include integration and co-ordination of services. Without such integration and co-ordination, it can be very difficult and frustrating for parents seeking services to find the right service at the right time. Without integration and co-ordination, parents often find that they have to learn about services in a piecemeal fashion; that it is difficult to access services due to confusing eligibility criteria and participation requirements, and that they have to spend hours completing application and intake forms (Hanson and Lynch, 1995).

In many communities, parents are asked to complete detailed forms for each agency from which they may be receiving services. In addition to information about the child's history and developmental status, many agencies also ask questions about the parents' health, education, employment, family routines and style of interacting. They may even ask for information about the family's financial resources. After several different agencies have asked for the same or similar information, it is easy to understand how some families become quite frustrated with this time-consuming and intrusive process. Community collaboration, or collaboration across agencies, can reduce this duplication and make the process of accessing services easier and friendlier for the families involved. One way to do this is to adopt a common intake form (i.e. the same form used by multiple agencies). After a family completes this form for one agency, it can then be shared with other agencies as well. Of course, parent permission for the sharing of such information is vital.

If services for young children with special needs are not organized in a coherent manner, the co-ordination of services to meet the needs of an individual family and the transition of the child from one intervention programme to another can become major problems. In addition, the family might be faced with incomplete, fragmented and even conflicting information about their child's disability and ways to facilitate his or her development. For example, an occupational therapist working with a 6-year-old who has hand control difficulties may suggest that the parents use mealtimes to stress independent use of eating utensils. A physician treating this same child, however, may be more concerned about the child's tendency to be undernourished and suggest that the parents make mealtimes as relaxing and enjoyable as possible. A third opinion might be presented by the child's teacher who believes that mealtimes offer the best opportunity for the child to learn social and communication skills. The parents, in this case, may feel frustrated and confused as to how to proceed in meeting their child's needs.

In addition to co-ordination across agencies within a community, co-ordination must also occur across levels of government, with consistency assured between policies developed at state and local levels. According to Wolfendale (2000), 'recent government and local initiatives now acknowledge explicitly that provision targeted at young children and their families (Carpenter 1997) cannot effectively be uni-dimensional, that is, the monopoly of one statutory service' (p. 4). She goes on to say that this 'idea of "joined up" policies epitomises joint service planning and delivery, with the full inclusion of all partners' (p. 4).

While the complexity of government and the diversity of communities suggest that some inconsistencies and contradictions are inevitable, they need not be extreme. Questions proposed by the European Commission Childcare Network (n.d.) that might be used in studying the integration and co-ordination of services across differing policy-making units include the following:

- What contradictions about policies and priorities exist between departments at the national level?
- What contradictions about policies and priorities exist between departments at the regional or local level?
- How do national and local policies relate to one another?
- What contradictions exist within departments (such as education) about the priority given to services to young children?
- What contradictions exist between the aims and objectives of services at a local level?
- What strategies exist to address these contradictions?
- How do services for young children link up with systems of healthcare?
- How do fiscal policies affect families with young children?
- How do employment policies relate to families with young children?
- How do environmental policies relate to the needs of young children?

The European Commission Childcare Network is an interagency and interdisciplinary group concerned with the protection of the rights and well-being of children. This group, established in 1986, focuses primarily on childcare issues. From its beginning, the Network has emphasized that childcare services must be of good quality as well as sufficient in number. As outlined by the European Commission Childcare Network, high-quality services for young children provide the opportunity for children to experience the following:

- a healthy life
- spontaneous expression
- esteem as an individual
- dignity and autonomy
- self-confidence and zest in learning
- a stable learning and caring environment
- sociability, friendship and co-operation with others
- equal opportunities irrespective of gender, race and disability
- cultural diversity
- support as part of a family and a community
- happiness.

If a community can ensure that each of these opportunities is available for young children and their families, chances are that the community has a healthy network of comprehensive services. Once these opportunities are in place, the next challenge is to see that they are integrated and co-ordinated in a consumer-friendly format. Community collaboration is the key to achieving the necessary integration and co-ordination of services.

Community collaboration occurs when two or more programmes or agencies establish an ongoing working relationship to achieve common goals. A truly collaborative relationship goes beyond co-operation and co-ordination in that it involves a greater commitment of time and resources than that which co-operation and co-ordination alone would require (Bruder, 1994). Interagency team models based on co-operation and co-ordination allow separate agencies and staff to maintain their own autonomy as well as their own philosophy and goals. There are serious limitations to this approach. In fact, 'differing philosophies' and 'distinct goals' have been identified as common barriers to interagency collaboration (Bruder, 1994).

Gaps, overlaps and other concerns

Without co-operation and collaboration, gaps and overlaps in services for young children with special needs often occur. A gap occurs when a service that is needed is not available in a given community. Quality childcare for young children with special needs represents a gap in some communities. A 4-year-old child who is blind may attend a school-based programme from 9 a.m. to 3 p.m. each day. Because his parents work until 5 p.m., they need after-school care for their son as well. They also need childcare during school holidays and summer breaks. After numerous phone calls, they find that the childcare programmes in their community do not accept children with disabilities. The parents respond to the situation by trying to take turns with childcare responsibilities – either by taking time off work or finding neighbours and/or extended family members to fill in for them. Obviously, this gap in needed services puts a great deal of strain on the parents and can be a source of emotional stress for the child.

Overlaps in services can also be a concern. Overlaps occur when the same services are provided through multiple agencies in communities where the need or demand for the services fails to warrant such duplication. Overlaps in such cases can put an unnecessary strain on the financial resources of the community and can lead to unhealthy competition for clients and qualified personnel. An overlap in services might occur in a community if the schools decide to establish assisted-living arrangements for young adults with autism when such services are already being provided through a mental health agency.

Parents of young children with special needs have identified transitions from one programme to another as times of particular stress for their families (Haines *et al.*, 1988). The nature of the difficulties involved during transitions suggests that co-operation and collaboration across providers and agencies are especially needed at this time. Educators and researchers have begun to address the issues of transition for children with special needs and their families and to develop models for easing the process. Further discussion about the transition process is presented in Chapter 10.

Team models

Members of a team can work together in several different ways. Three basic models have been identified for the way early intervention teams might work together. These three models are: multidisciplinary, interdisciplinary and transdisciplinary.

In a *multidisciplinary* team, members work independently within their own disciplines. They each provide assessment and direct services to a child and then meet as a group to share assessment findings and progress reports. With this model, there is little co-ordination of efforts. In an *interdisciplinary* team, members often conduct their assessments and plan goals together, but provide direct services independently of each other. In a *transdisciplinary* team, professionals share roles and may even combine their assessment and treatment tasks, so that any one member may be performing responsibilities and tasks usually associated with a discipline other than his or her own. There follows an example of how the role of Lonnie, a speech/language therapist, might differ according to the team model being implemented.

When working within the multidisciplinary model, Lonnie contacts the Year 1 teacher to schedule a time when she can conduct an assessment of a child's communication skills. She then conducts the assessment in her speech therapy room, tabulates the results, and shares a report at a 'staffing' for the child. Lonnie develops and implements a speech/language intervention plan for the child, which involves individual therapy on a schedule of thirty minutes twice a week. At the next staffing three months later, Lonnie shares a report on the child's progress as she sees it in her therapy sessions.

When working within the interdisciplinary model, Lonnie and the classroom teacher observe the school psychologist as she conducts an assessment of a child's cognitive skills. During the assessment, Lonnie records language samples and information about the child's speech sounds and language use. In this way, Lonnie is able to complete a large part of her speech/language assessment without duplicating the testing in a separate session. Lonnie also talks with the school psychologist and the classroom teacher about how they might combine intervention goals and activities across domains or areas of instruction.

When working within the transdisciplinary model, Lonnie meets the classroom teacher to discuss how they might assess a child's pragmatic language skills within the context of the regular classroom activities. Lonnie also works with the teacher on how to make her (i.e. the teacher's) lessons more language focused, with special attention on how to address the speech and language goals of the target child and other children with SEN within the context of the classroom.

The team model used in a particular situation depends on the administrative policy of the school and service agencies involved. It also depends on the philosophical orientation, professional expertise, and cohesiveness of the professionals serving a particular child. Regardless of which model the intervention team follows or represents, collaboration among team members with information sharing and consensus decision making is crucial for quality intervention services (McLean and Odom, 1996).

Building and maintaining effective teams

Meaning of team

While 'team' can be defined as a noun (i.e. a group of people working or acting together), it can also be defined as a verb (i.e. to join forces). The most effective teams are those that focus on the verb-related aspects of teaming. They view themselves as a team in relation to what they do (i.e. they team; they work together) versus something they are (i.e. a group by association). They recognize that 'teams do not naturally fall together; groups can, but teams cannot' (Howard *et al.*, 1997, p. 415).

Developing effective interdisciplinary and interagency service delivery teams is a complex and challenging task. Philosophical, professional, interpersonal and administrative issues often hinder the process. A listing of some of the most common barriers to collaboration in early intervention services is presented in Box 7.2.

Box 7.2 Common barriers to collaboration in early intervention

- staff, time and budget limitations
- poor communication skills
- competitiveness
- narrow or self-serving interests
- lack of incentive
- lack of training and skill in co-ordinating efforts
- preoccupation with administrative structure rather than the function of the agency
- general resistance to change
- lack of political awareness and other political issues
- turf issues and territoriality
- lack of information about other agencies' mission and function
- haphazard team process
- lack of planning
- lack of monitoring of the collaborative process
- distance and other related logistical concerns
- questionable administrative support
- discipline-specific jargon and perspectives

Some typical Western culture perspectives conflict with effective team behaviours. Competitiveness, for example, can serve as a major barrier to effective teaming. It has been suggested that early childhood professionals could benefit from specific instruction on how to move away from competitive work and towards collaborative efforts if they are to be effective members of an interdisciplinary team (Kagan, 1991).

Strategies to enhance collaboration

There are steps that can be taken to minimize the barriers to interdisciplinary and interagency collaboration. The following five strategies, focusing primarily on interagency collaboration, have been suggested by Hanson and Lynch (1995).

1 Develop new ways to meet community needs. Rather than getting trapped in bureaucracies or current administrative structures, communities would do well to find new ways to deal with identified

needs. Communities might start by: (1) conducting a community needs assessment to determine how the community has changed over time; (2) helping agencies or groups write small grants to fund new projects, and (3) using faculty and students at nearby colleges to solve problems in new and creative ways.

2 Increase community awareness about the issues and needs relating to young children who are at risk or disabled. Networking to increase awareness can facilitate collaboration. Forums for networking could include a series of meetings where professionals from different agencies get together to discuss current issues and practices, or be as simple as meeting periodically for a more social lunch.

3 Be responsive to people and agencies throughout the change process. 'Being responsive', in the context of teaming, means about the same as it does in the context of interpersonal relationships. In fact, 'many of the behaviours that people view as responsive are simply good manners' (Hanson and Lynch, 1995, p. 284). Examples of being responsive include acknowledging people's and agencies' accomplishments and following through in a timely manner on commitments. An expression of congratulations through telephone calls, written notes and public recognition can do much to foster collaborative relationships, as can willingness to share responsibilities on tasks to be completed.

4 Acknowledge and respect turf and territorial issues while working to decrease them. Territorial issues usually reflect what has occurred in the past and 'the rules' (spoken and unspoken) which tend to govern the present. While members of interagency teams should be aware of these territorial issues, they can prevent such issues from becoming barriers to collaboration by focusing on a common vision for the future.

5 Maintain frequent, open communication. A breakdown in communication is one of the most common barriers to effective teaming. It is important, therefore, for interagency teams to seek out ways to keep the lines of communication open. At times, outside group facilitators can be helpful in bringing groups together and establishing procedures for ongoing communication. Regularly scheduled meeting times, with a commitment from all involved to participate on a regular basis, can also be crucial to establishing and maintaining effective interagency communication.

There is a considerable amount of literature on the team-building and team-functioning process, much of which may be found in publications developed for the business community and/or business education purposes. Many of the specific team-building strategies that are used in business can also be used to build and maintain early intervention teams. Some such strategies include the following:

- Establish regular meeting times with all staff involved. Staff should make participation in these meetings a priority.
- Clarify roles and responsibilities for all members of the team.
- Establish and maintain ongoing communication mechanisms among everyone involved. Such mechanisms should include oral and written communications.
- Establish a shared system of decision making and accountability. Each member of the team should understand and be committed to an organizational structure that includes such components as leadership selection, role assignments, agendas, and individual and group evaluation.

For professionals and agencies serving young children with disabilities, the following suggestions are also offered:

- Each member of the team should become familiar with the special education and related service personnel available to children with special educational needs. Not only should team members be familiar with the special services and service personnel within their own agency, but they should also have familiarity with such services and service personnel in other community agencies.
- Philosophies or mission statements regarding collaborative teaming should be developed and adopted at the regional level, in local or smaller communities, and even within a particular service agency (e.g. school, hospital, specialized clinic). Individual teams should establish their own philosophy or mission statement, and, once this is in place, all other decisions (personal and team) should be measured against the intent of this statement.
- Specific strategies for accomplishing goals should be discussed and agreed upon. Because members of an intervention team not only come from various disciplines, but also from various professional training backgrounds, they are often guided by differing theories, methods and models. Finding common ground on a method or approach to intervention can be a challenge. Advance planning regarding specific strategies to be used is important to ensure instruction that is intentional and sufficiently intensive to meet individual learner needs.
- Establish and maintain meaningful connections with the community. Working on joint projects can often serve as a vehicle for bringing individuals and groups together in a meaningful way. Examples of joint projects that some communities have initiated for young children and their families include: (1) offering developmental and health screenings in public areas, such as shopping malls and community fairs; (2) organizing information forums addressing issues relevant to new parents, such as health and safety, age-appropriate toys, behaviour

management, and (3) developing community playgrounds, after-school childcare programmes and summer recreation opportunities.

- Respect the contributions of all team members, recognizing that each individual and discipline contributes unique insights and skills to programme planning and implementation. No one discipline or individual should be viewed as 'more right' or 'more of an expert' than any other discipline or individual. The sharing of multiple perspectives and the merging of skills and differing knowledge bases should be valued by all members of the team.
- Ensure that all members of the team are familiar with each child's individualized objectives. It is important to recognize that neither teachers nor specialists own particular objectives. Instead, all team members share responsibility for the total educational programme for individual children.

Working in the early years classroom

There was a time when to be a teacher meant working as the single adult with a group of between fifteen and twenty-five children. It meant planning and directing large group activities for the majority of the day. As children with disabilities were not expected to be able to keep up with the rest of the class, they were often served in separate classrooms or groups with a special educator filling the role as teacher. There was usually little communication between the regular education and the special education programmes within a school. Children from the two different programmes usually had lunch separately, went on separate field trips and had few opportunities to get to know each other.

Today, with an emphasis on the least restrictive environment for children with disabilities and a recognition of the value of transdisciplinary teaming, teachers are beginning to work as members of a team. While some teachers may still be the one adult in a room with a group of children for part of the day, it is becoming increasingly common for several adults to be working in the same classroom at the same time. These other adults often include learning support assistants (LSAs), specialized staff (i.e. speech/language therapists, physiotherapists), parents and volunteers. Recommended practices call for a co-ordination of the efforts of these other adults in the classroom rather than having each of them work in relative isolation from each other. The following discussion addresses such co-ordination.

Working with learning support assistants (LSAs)

To facilitate the inclusion of children with disabilities, many schools are introducing learning support assistants (LSAs) into classrooms. Because

LSAs do not usually have the same grounding in early childhood development or an understanding of young children with disabilities as the classroom teachers, initial and ongoing training and supervision are critical to their effectiveness as a member of the educational team. Much of this training and supervision becomes the responsibility of the school and local education authority.

The professional development process

As stated above, personnel working with young children with disabilities need information and skills from both early childhood education and early childhood special education. As such, their professional programme should focus on both typical and atypical early childhood growth and development. Their professional development programme should also address teaming and collaboration and reflect a family-centred orientation.

Ideally, preparation programmes designed for personnel working with young children with disabilities should be interdisciplinary in nature. To be interdisciplinary is not the same as being multidisciplinary. Multidisciplinary programmes are often pieced together by taking existing courses from various departments and listing them as programme requirements or electives. For example, a student majoring in early childhood education may take a special education course from one department, a communication disorders course from another, and the majority of his or her courses from the early childhood department. This programme can be considered as multidisciplinary, in that it incorporates courses from more than one discipline. The content across the various courses, however, may be fragmented and contradictory.

An interdisciplinary programme, on the other hand, involves a greater degree of collaboration between disciplines. While the interdisciplinary curriculum is derived from several related disciplines, it is planned and implemented jointly. The result is a unified programme versus a piecing together of existing courses. Interdisciplinary programmes are usually developed, implemented and evaluated by a team of faculty from different departments.

As preservice preparation can usually provide only entry level knowledge and skills for a profession, inservice programmes are needed to continue the professional development process. Quality inservice programmes are especially important for professionals serving young children with disabilities, since the field of early childhood special education is relatively new and evolving quickly. Inservice programmes can serve as a vehicle for professionals to keep up to date in a changing field.

Changing practices in early childhood special education necessarily result in changing roles for personnel involved in the process. These personnel are not only teachers, but other members of the team as well, including speech/language therapists, physiotherapists, school psychologists, supervisors and others. To work together effectively, all members of the team should receive specific training in providing family-centred services, in collaborating as team members, and in providing consultant or direct services in inclusive settings (Miller and Stayton, 1996).

Recommended practices indicate that inservice programmes should be based largely on a 'needs-based' approach (i.e. from the assessed needs of the participants). To be most meaningful and effective, the needs assessment should address competencies that are directly applicable to the individual's professional role. Needs-based inservice acknowledges the experiences of the participants and builds upon those experiences that are relevant to the learner's situation. Needs-based inservice also recognizes the learner's own goals as the primary incentive for participation.

One programme, committed to a more unified approach to intervention, developed its own 'self-rating scale' to evaluate individual performance in relation to programme priorities. Staff from this programme then used the results of this evaluation to identify specific areas for inservice. According to staff reports, this form of self-evaluation was far less intimidating and much more affirming than an evaluation based on a more generic scale and conducted by a programme supervisor (Wilson, 1991). Staff also reported that another positive outcome of this process was the development of an inservice plan that was meaningful to them and which they felt confident would address their most immediate professional development needs.

Case study – Terry

Background information

Due to a serious health condition, 7-year-old Terry is scheduled for a variety of medical tests and treatments on Tuesdays and Thursdays after school. Terry usually gets less sleep on the nights of the treatment, due to the travel time and other scheduling complications involved, as well as her physical and emotional reaction to the treatment. The mornings following the treatment are also hard for Terry – she does not want to get up and usually refuses to eat breakfast. A physical therapist, who has been working with Terry at school, sees her early every Friday morning for forty-five minutes. Since the medical tests and treatments have started, Terry has been unco-operative and whiny during her physical therapy sessions.

The classroom teacher and the physical therapist make arrangements for a behavioural specialist to come in to observe Terry during these sessions. A behavioural management plan (based on rewards and penalties) is developed and scheduled to begin the following week.

Discussion

Terry's unco-operative behaviour during her physical therapy sessions may be due to 'treatment overload'. Involving a behavioural specialist and adding another treatment (i.e. 'behaviour therapy') could easily result in more stress and discomfort for Terry, as well as for her parents. While the behaviour management techniques may modify her behaviour over the short term, they will probably not alleviate her stress.

A team approach to the concern might have led to an entirely different plan of action. If members of the intervention team (i.e. teacher, medical personnel, physiotherapist and parents) had first met to discuss the situation, they may have been able to adjust Terry's schedule in a way that would be less stressful for her. The physiotherapist, for example, may have been able to work with Terry on another day or at a later time on Friday. Terry's parents may have been able to rearrange things at home to make it possible for Terry to go to bed earlier on Thursday and perhaps make it a more soothing time for her. Terry's teacher may have been able to give Terry more rest time and reassurance. In addition, the physiotherapist, the classroom teacher and the parents may have developed a plan for incorporating more of Terry's physiotherapy activities into the classroom and home routines, perhaps resulting in less need for intensive therapy in an isolated setting. This arrangement would probably be a lot less stressful for Terry and more conducive to her positive emotional and behavioural development.

8

PARTNERSHIP WITH FAMILIES

Rationale for a family-centred approach

Early childhood education has a history of being committed to parent involvement and family support. Thus it should not be surprising that parent education and involvement are also integral to services for young children with disabilities. Unfortunately, this family-focused approach has been relatively slow to develop in the field of early intervention/early childhood special education. Historically, the focus in programmes serving young children with disabilities has been on the child and his or her areas of deficit. Even programmes serving children at risk due to poverty have tended to focus more on enrichment for the child versus services for the family.

The trend in recent years, however, is to view the child within the context of the family and to consider working with families to be an essential aspect of early intervention (Wolfendale, 1997). Factors contributing to this more family-centred approach include research findings, shifting philosophical and theoretical assumptions, and parental dissatisfaction with traditional parent–professional relationships (Bailey, 1994).

A family-centred approach to serving young children with special educational needs is based on the understanding that parents are the managers or decision makers for their children, and that the role of professionals is to provide guidance and assistance to the parents in this process. The earlier approaches sometimes viewed parents as incompetent, dysfunctional or irrelevant, and viewed professionals as the experts and leaders of the intervention team. Parents were often relegated to passive roles in the intervention process (e.g. receivers of information, implementers of activities developed by the therapists, and supporters of school-sponsored initiatives, such as fund raising, holiday parties and so on.)

A family-centred approach, in contrast, views parents as equal-status partners in planning, implementing and evaluating intervention services for their children (Vincent and McLean, 1996). This approach recognizes the importance of enabling parents to become long-term advocates for their children and provides them with the necessary information and skills to be confident and competent in this role (Howard *et al.*, 1997). A family-centred approach goes beyond 'helping' families to 'enabling and empowering' them, so that they need not be dependent upon professionals for decisions regarding the education, care and future of their children (Bailey, 1994).

As evident from the following excerpts, the *Special Educational Needs Code of Practice* (DfES, 2001a, p. 16) clearly calls for active, meaningful partnerships with parents.

> Parents hold key information and have a critical role to play in their child's education. They have unique strengths, knowledge and experience to contribute to the shared view of a child's needs and the best ways of supporting them. It is therefore essential that all professions (schools, LEAs and other agencies) actively seek to work with parents and value the contribution they make. The work of professionals can be more effective when parents are involved and account is taken of their wishes, feelings and perspectives on their child's development. This is particularly so when a child has special educational needs. All Parents of children with special educational needs should be treated as partners.

The early intervention and early childhood education literature also indicates that the impact of educational programming is likely to be 'more profound and lasting if the whole family . . . is involved' (Nickse, 1990, p. 3). Because the family often consists of more than the parent–child dyad, a number of family involvement programmes have initiated ways to involve siblings, grandparents and other individuals within or close to the family unit. Such programmes reflect an understanding of systems theory and the influence of one's community on child growth and development. This ecologically based approach to family services views 'the family from its center (the child) through the family system (a circle around the child) to the community (a circle around the family)' (Howard *et al.*, 1997, p. 330).

There is no doubt that having a child with a disability places unique demands and stressors on a family. The presence of such demands and stressors, however, does not make the family dysfunctional, heroic or incompetent; nor does it make all families with children with disabilities alike. Accordingly, parent education and involvement programmes should reflect understanding and respect for diversity across families and should provide options for when, how and to what extent parents wish to be involved with their child's educational programme.

Options for families

Partnerships between parents and professionals can focus on an individual child and his or her family and/or on issues related to the educational/intervention programme as a whole. While many families may not choose to be involved at the systems level of decision making (i.e. with issues affecting the programme as a whole), professionals and agencies should be prepared to build such collaborative partnerships with the families who are interested (Vincent and McLean, 1996). Professionals should encourage systems-level involvement and offer more options at this level than just inviting parents to serve on a formal board or committee. Other options for systems-level involvement might include: (1) assisting in planning and conducting orientations for parents and staff new to the programme, and (2) reviewing written materials and other publicity about the programme.

Family involvement at the level of the individual child and his or her family is often categorized into two broad types: educational enhancement and family support. A third type, however, should also be carefully considered. This type directly involves parents in the assessment, educational planning and monitoring process, as these relate to their child's educational programme. There follows a brief discussion of each of these three types of family involvement.

Educational enhancement

Generally, the goal of educational enhancement activities is to help parents improve their parenting skills and become more effective in fostering their child's development. As such, educational enhancement programmes designed for groups of parents may be devoted to such specific concerns as helping parents become more effective communication partners, managing child behaviour and fostering family literacy. At times, educational enhancement programmes are conducted with individual families versus groups of parents. For children with special needs, such programmes often focus on therapeutic activities (designed by specialists) that parents can do at home.

Family support

The second type of family involvement is designed to provide support to the family in raising a child with a disability. This type of family involvement programming was developed in response to a concern for the special demands and stressors experienced by parents of children with disabilities. Family support programmes tend to focus on: (1) parent-to-parent interactions for mutual support, (2) personal reflections, and

(3) assistance in learning about and accessing family support services in the community, such as respite care and resource-and-referral programmes.

Parental involvement in assessment, planning and monitoring

As articulated in Chapter 7, a team approach to intervention is essential for serving young children with special needs. Parents should be considered an integral component of this team. The *Special Educational Needs Code of Practice* (DfES, 2001a) indicates that 'the parents' perspective is particularly important when assessing the special educational needs of young children' (p. 39).

While the above excerpt from the *Code* addresses parental involvement during the assessment phase of intervention, the *Code* also makes it clear that there should be close consultation and partnership with the child's parents throughout all of the school-based stages. At no part of the process should parents be excluded. Not only should parents be informed all along the way, but the expression of their wishes, feelings and knowledge should be encouraged, respected and responded to.

Many parents may need assistance in learning how to be meaningfully involved throughout the assessment, planning and monitoring process as these relate to their child's educational programme. They may also need information, advice and encouragement on how to be effective advocates for their child. Professionals can help parents by sharing with them some basic understandings about what it means to be an advocate. A listing of some of these basic understandings is presented in Box 8.1. As some parents may feel intimidated when talking with a team of professionals, some suggestions for making them feel more comfortable are presented in Box 8.2.

Box 8.1 Characteristics of an effective advocate

- An advocate communicates effectively and is assertive.
- An advocate believes that he/she is an equal partner in planning and evaluating services for a child.
- An advocate is not afraid to ask questions.
- An advocate communicates effectively by documenting in written form and by keeping good records.
- An advocate is involved in the education process of his/her child.

Source: Adapted from the Family Collaboration module developed by Project PREPARE, Columbus, OH (USA): Ohio Department of Education.

Box 8.2 Communicating with professionals – some suggestions for parents

1 Before each meeting or contact with a professional, remind yourself that you are an important part of the intervention team and that you have a right to be involved.

2 Prepare for meetings by planning in advance the important points you want to make. A written list may be helpful.

3 Feel free to take someone with you. Another person might take notes, help you make a point and provide support.

4 When you don't understand something, ask questions.

5 Communicate assertively, rather than passively or aggressively.
   - An assertive person clearly states his or her point of view, while being open to what others have to say.
   - A passive person discounts his or her own ideas and needs, while deferring to the other person.
   - An aggressive person discounts the ideas and needs of others. Assertiveness can be expressed both verbally and nonverbally. Nonverbally, assertiveness can be expressed by taking notes and looking at people when you talk to them. Verbally, assertiveness can be expressed by clearly stating your needs and ideas. The ideas following are several examples of assertive statements: 'I see the situation differently.' 'I would like to make a point.' 'I have a question.'

6 When you have a complaint, discuss it first with the person most directly involved. If the problem still goes unaddressed, take your complaint to the next level (e.g. supervisor, administrator, etc.).

7 In addition to expressing concerns, it is also important to share compliments and to show appreciation for what goes right.

Source: Adapted from the Family Collaboration module developed by Project PREPARE, Columbus, OH (USA): Ohio Department of Education.

The option of non-involvement

Some parents may decide not to be involved with their child's programme at all. This choice should be allowed and respected (Howard *et al.*, 1997). An important concept to bear in mind is that not being involved with their child's programme does not mean that the parents are not involved with their child. Parents can be emotionally close to and interactive with their child and still choose not to participate in school-related functions. Parents may have needs and priorities not shared by professionals on the intervention team. Parents should not be made to feel uncomfortable or guilty about this.

Family assessment and parental involvement

The *Special Educational Needs Code of Practice* (DfES, 2001a) offers 'key principles' on how to communicate and work in partnership with parents (p. 17). It specifies that to make communications effective professionals should:

- acknowledge and draw on parental knowledge and expertise in relation to their child;
- focus on the children's strengths as well as on areas of additional need;
- recognize the personal and emotional investment of parents and be aware of their feelings;
- ensure that parents understand procedures, are aware of how to access support in preparing their contributions, and are given documents to be discussed well before meetings;
- respect the validity of differing perspectives and seek constructive ways of reconciling different viewpoints;
- respect the differing needs which parents themselves may have, such as a disability, or communication and linguistic barriers;
- recognize the need for flexibility in the timing and structure of meetings.

Every effort to encourage parental involvement includes offering options that are individualized to reflect each family's own culture and unique set of strengths, values, skills, expectations and service needs (Bailey, 1994).

A prerequisite to developing such individualized options is an understanding of the family's unique characteristics. Both formal and informal family assessment procedures may be used to arrive at this understanding. Professionals should take great care, however, in conducting any type of family assessment to safeguard the family's privacy and to avoid unwelcome intrusions.

A family assessment should be an interactive process involving parents and professionals, rather than an activity conducted by the professional(s) on the family. This assessment should focus on family strengths as well as needs. Consideration of the following definitions developed by Bailey (1991, p. 27) may be helpful in conducting family assessments and setting up family involvement programmes that reflect a family-centred approach.

- *Family assessment*: the ongoing and interactive process by which professionals gather information in order to determine family priorities for goals and services.
- *Family need*: a family's expressed desire for services to be obtained or outcomes to be achieved.
- *Family strength*: the family's perception of resources that are at its disposal which could be used to meet family needs.

The definition of 'parent' as outlined in the *Special Educational Needs Code of Practice* (DfES, 2001a) should also be considered. In addition to the child's birth parents (i.e. natural parents), 'parents' should be taken 'to include all those with parental responsibility, including corporate parents and carers' (p. 16). It is important for the school to know in each instance who should be regarded as a parent of a particular child and who should therefore be consulted regarding the child's needs and progress. In some cases there are adults in more than one household who qualify as parents. Schools should be aware of this and attempt to involve all those with parental responsibility as much as possible in the child's education.

Related issues

There has clearly been a shift in early intervention services from viewing parents as clients and recipients of services towards a view that they should be partners in the planning and delivery of services (Wolfendale, 2000). The philosophy of partnership with parents is also evident in the *Special Educational Needs Code of Practice* (DfES, 2001a). There are concerns, however, about how this partnership model actually works (or does not work) with the widely diverse parent population involved in SEN programmes. In many instances, the vision of collaborative relationships and family-centred practice continues to remain elusive, particularly for low-income and culturally diverse families (Kalyanpur *et al.*, 2000).

This failure to engage parents as equal and full partners is often attributed to the way professionals implement the programmes and/or to family circumstances. Some of the issues relating to professional implementation include: (1) little effort on the part of professionals to seek families' input when making decisions about their child's education; (2) scheduling meetings at times inconvenient for parents; and (3) providing information about services and parents' rights through written materials that many families are unable to understand. Family circumstances sometimes identified as barriers to active parental involvement include (1) lack of transportation and/or childcare; (2) communication and language barriers; (3) a history of poor relationships with schools; (4) beliefs about disability; and (5) perceptions about professionals as experts whose views should not be challenged (Kalyanpur *et al.*, 2000).

The idea that poor implementation and logistical constraints contribute to a lack of collaboration between parents and professionals is not new. The related issues (as articulated above) have often been presented in the literature, and efforts to work around these barriers have been numerous and diverse. Yet, parental/professional collaboration often remains less than satisfactory.

Kalyanpur and colleagues (2000) suggest that the root problem impeding the collaborative process rests in certain cultural assumptions that conflict with the professionals' (and system's) expectations for such collaboration. The poor implementation and logistical constraints, they suggest, are merely outcomes of the 'contextual barriers' which exist within the cultural assumptions. They go on to explain that the expectation (and sometimes requirement) of parental participation is based on the understanding that equity, individual rights and freedom of choice are valued highly. They discuss two problems related to this understanding. First, 'the expectation of equity directly contradicts the hierarchic structure of knowledge and status imbedded in the positivist paradigm of professionalism'; and second, 'the expectation of advocacy assumes that all families believe in individual rights and freedom of choice' (p. 120). There follows a brief discussion of each of these problems.

The 'contextual barrier' relating to the expectation of equity rests, in part, on the dissonance between this expectation and a professional system based on the model of technical rationalism (Kalyanpur *et al.*, 2000). Education, like other modern professions, is based on a positivist model of Western rationalism that values objectivity and professional distance. In this model, professional knowledge (which is scientifically based) is more highly valued than anecdotal or subjective knowledge. An expectation of equity in a system that is hierarchical leaves many professionals and parents feeling quite bewildered. 'Professionals, trained to believe that their knowledge gives them authority to make decisions about a student's education, must now grapple with the seemingly radical idea that parents can be experts too' (Kalyanpur *et al.*, 2000, p. 123).

The idea of the professional as expert also impacts on the parents' response to collaboration. The lack of participation by parents from culturally diverse or low socio-economic backgrounds may relate to their feelings of 'being different', having little to offer and not measuring up to the professionals' expectations. They may also feel vulnerable – concerned that any signs of non-compliance could result in a withdrawal of resources for their child (Kalyanpur *et al.*, 2000).

The 'contextual barrier' relating to the expectation of advocacy is imbedded in different value systems. Some families from culturally diverse backgrounds may not place the same value on individual rights and freedom of choice as families representing the dominant culture. In fact, 'the principle of parent participation is based on ideals that are highly valued in the dominant culture' (Kalyanpur *et al.*, 2000, p. 122), but may not be so valued in other cultures. The advocacy expectation assumes that parents share the understanding that they can and should 'challenge the system' when they believe change would benefit their child. But not all parents feel this way. Some parents believe that authority should not be challenged, that individual needs are subservient to those of the community, and that parents should wait for professionals to initiate communication. They may be 'both unfamiliar and uncomfortable with the prevailing "culture of rights"' on which parental participation policy is based (Kalyanpur *et al.*, 2000, p. 128).

Improving parent/professional collaboration

Professionals committed to working with families as equal partners in the intervention process often face the question of *how* to implement a family-focused intervention programme. It is hoped that the following suggested guidelines and related discussion will be helpful to professionals in moving towards a more family-focused approach to early intervention.

- Work to develop an awareness of your own cultural and ethical values and recognize the assumptions and taken-for-granted beliefs imbedded in your professional practice. Without this awareness, collaboration with parents, especially parents from low-income and culturally diverse backgrounds, will remain elusive (Kalyanpur *et al.*, 2000).
- Make family support and involvement primary goals of early intervention. As professionals involved in direct service to the child and family cannot institute a family-focused programme alone, administrative support and resources (e.g. adequate time and money and sufficient staff) must be provided.
- Expand the traditional concept of successful parental involvement. Instead of defining and evaluating parental involvement *for* families, professionals should enable parents to *self-define* family participation in ways that are meaningful to them. Parents should be able to determine what would be helpful to them and professionals should support the parents' decisions about how they wish to be involved with their child's programme. This approach is different from the traditional concept of 'professionals as experts'. It requires professionals 'to shift from involving families in the approval of professionally determined intervention plans to involving families as partners throughout the entire assessment and intervention process' (Vincent and McLean, 1996, p. 67).
- Encourage and support the family's dreams and visions for the future. Allow parents to feel hope. Without hope, it can be difficult for parents to face the demands of the present, even in such routine concerns as getting to their next appointment or helping their child with reading or maths homework. Dreams and visions for the future can also help parents make decisions in relation to life-span planning (e.g. what skills are necessary for my child to make friends, function independently and so on?).
- Work with the family in identifying their needs and concerns. Too often, family involvement programmes have been designed around family needs or deficits *as perceived by the professionals*. This approach

contributes to the pathology model that assumes deficits in families of children with disabilities. For example, having a child with a disability was assumed to be a burden with few positive outcomes for the family (Kalyanpur *et al.*, 2000). Recommended practices in early intervention/early childhood special education, however, indicate that the *family's perspective* on what they need must be an essential consideration in the design of family involvement programmes (Dunst, 2000).

- Emphasize strengths rather than weaknesses or deficits as the focus of intervention practices. With this approach, it is also important to involve families in identifying their own resources and strengths and then provide the necessary assistance to capitalize on them. This approach leads to empowerment where families exercise control over and access to desired resources (Dunst, 2000). This empowerment model has proven to be more effective in producing positive benefits than have more traditional practices which depend on professional expertise to solve problems for people (Dunst, 2000).
- Emphasize support from informal network members rather than relying solely or primarily on formal supports from professionals and professional help-giving agencies. Informal supports include family members, friends, neighbourhood, church and so on. The mobilization of informal supports has proven effective in enhancing personal and family well-being, parenting attitudes, parenting interactional styles, and various aspects of child behaviour and competence (Dunst, 2000).
- Identify the family's preferred method of maintaining healthy home–school communications. Many parents prefer informal versus formal avenues of communication (Mandell and Johnson, 1985). Parents have indicated, for example, that they find frequent short conversations (either face-to-face or on the phone) with professionals just as meaningful as scheduled parent/teacher conferences, parent meetings at school, or home visits. Parents have also indicated that they learn as much about instructional and/or therapeutic techniques to use with their child by watching teachers and therapists as by attending informational meetings about such techniques. Some parents prefer short written notes about their child's performance, while others prefer phone or face-to-face communication (Mandell and Johnson, 1985). Of particular note is the importance of being aware of parents' oral and written language status. Do the parents speak English, Welsh or any other language as their first language? Can they read, and, if so, at what level?

Sure Start

Sure Start is an early years intervention programme designed to improve the life chances of young children through better access to early education, health services, family support and advice on nurturing (Wolfendale, 2000). Sure Start, with a focus on parents as 'first educators', provides outreach and home visiting, advice about child and family health, and support for families with young children with special needs. Services focusing specifically on the young child are also provided, including support for good-quality play, learning and childcare experiences. The primary focus of the programme, however, is on parents of newborn and preschool children.

While Sure Start ascribes to a philosophy of partnership with parents, concerns have been expressed in the literature as to the realization of this goal. As expressed by Wolfendale (2000), 'it remains to be seen as to whether this governmental flagship enterprise [Sure Start] will epitomise a real partnership with parents by consulting with and including them from the earliest planning stages, through service delivery to evaluation' (p. 8).

Sure Start, then, represents an example of a family-centred early intervention programme. It is also an example of a cross-departmental (Education, Health, Home Office) initiative. The hope for this recently established programme is for the principles and policies on which it is based to '"trickle down" to where practitioners and children spend their working days' (Wolfendale, 2000, p. 4).

9

CHILD FIND

'Child Find', in the context of this chapter, refers to the identification of children with special educational needs. Unless such children are identified and assessed, their special needs may not be understood or attended to. The result may be the development of secondary handicaps and negative impacts on learning and development which may have been avoided if appropriate adaptations had been made. As emphasized in Chapter 1 and discussed in other sections of this book, children with disabilities are similar in many ways to their typically developing peers and should always be viewed as such. Yet an awareness and understanding of their special needs are also important for planning and implementing educational experiences which maximize their chances of success.

Identifying children with special needs is often a complex and multifaceted task. The challenge is even greater at the early childhood level, in that many of the screening and assessment tools and procedures used with older children are not appropriate when working with young children. This chapter gives an overview of the different aspects of assessment and a discussion of the special challenges involved in assessing young children. Presented first, however, is a clarification of the reasons for conducting different types of assessment.

Meaning and purpose of assessment

The term 'assessment', when used in relation to educational programming, may in some people's minds mean the same as testing. In fact, the terms 'assessment' and 'testing' are sometimes used interchangeably by the general public. For example, a parent may say, 'My child is having her hearing tested today', while the audiologist may refer to the process as an assessment of the child's hearing ability. The term 'assessment' actually has a broader meaning than the term 'testing'. Assessment refers to the process of systematically gathering information about a child. Its primary purpose is to help professionals to 'really know' the child (Neisworth and

Bagnato, 1996). Testing, which involves the use of specific instruments and/or procedures to gather information about a child, is often part of an assessment, but is not the same as the total assessment process.

There are several different reasons for assessing young children. One is to screen them for possible developmental delays and disabilities. Other reasons for assessing children include: (1) determining whether they should be given a specific diagnosis (e.g. hearing impaired, visually impaired, attention deficit disorder); (2) deciding if they are eligible for special services (e.g. speech/language therapy, special education services); (3) planning their instructional programmes; (4) determining their educational placements; (5) monitoring their progress; and (6) evaluating the effects of the early childhood services. It is important to note that the information gathered for one of these purposes (e.g. screening) may not be useful for another (e.g. planning instructional programmes). Thus decisions about which procedures and tools to use for any type of assessment should be determined by the purpose of the assessment itself (Wolery, 1994a). Early childhood educators need to be clear as to why information on a child is being gathered and to know which assessment strategies are appropriate for that purpose. Unless the purpose is clear and the strategies appropriate, assessments should not be done (NAEYC and NAECS/SDE, 1991).

Screening

Screening refers to an assessment conducted to determine whether the child should receive further, more in-depth evaluation. Screening results can indicate possible cause for concern, but cannot be used to confirm a disability or a specific diagnosis. Screening procedures are not appropriate for planning instructional programmes; nor should they be used for grouping children for instructional purposes. Some screening programmes focus on the developmental status of a child; others on physical and health concerns and/or sensory functioning (i.e. sight and hearing).

Assessment strategies appropriate for screening include the use of specific screening instruments and systematic observation over time. Screening should not be done without the consent and involvement of the parents. Parent involvement often includes a parent questionnaire and/or interview which can provide valuable data for the screening process. Box 9.1 gives an example of a parent questionnaire that might be used for screening purposes. As illustrated, this questionnaire is designed to be brief and open-ended. At this point, there is no need to alarm the parents or to subject them to a lengthy process.

Children who are identified by screening efforts as possibly having special learning needs should be scheduled for further assessments without undue delay. Appropriate follow-up assessment procedures

Box 9.1 Parent questionnaire for assessment

A THE EARLY YEARS

1 What do you remember about the early years that might help?
2 What was he or she like as a young baby?
3 Were you happy about progress at the time?
4 When did you first feel things were not right?
5 What happened?
6 What advice or help did you receive – from whom?

B WHAT IS YOUR CHILD LIKE NOW?

1 **General health** – Eating and sleeping habits; general fitness, absences from school, minor ailments – coughs and colds. Serious illnesses/accidents – periods in hospital. Any medicine or special diet? General alertness – tiredness, signs of use of drugs – smoking, drinking, glue-sniffing.
2 **Physical skills** – Walking, running, climbing – riding a bike, football or other games, drawing pictures, writing, doing jigsaws, using construction kits, household gadgets, tools, sewing.
3 **Self-help** – Level of personal independence – dressing, etc.; making bed, washing clothes, keeping room tidy, coping with day-to-day routine; budgeting pocket money, general independence – getting out and about.
4 **Communication** – Level of speech, explains, describes events, people, conveys information (e.g. messages to and from school), joins in conversations; uses telephone.
5 **Playing and learning at home** – How . . . spends time watching TV, reading for pleasure and information, hobbies, concentration, sharing.
6 **Activities outside** – Belonging to clubs, sporting activities, happy to go alone.
7 **Relationships** – With parents, brothers and sisters; with friends; with other adults (friends and relations) at home generally, 'outside' generally.
(a) Is . . . a loner?
8 **Behaviour at home** – Co-operates, shares, listens to and carries out requests, helps in the house, offers help, fits in with family routine and 'rules'. Moods good and bad, sulking – temper tantrums; demonstrative, affectionate.
9 **At school** – Relationships with other children and teachers; progress with reading, writing, numbers, other subjects and activities at school. How the school has helped/not helped your child. Have you been asked to help with school work – hearing child read – with what result?
(a) Does . . . enjoy school?
(b) What does . . . find easy or difficult?

C YOUR GENERAL VIEWS

1 What do you think your child's special educational needs are?
2 How do you think these can be best provided for?
3 How do you compare your child with others of the same age?
4 What is your child good at or what does he or she enjoy doing?
5 What does . . . worry about – is . . . aware of difficulties?
6 What are your worries, concerns?
7 Is there any other information you would like to give
(a) about the family – major events that might have affected your child?
(b) reports from other people?
8 With whom would you like more contact?
9 How do you think your child's needs affect the needs of the family as a whole?

Source: DFE, 1994, pp. 72–73. Crown copyright is reproduced with the permission of the Controller of Her Majesty's Stationery Office.

should include teacher and parent consultation, observation and test-based assessments. Screening results relating to specific physical conditions (e.g. hearing, vision or health concerns) may require referral to medical specialists. The primary purpose of this follow-up assessment is to thoroughly identify and describe the child's special needs and to develop appropriate interventions. It is important to remember that screening results cannot be used to positively identify a child as being handicapped or in need of specialized interventions; nor should screening results be used to exclude children from participating in a programme or service. When sharing screening results with parents, professionals should take great care to emphasize the tentative nature of the screening decision.

Box 9.2 presents a number of problems and concerns related to the process of screening. These should be kept in mind when planning, implementing and interpreting the screening process.

Box 9.2 Screening-related problems and concerns

- Limiting screening activities to 'tests', rather than incorporating a range of approaches
- Neglecting to involve parents before, during, and after the screening procedures
- Using a locally developed screening instrument that is of poor technical quality
- Using a screening facility or approach that is not comfortable for young children
- Using screening personnel who are not knowledgeable about young children and are unable to facilitate their best performance
- Interpreting screening data as diagnostic information for making educational placement and program planning decisions

Source: Adapted from Ohio Department of Education (1989).

Diagnosis

Assessments used to determine a diagnosis indicate whether or not a child has a developmental delay or disability. Such assessments may also provide information about the nature and extent of the delay or disability. It is important to note that a medical diagnosis and a developmental/educational diagnosis, while related, are not the same. A medical diagnosis is conducted by medical and other healthcare professionals. The presence of a medical diagnosis does not confirm a disability. For example, a medical diagnosis of recurrent otitis media (middle ear infection) does not necessarily mean that a child has or will have related language and learning disabilities. Although the medical condition places the child at greater risk of such problems, further diagnostic assessments are required to determine the presence of a disability.

Diagnostic assessments should be conducted by a multidisciplinary team of individuals. This multidisciplinary model offers several advantages over a single-discipline approach. For example, it provides a way of checking information across several data sources and settings. Such validation can play a crucial role in analysing strengths and weaknesses needed to plan appropriate interventions.

Perhaps the best way to implement a multidisciplinary model is to employ a core team with consistent membership. This core team should include three professional disciplines: school psychology, speech/language therapy and early childhood education. One member of the core team usually assumes the role of case co-ordinator and assumes responsibility for compiling all the information pertaining to the child and serving as the primary contact for parents and other personnel involved with the child. The composition of the rest of the team and the assessment measures used vary in relation to the diagnosis being considered. For example, a physiotherapist would be involved and make diagnoses in relation to gross motor concerns, while an audiologist would be involved and make diagnoses for a hearing impairment.

It is important to note that early childhood personnel should also be involved in diagnostic assessments. The role of the early childhood educator is to provide relevant information about a child's performance across developmental domains to the other team members. Parents, too, should be considered as an integral part of the assessment team. Their input is crucial for information about the early history of the child and the child's current level of functioning at home and within the family structure. Collecting this information is often by way of a parent questionnaire and/or interview. Questions asked during the assessment are usually more in-depth than the questions for screening. The purpose here is to collect more comprehensive and detailed information about the child. The following are several examples of questions which may be included on a parent questionnaire for assessment:

- What was your child like as a baby?
- Can you tell me about your child's general health?
- Can you describe how your child communicates?
- How does your child spend most of her time? What does she like to do?
- What special concerns might you have about your child's development?
- Do you have any special concerns about your child's behaviour?
- How do you think your child compares to other children of her age?

Wolfendale's developmental profile, *All About Me* (Wolfendale, 1998), involves parents and young children jointly in eliciting views about home events and relationships. It is an excellent resource for use during the assessment process.

To receive special services through the schools, children must meet certain criteria. Diagnostic assessments confirming the presence of a disability often play an important role in determining such eligibility. The eligibility role of assessment is not without controversy. In fact, this role of assessment, sometimes referred to as 'gatekeeping', probably provokes the greatest dispute in relation to diagnostic assessments (Neisworth and Bagnato, 1996).

The completion of assessment activities should be viewed as the beginning of important interventions for children. Without follow-up, screening and assessment are of little value. Follow-up should include communicating with parents, planning appropriate interventions, keeping other professionals informed and conducting periodic reviews. At times, assessment for diagnosis results in applying a diagnostic label to a child (e.g. deaf, autistic, mentally retarded). There are both concerns and advantages associated with labelling. Applying diagnostic labels to young children is a serious matter, whether these labels are special education categories or clinical terms. At times, diagnostic labels may restrict opportunities available to children and/or result in bias, low expectations and self-fulfilling prophecies.

Diagnostic labels, however, can also produce some positive results. They can 'open the door' for children to receive appropriate intervention services and be helpful to parents in understanding their child's behaviour. To emphasize the positive and minimize the negative aspects of labelling, the following suggested practices are offered:

- Communicate clearly to parents the meaning of a label and the reasons why it applies to their child.
- Work from the premise that the diagnostic label represents the team's current judgement and, except in rare cases, should not be interpreted as being permanent.
- Review the use of a diagnostic label regularly and change it, as appropriate.

Assessment strategies

Information about a child can be gathered in a variety of ways. To fulfil the needs of an assessment, however, such information should be gathered in a systematic way. For a valid assessment, it should also involve more than one tool and/or strategy. The goal of this multiple-data approach is to sample many different types of behaviour in a variety of ways. There are a number of different information-gathering methods that may be used during the assessment process. These include testing, direct observation, interviews, anecdotal and running records, work samples, questionnaires, and rating scales completed by a professional or someone familiar with the child. Assessment strategies appropriate for diagnosis are presented in Box 9.3, along with a brief statement about the benefit(s) of each.

Box 9.3 Assessment for diagnosis: sources of data

1 Parent interviews
- provide critical information that only a parent may be able to provide
- provide insights about the child within the family context

2 Parent questionnaires
- complement information from direct assessment by providing a more comprehensive view of the child's behaviour

3 Teacher interviews
- contribute to a complete assessment by adding information about the child's classroom performance

4 Teacher checklists
- quantify teachers' observations about a child

5 Work samples (e.g. art work, reading and/or maths worksheets, etc.)
- contribute to a complete assessment by adding information about the child's academic performance

6 Systematic observations
- provide information about a child's behaviour that may not be gained from other procedures (e.g., interactions with peers and adults, adaptability to differing situations, use of language, etc.)

7 Data from other professionals
- contribute to a complete assessment by adding information about the child from other disciplines (e.g. physicians and therapists) and other child experiences (e.g. daycare)

8 Structured testing
- provides information about a child's knowledge and skills that may not be assessed through other means
- provides information about a child's behaviour in a structured context
- provides information about a child's knowledge and skills in relation to age expectations and/or established criteria

A combination of strategies tends to result in a more valid assessment of the child than any one strategy used in isolation. It should also be noted that there is often more than one way to use an assessment strategy, and, as indicated above, the purpose of the assessment should determine the tools and procedures to be used. At times, certain tools and methods used for one type of assessment may also be used for another purpose (e.g. tools and procedures used for programme planning may also be used for monitoring child progress) (Neisworth and Bagnato, 1996). There follows a brief discussion of interviews, observations and tests, as these three information-gathering formats represent the most commonly used assessment strategies at the early childhood level.

Interviews, as an assessment strategy, involve asking others who know the child well to provide information about how they perceive the child and his or her level of functioning. Interviews can be quite structured, with questions to be asked determined in advance. When interviews are part of a formal assessment tool, the questions may have to be asked in a specific way and the interviewee given limited choices of specific responses. For example, a parent or teacher may be asked to describe a child's level of independence during mealtimes but be limited to one of the following three responses: 'independent', 'needs some help', 'needs a great deal of help'. Other interviews may be quite open-ended, allowing for more detailed information and addressing a wider range of issues. In an open-ended interview, a parent or teacher may be asked, 'How does Jimmy do at mealtimes? Could you talk about how well he does in trying to feed himself?'

There are, of course, a number of different interview formats that fall between the two examples presented above. The purpose of the assessment should determine the format used. If the interview is part of a screening to determine possible developmental delays, the more structured interview would usually be more appropriate. If the purpose of the interview is to determine the child's special interests or to 'fill in the picture' of what he or she likes to do at home, the open-ended format would be more appropriate.

Observation, when used for assessment, entails gathering information by watching and listening and then making a record of what is observed. There are a number of different observational systems that may be used for assessment purposes. One type consists of printed rating scales that the assessor completes during or after an observation. The following is an example of an item that may appear on such a scale: 'Engages in simple make-believe activities.' Other observational systems involve counting and/or timing specific child behaviours. Such systems may be as simple as recording the length of time a child stays with a chosen activity during learning centre time. Observational systems can also be quite complex, such as recording not only the frequency and type of a child's disruptive outbursts during a specified period of time, but also the antecedents of such outbursts (i.e. events that happen before).

Observation, as an assessment tool, has rich potential. Observation may occur in the child's natural environments (e.g. classroom or home) and provide information about how a child usually functions. Observation may be used to gather information that is difficult to obtain in other ways, such as how children interact with peers, how they respond to frustration and how they play.

In spite of its rich potential, systematic observations seem to be used less frequently for assessment purposes than either interviews or testing. This is due perhaps to the complexity of the task and the skill required for analysing and interpreting the data. Some noteworthy attempts have been made to provide an organizational framework for conducting ongoing systematic observations in natural settings. The 'arena assessment' represents one such system. With this approach, one member of the team interacts with a child in a play-based setting, while other members of the multidisciplinary team observe and record observations of the child.

Tests tend to be less useful than interviews and observation when working with young children, especially young children with disabilities. The following are some of the limitations associated with testing, as outlined by Wolery (1994b): (1) tests rarely include adaptations to accommodate to children's disabilities; (2) tests often contain items or sequences of items that are not instructionally relevant; and (3) tests are frequently administered in artificial situations rather than in natural contexts.

There are generally two broad types of tests: norm-referenced and criterion-referenced tests. Norm-referenced tests indicate how a child performs in comparison to the group on which the test was normed. These tests are often used for screening purposes and for making diagnoses related to special needs. To be valid, such tests must be administered according to the developers' specifications. Criterion-referenced tests indicate how a child performs in comparison to specific criteria for each item, and scores for each item are reported in relation to a specified level of performance or knowledge.

Curriculum-referenced tests, a type of criterion-referenced test, compare children's performance to the objectives of a specified curriculum. Some tests address a specific area of child development, such as motor development or language development. Other tests focus on multiple aspects of child development and address all the major developmental domains (e.g. cognitive, motor, communication, social/emotional, adaptive). Many tests can be administered by early childhood personnel who are familiar with the tests; others must be administered only by specifically trained professionals, such as psychologists or speech/language pathologists.

Some types of structured testing are often included in assessment for screening and for diagnosis. Serious concerns associated with the use of structured testing for young children necessitate careful consideration when choosing which tools and procedures to use. While there are a number of variables to consider, including complexity and cost, the following variables warrant special consideration:

- *Reliability*: Reliability refers to the degree to which test results can be trusted in relation to accuracy. Every test has some degree of error, with measures of young children's performance more susceptible to error than those designed for older children and adults. A test that is characterized by too much error is unreliable and should not be used.

- *Validity*: Validity refers to the degree to which an instrument measures what it is designed to measure. For example, a test of cognitive functioning that actually measures the child's cognitive skills rather than skills in other domains is said to be valid. If a test of cognitive functioning relies heavily on a child's receptive and expressive language skills and the child is weak in these areas, the results may not be a true indicator of the child's cognitive abilities. A test lacking in respectable test validity may not provide a fair assessment of the child's true abilities and may thus be discriminatory against the child.
- *Standardization and norming*: Assessment instruments should be critiqued in relation to the normative population used for standardization. It is important that the group on which the assessment instrument was normed matches the group on which the instrument is used, especially in relation to such factors as ethnic background, socio-economic level, geographic region, age and special needs. While some programmes like to use locally developed instruments for screening, such instruments are rarely of adequate technical quality, due in part to problems with standardization and norming.
- *Administration time*: Long structured testing situations are usually not a good match to the characteristics of young children. Thus administration time should be considered carefully when making choices about which assessment tools to use. Screening is designed to be a brief process and should usually require no more than fifteen to twenty minutes for administration. Assessment for diagnosis may take longer to administer, but should not exceed the child's tolerance level. Child-friendly materials and procedures can minimize some of the concerns associated with longer administration time.
- *Personnel*: Some assessment instruments and procedures require a trained or certified individual to administer them. Others require the involvement of a team of individuals. Because both screening results and assessment for diagnosis should be as accurate as possible, anyone involved in the assessment process should be knowledgeable about young children and be able to facilitate their best performance. They should also be aware of the purpose of the assessment and familiar with the instruments and procedures being used.
- *Appeal for children*: Ideally, assessment activities should be pleasant for children, since they are more likely to demonstrate their best performance when they are comfortable and interested in the activities.
- *Setting*: Some assessment instruments and procedures require a specific type of environment (e.g. a sound-proof room, a quiet place for parent interviews, individual workstations for children). Such

requirements should be attended to, as should considerations relating to parent and child comfort and accessibility in terms of location and special needs (e.g. wheelchair accessibility, adaptive equipment available).

- *Cost*: Screening and assessment instruments tend to vary considerably in cost. As there may be no direct relationship between price and quality, purchasers should take care not to equate the two. Some screening instruments have certain 'hidden costs' that should be taken into consideration. These may include individual record forms, training requirements or essential computer scoring.
- *Multiple sources of information*: Effective assessment requires the collection of information from multiple sources. In addition to using a combination of the assessment strategies outlined above (i.e. interviews, observation and testing), it is crucial that expressions of concern and information provided by parents be viewed as valuable assessment data. It is also important for schools to make full use of information passed on to them when the child transfers from one classroom or programme to another.

Special issues and concerns

As indicated above, there are some special issues and concerns relating to the assessment of young children that go beyond the concerns associated with assessment of older children and adults. The following is a discussion of some of these issues and concerns.

- *Intrusiveness*: While assessment plays a pivotal role throughout the early intervention process, considerable debate and concern surrounds the process (Neisworth and Bagnato, 1996). Part of the debate centres on the 'intrusiveness' of the assessment procedures. Assessment can be intrusive to the child, his or her family, and to the professionals involved. Some assessment procedures subject the child and his or her family to invasions of privacy, to inconvenient scheduling, and to assessment-related demands (or tasks) that threaten their feelings of confidence and trust. Assessment procedures can also be intrusive in terms of time constraints, experienced by both professionals and parents.
- *High-stake considerations*: Neisworth and Bagnato (1996), in discussing assessment-related concerns, suggest that professionals involved in making assessment decisions should take care to gather, synthesize and interpret enough information to serve the intended purposes of assessment while avoiding 'over-assessment'. They refer to 'low-stake' and 'high-stake' assessment decisions and suggest that the higher stake decisions should be based on greater sampling and include low

inference measures. Deciding which of three acceptable goals for the child should be worked on first is an example they use of a 'low-stake' decision. Diagnosing the presence of mental retardation and determining eligibility for specialized treatment are examples they use of 'high-stake' decisions. It should be evident from these examples that 'low-stake' and 'high-stake' considerations relate to the potential social consequences of the assessment results.

To help professionals weigh 'high-stake' and 'low-stake' considerations, Neisworth and Bagnato (1996, pp. 25–26) offer the following implications for practices:

1 Strive to obtain the best and closest descriptions of child status when decisions to be made are not trivial.
2 Decisions that are not high stake need not be made with the same set of assessment materials, crew of professionals and expenditures of times [as decisions that have high-stake implications].
3 The possible use of a given assessment instrument and approach should be pitted against alternative assessment or means to achieve similar outcomes, including no assessment.

- *Appropriateness*: It is generally not appropriate to use a 'downward extrapolation of school-age practices' to test young children (Neisworth and Bagnato, 1996, p. 26). This is because assessment methods used with older children often do not match the developmental characteristics of younger children. This mismatch is especially evident when norm-referenced assessments are being used. 'The expectations of most norm-referenced standardized assessments run counter to the realities of the behaviour of young children' (Neisworth and Bagnato, 1996, p. 26). Some of the 'realities of behaviour' that get in the way of standardized testing include 'the child's distractibility, lack of interest in the standard objects in the test kit, oppositional behaviour and non-compliance, lack of endurance, persistence at other competing (more interesting) activities, and frustration with test tasks' (ibid.).

The process of early development represents another concern that needs to be considered in relation to appropriateness in assessing young children. Normal early development tends to be nonlinear and intermittent. These characteristics make prediction and inferences related to assessment problematic (Neisworth and Bagnato, 1996). Transitional phases in early child development add to the concern. If a child is assessed during a transitional phase (i.e. a time characterized by emerging and fluctuating skills), conclusions about the child's current level of functioning may be either exaggerated or depressed. During the early childhood years, it is not unusual for children to exhibit a more advanced skill and then return to a former, less skilled performance. A skill that is 'emerging' may be evidenced or 'previewed' a month or so before it becomes part of the child's daily repertoire of skills. It is thus quite difficult to build an accurate picture of the child's current level of functioning, as this level may fluctuate from week to week or even day to day.

Uneven or nonparallel development, which is characteristic of very young children and children with disabilities, also causes a mismatch between the characteristics of young children and the demands of standardized assessments. With young children and children with disabilities, 'parallel development across the interrelated and interactive developmental domains cannot be expected' (Neisworth and Bagnato, 1996, p. 27). Making decisions about a child's cognitive functioning based on his or her language skills illustrates the type of problem encountered with uneven or nonparallel development. A 4-year-old who is deaf, for example, will not be able to use age-appropriate language skills, even though his or her cognitive functioning may be at or above age expectations.

- *Non-discriminatory practices*: Discrimination can enter into assessment practices in a number of ways. One way is through the disregard of a child's communication status when his or her first language is not English or Welsh. Lack of competence in English or Welsh must not be equated with learning difficulties. Non-discriminatory assessment 'takes into consideration children's ability in English, their stage of language acquisition, and whether they have been given the time and opportunity to develop proficiency in their native language as well as in English' (NAEYC and NAECS/SDE, 1991, pp. 32–33).

  To be non-discriminatory in assessment, care must also be taken to consider the child within the context of his or her home, culture and community. If necessary, bilingual support staff, interpreters and translators should be used to help the child and his or her parents to understand fully the assessment measures the school is taking. It is also important for assessment tools to be culturally neutral and useful for a range of ethnic groups. In addition, when assessing children from minority ethnic groups, it is recommended that schools make use of any local sources of advice relevant to the ethnic group concerned.

  Discrimination can also enter into assessment practices due to a child's disability or special needs. Some tests of cognitive functioning involve the manipulation of materials such as puzzle pieces or paper and pencil. In such instances, a child's inability to score well on a particular test item may be due to cerebral palsy or some other condition relating to poor muscle control rather than delayed cognitive functioning.
- *Appropriate interpretation*: Assessment data should never be viewed as the 'total picture' of a child; nor should it be used to predict future performance. At best, assessment data – particularly in the case of

young children – should be viewed as 'a picture in time' of the child's performance. People perform differently at different times and under different circumstances – again, this is especially true in relation to young children. Appropriate interpretation of assessment data is complicated further by the fact that the expression of handicapping conditions and special educational needs may be very different in young children than in older children and that differentiating between a handicapping condition and inexperience can be difficult in young children. Thus making predictions about a child's subsequent adjustment is not recommended.

Approaches and recommendations

How professionals approach the assessment of children depends to a large extent on their general philosophy about how young children learn and develop. This, in turn, is usually a result of their professional training (Zirpoli, 1995). Historically, assessment of children for educational purposes has followed a medical model approach. The traditional medical model is characterized by various professionals conducting their assessments in isolation, with little communication among the professionals and caregivers involved. More recently, the educational assessment of children has been moving away from this medical model to a more collaborative approach.

In early childhood education and early childhood special education, this move has resulted in the development of an 'arena approach' to assessment. With this approach, assessment is completed by one professional who acts as a facilitator, while other members of the team, including the parents, observe and record observations relevant to their discipline. The role of the facilitator in an arena assessment is to engage the child in activities that demonstrate the child's developmental strengths and weaknesses. Prior to the assessment, team members often meet and identify the facilitator behaviours they would like to see for their individual evaluations. This information helps the facilitator to make decisions about the kinds of activities and materials to introduce with the child.

An arena assessment is usually conducted in a creative play environment, where materials invite expression in all areas of development, including exploratory, manipulative and problem-solving behaviours, emotional expression and language skills (Linder, 1990). Two or three children are often observed at one time, allowing for observations about child-to-child interactions. A play-based arena assessment is generally appropriate for all children who are developmentally functioning between 6 months and 6 years of age. It can be used effectively with children who are typically developing, those who are at risk, and for children with disabilities (Linder, 1990).

Parents are involved in the arena assessment process prior to, during and after the observation period. Before the observation, parents complete developmental checklists and/or participate in an interview to share information about their child's history and level of performance at home. During the observation, parents observe along with the professionals. At times, they may help facilitate their child's play. After the observation, parents are involved in the discussion of their child's performance and in planning an appropriate programme for their child.

The arena assessment receives generally positive reports. 'Professionals who use arena assessment indicate that it saves time, and that with training they can see what they need for their discipline-specific evaluations while also seeing the whole child' (Raver, 1991, p. 34). It has also been observed that 'children who were previously deemed untestable played and interacted comfortably in the play-based [arena] assessment' (Linder, 1990, p. ix). Parents, too, have indicated that they prefer the multidisciplinary arena approach to separate (single-discipline) assessments (Linder, 1990). The arena assessment approach, then, has advantages for the family, the child and the team. A listing of some of these advantages is presented in Box 9.4.

Recommendations

In response to the many concerns relating to traditional approaches to assessment with young children, a number of professional organizations, researchers and practitioners have worked to develop recommendations regarding appropriate assessment practices. Such recommendations have been outlined in a number of publications, including a Position Paper developed by the National Association for the Education of Young Children and the National Association of Early Childhood Specialists in State Departments of Education (NAEYC and NAECS/SDE, 1991). The following recommendations are based on this Position Paper. While the Position Paper addresses all aspects of assessment, the following selected recommendations relate primarily to the identification of young children with special needs. Several of these recommendations have already been discussed, and some overlap between them will be evident.

1 Child assessment should address all domains and aspects of child development. As a disability seldom affects only single areas of development, assessment should address all the developmental domains.
2 Assessments should be conducted, as far as possible, in natural settings and through procedures that are familiar and meaningful to the child.
3 Assessments should use an array of different assessment techniques.

Box 9.4 Advantages of the arena approach to assessment

For the family
- Includes the family as fully functioning members of the team
- Avoids duplication of assessment questions and procedures addressed to or involving them
- Leads to a better understanding of specific skills that are being addressed
- Tends to be less stressful and intimidating for the parents

For the child
- Provides a more comfortable environment, in that the child's parents are present, the facilitator is a play partner versus an examiner, and the materials are fun and interesting
- Participates in one assessment session, versus several domain-specific or discipline-specific assessments
- Provides the opportunity to demonstrate strengths and functional skills in a natural context
- Provides information about a child's learning style, interests and interaction patterns
- Allows flexibility in testing, thus avoiding assessment bias in relation to a child's disability
- Provides qualitative information about the child's functioning, not just quantitative (e.g. information about how a child performs a task, not just the number of tasks he or she can perform)

For the team
- Allows for immediate access to the skills and knowledge of their team mates
- Results in a comprehensive, integrated assessment of the child
- Provides the opportunity to share information based on simultaneous observations of the child, leading to easier consensus
- Expands the knowledge of all team members as they share information from the perspective of various disciplines
- Represents a less costly and less time-consuming process than traditional assessments

Source: Material adapted from Linder (1990) and Raver (1991).

4 Assessment procedures should be sensitive to individual diversity including differences in styles and rates of responding, as well as in children's use of language.
5 Assessment procedures should avoid situations that threaten children's psychological safety or feelings of self-esteem. Children's usual behaviour in natural situations can be assessed easily without causing children undue stress.
6 Assessments should focus on children's strengths and what they can do – not just their weaknesses or areas of deficits.
7 Assessment should be a collaborative process, involving parents and a multidisciplinary team of professionals.

8 The choice of which assessment tools and procedures to use should be given careful consideration. Some questions which may be used to guide the selection process are presented in Box 9.5.

Box 9.5 Selecting assessment tools and procedures

1 Are the materials and procedures reliable and valid?
2 Are the materials and procedures child friendly?
3 How much training is required to administer the assessment?
4 What adaptations, if any, are provided to meet the needs of children with physical, sensory, or other impairments?
5 What role do parents have in administering this assessment?
6 What was the cultural orientation of the normative sample (if norm-referenced)? Were efforts made to provide norms on a separate sample or to include minority cultural groups in the sample? Are non-English forms available?

Case study – Amanda

Background information

Amanda is 4 years old and has been participating in a Reception year class for about three weeks. Her teacher, Ms Lane, is concerned about Amanda's continued 'shyness' and limited use of expressive language. Amanda rarely speaks to anyone except to answer direct questions, and then her responses usually consist of one- or two-word utterances. She often responds with gestures instead of words and seems to avoid contact with others as much as possible. Ms Lane called Amanda's parents, Mr and Mrs Smith, to discuss her concerns, but they indicated that Amanda does not talk much at home either. She likes to watch television and usually plays by herself.

Ms Lane talked to Mr and Mrs Smith about doing a screening with Amanda. She explained to them that she does not really know if Amanda will need special help, but that she is concerned about Amanda's speech, language and social skills. Mr and Mrs Smith agreed to the screening and completed a questionnaire about Amanda's early child development and current functioning at home.

In addition to the parent questionnaire, other components of the screening process included an observation by the speech/language therapist, a hearing acuity screening and a developmental checklist completed by Ms Lane. The speech/language pathologist found it very difficult to get Amanda to respond to any prompts or other screening activities. Amanda would not talk beyond giving a whispered 'yes' or 'no' to direct questions. For the hearing screening, Amanda would sometimes look towards a source of sound (e.g. a bell ringing) but would not raise her hand to show that she had heard the sound; nor would she repeat words and sounds as she was requested to do. Ms Lane had to score many items on the developmental checklist as 'don't know' or 'not observed', since Amanda's participation in classroom activities was quite limited, and direct prompts were usually ignored.

After reviewing all the screening information, Ms Lane asked Mr and Mrs Smith to meet with her at their earliest convenience. They came to school the following week. At this conference, Ms Lane shared her observations and concerns with Amanda's parents and said that she would like further assessments done to determine whether or not Amanda might need special services. While reluctant, Mr and Mrs Smith did agree to follow-up assessments.

These assessments started three weeks later. First, the speech/language therapist took Amanda with her to a therapy room to administer a communication assessment in both the receptive and expressive language domains. As she had done during the screening process, Amanda gave very limited responses to items on the assessment measure. Her score placed her at about a 26-month level of functioning.

The next assessment was conducted by the school psychologist in his office. This assessment focused on cognitive functioning. Again, Amanda responded with very little verbal interaction and minimal attempts to complete tasks as requested (e.g. draw a circle). The psychologist also concluded that Amanda was functioning somewhere between 24 and 26 months of age.

Finally, an audiologist conducted an assessment of Amanda's hearing. She found her hearing to be normal. Using a norm-referenced test, Ms Lane completed an assessment of Amanda in the areas of social/emotional, motor and adaptive skill development. While her social/emotional score on this test was around the 3-year level, scores in the motor and adaptive skill areas were closer to the 4-year level. Reports from the family doctor indicated that there were no health-related concerns at the time.

A case conference was held to compare assessment results and to develop a 'combined report' that would then be shared with the parents. Attending the staffing were Ms Lane, the school psychologist, the headteacher at the school and the speech/language therapist. The team decided that Amanda was developmentally delayed and needed special education services.

Ms Lane scheduled another conference with Mr and Mrs Smith to share this report with them. They were quite upset with the team's findings, which were reported in age-equivalent terms (as indicated by the test scores). Mrs Smith cried, while Mr Smith argued. Both felt the team's report was not an adequate reflection of Amanda's skills. Their decision was to take Amanda out of school for now and work with her at home.

Discussion

The Smiths had moved from France to England three months before Amanda started Reception year at school. In France, the family were living with a maternal grandmother who was Amanda's primary caregiver while both her parents worked. French was the primary language used in the home, since Amanda's grandmother spoke very little English. After Amanda's grandmother died suddenly, Mr and Mrs Smith decided to move to London where Mr Smith's company had a second office. Mrs Smith also had a sister living in London and looked forward to living closer to her. Amanda's parents enrolled her in the Reception year class, believing that it would be a good way for Amanda to make friends and become more skilled in using English.

Amanda, however, was not doing well with the move to England. She missed her grandmother greatly and had had very little experience playing with other children. Amanda's response to the differences in language and customs, along with the trauma of losing her grandmother and moving to a new country, was to retreat within herself. These considerations were not addressed during the screening and assessment process. The procedures used were discriminatory against Amanda in that they failed to consider the context of her language, culture, home and community. Had the process been conducted in a non-discriminatory manner and with more involvement on the part of the parents, the outcome might have been quite different. Amanda might not have been labelled 'developmentally delayed', and appropriate supports might have been identified to make her school experience more positive. In addition, Mr and Mrs Smith might have felt themselves to be a valuable part of the intervention team and become actively involved in Amanda's educational programme.

10

PROGRAMME AND COMMUNITY RESPONSES

To serve children well, it is important for service providers representing different disciplines and agencies to work from a common understanding about young children and how they learn, and to work together within an inclusive setting. As previously expressed, it is also important for members of an intervention team to work together towards common goals. Common understandings and common goals take on added significance as young children with special needs move from one programme to another. Unified planning and support play crucial roles in helping young children and their families navigate such transitions successfully.

This chapter addresses three interrelated topics:

1 a common philosophy and curricular approach;
2 a common programme;
3 working together during times of transitions.

Common philosophy and curricular approach

Within a programme, understandings about how to best serve young children are sometimes articulated in the form of a philosophy statement. Without a common philosophy, team efforts (both within and between different disciplines and agencies) can be seriously jeopardized.

A programme philosophy may be viewed as the framework of a programme. It provides information about the programme's goals, priorities and practices. A programme philosophy can also provide guidelines for decision making and help to sensitize staff to key educational issues. In addition, a written programme philosophy tends to facilitate team building (especially if the staff and parents are included in the development of the philosophy), establish consistency in approaches and practices, and help identify unique characteristics of the programme to other service agencies. Finally, a programme philosophy can assist parents in making informed choices about programmes for their children. While a common philosophy is certainly desirable within a programme, a common philosophy across programmes – while often difficult to achieve – is a vision that some communities are committed to as a means of providing more effective services to young children and their families.

A programme philosophy should reflect sound practice, research and theory related to young children and their unique characteristics. For inclusive programmes (i.e. early childhood programmes serving children with disabilities), the programme philosophy should address the rationale for including young children with special needs. As such, it should address educational, exceptionality and developmental issues. It should also include statements about the purposes of education, the nature of learning and the nature of the learner. The following are some of the specific items that might be included in a programme philosophy statement:

- a rationale for the inclusion of children with disabilities
- the role and involvement of families
- the curriculum model or approach used in the programme
- the nature and composition of the educational team
- the value of play and peer interaction.

A sample philosophy statement is presented in Box 10.1 which would be appropriate for a programme serving children with special needs in an inclusive setting. In addition to having a common philosophy, it is also important for a team to agree on how to translate this philosophy into practice. Fortunately, clear guidelines for practice in the field of early childhood education have been developed and articulated in the form of developmentally appropriate practices (DAP) (Bredekamp and Copple, 1997). All team members should work from the understanding that the

Box 10.1 Sample programme philosophy

The Forest School programme is designed to provide children of varying abilities with the following opportunities:

- to learn and grow to their maximum potential
- to feel safe and cared for by responsive and competent adults
- to play and learn in an environment that helps them understand that they are a valued part of a group
- to have their parents involved in their educational programme to the extent possible and desired by each parent
- to play and work with their peers and teachers in situations that are appropriate to each child's needs and abilities
- to learn about their world in a way that allows for each child's differences and strengths to be recognized and valued.

DAP approach is considered an appropriate framework in which intervention for children with special needs can be embedded. They should also know that, at times, the special needs of children with disabilities may necessitate adaptations and modifications of the DAP approach. Special adaptations and modifications (sometimes referred to as 'exceptionality appropriate practices') will be addressed in greater detail in Chapter 12.

Common programme

The *Special Educational Needs Code of Practice* (DfES, 2001a) outlines a number of 'fundamental principles' that serve as a basis for the practices and regulations concerning the education of children with disabilities. One such principle is that 'the special education needs of children will normally be met in mainstream schools or settings' (p. 7). A 'common programme', or a mainstream experience, also represents recommended practices as outlined in the early childhood special education literature (Odom and McLean, 1996).

Definitions

There are several different terms often used in relation to the placement of children with disabilities in the same physical setting as children without disabilities. These terms include mainstreaming, least restrictive environment, integration, inclusion and normalization. Using these terms interchangeably, as is sometimes done, tends to generate confusion. The following definitions are offered in an attempt to define them in relation to discrete practices.

- *Mainstreaming*: The placement of a child with a disability in a programme designed for children without disabilities. Mainstreaming is generally considered appropriate in situations where a child with a disability can participate in the regular programme with the same chances of success as his or her non-disabled peers. In other words, such children's disabilities are not expected to affect their performance as compared to the majority of their peers.
- *Least restrictive environment (LRE)*: The understanding that to the maximum extent appropriate, children with disabilities will be educated with children who are not disabled. LRE is also based on the understanding that special classes and separate schooling occur only when the nature or severity of the disabling condition is such that education in regular classes with the use of appropriate aids and services cannot be achieved satisfactorily. The least restrictive environment thus represents the most integrated or inclusive setting in which a child may function successfully.

- *Integration*: The practice of bringing together different groups which previously have been segregated. In early intervention or early childhood special education, the term 'integration' is used to refer to the practice of educating children with disabilities in specialized separate classrooms within a public school. This arrangement allows for a specialized programme and the opportunity to see and interact with other children without disabilities. This arrangement, however, still separates the children with special needs into a group of their own. It highlights their differences and distances them from others (Howard *et al.*, 1997). Integration often allows for the participation of children with disabilities in regular classroom environments for non-academic activities (e.g. recess, lunch, physical education, school assemblies). At times, it may also include participation in the regular classroom for part of the day (e.g. for reading or speaking and listening activities). This arrangement usually gives the child with a disability a 'visitor' status versus 'full member' status.
- *Inclusion*: The practice of including all children as full-time contributing members of a heterogeneous group of children. With inclusion, all students participate in all the regular daily routines of the classroom. These routines are modified to meet each child's individual goals and objectives. In addition, each child has multiple opportunities during the day for naturally occurring positive interactions with typically developing children. The classroom teacher, with support from educational specialists, serves as the primary interventionist. Full inclusion stands out as different from mainstreaming and integration, in that it represents 'not simply a child's placement, but has to do with the integrity of the placement. . . . Full inclusion occurs when a student with a disability becomes a full-time member of a programme the child might attend if he or she did not have a disability, and the child is not removed for the delivery of educational, social, or related services' (Howard *et al.*, 1997, p. 7). Inclusion assumes that membership of the group should be 'a given' versus something that is discussed and decided.
- *Normalization*: Refers to an approach (versus a placement) used by various providers which serve individuals with disabilities. This approach stresses that individuals with disabilities should experience patterns of life and conditions of everyday living which are as close as possible to the regular (i.e. normal) ways of life in their society.

Four different approaches

There have been major changes in attitudes and practices over the past fifty years relating to educational programming for children with disabilities. These changes have been described in relation to the following four different approaches: the denial approach, the box approach, the permission approach and the inclusion approach.

The *denial approach* failed to recognize individual differences and operated from the belief that 'one programme should fit all'. If a child was not succeeding in the regular classroom, this must mean that he or she was not trying hard enough. If a child was severely disabled and clearly not able to participate in the regular classroom in a meaningful way, he or she was denied access to educational programming. The parents could either choose to keep their child at home or place him or her in an institution that would take care of the child's physical needs. Educational needs were not even recognized, and children with special needs who grew up during the time of the denial approach rarely became a part of the mainstream of life.

The *box approach* focused on individual differences to the point of categorizing children as 'regular education' or 'special education' students. Each group was then assigned their own box (i.e. classroom). Children (and teachers) generally stayed in their own boxes throughout their educational experience. The message this approach gave to children with special needs was that 'You're different and you don't belong with "normal" children'. This approach often resulted in poor self-concept, low expectations and learned helplessness on the part of the children with special needs. For typically developing children, this approach failed to foster an appreciation of diversity and led to misunderstandings about individual differences.

With the *permission approach*, children with special needs were allowed to come into the regular classroom 'if they were ready' or 'if they passed the test'. The message to the children with this approach was that 'We hear you knocking, and we'll be nice enough to share our space with you, but only if you've learned the right skills. Can you communicate your needs and wants? Can you read and write? Can you work independently? Can you interact in a positive way with other children? Do you know all the right words?' Questions that were not asked included 'Do we know how to read the communicative attempts of the child with special needs?' and 'Do we really value diversity?' The permission approach often led to anxiety on the part of parents and pressure on the part of children with special educational needs. The children had to 'get ready' or 'prove themselves' in order to participate in the mainstream.

The *inclusion approach* is based on the understanding that everyone belongs, and that it is inappropriate to design a standard programme and expect it to suit every child. With the inclusion approach, the emphasis is on fitting the programme to what the child needs. No one is excluded, and every child is valued as an individual. The focus of this approach is on finding ways for every child to participate and to be successful. It assumes that all children have the right to attend the same neighbourhood schools and the same classrooms. It also assumes that children with disabilities can participate in the same extracurricular activities and community programmes they would if they did not have a disability. The inclusion approach is driven by a vision of unity, of 'being included'. With this vision, inclusion becomes much more than a placement; it becomes a way of being.

LRE controversy

Placing a child with a disability in the 'least restrictive environment' (LRE) tends to mean different things to different people. While, for some, the least restrictive environment is equivalent to mainstreaming, others maintain that only full inclusion can provide a child with a 'least restrictive' experience. Obviously, the concept of inclusion is not without controversy. To some, it represents no more than a current trend that will pass with time (Fuchs and Fuchs, 1994).

Strong justifications for full inclusion, especially in relation to young children, have been presented in the literature. There follow two of the arguments often used by proponents of full inclusion.

- When children with and without disabilities are educated together, they learn lifelong lessons and skills necessary for positive relationships with each other. This argument is backed by research data which indicate that supported inclusion leads to a higher frequency of interactions and fosters the development of social and adaptive skills of children with disabilities (Hanline, 1993; Kohler *et al.*, 2001). These findings apply to children with autism as well as children with other types of disabilities. The inclusion model is also more compatible with society's emphasis on pluralism.
- Young children with disabilities can achieve their highest potential only when they are provided with 'normal' opportunities. This argument reflects a philosophy of normalization, which has been promoted in the field of special education since the late 1960s. According to this philosophy, 'when persons are segregated, labelled, or treated in any way that sets them further apart for their differences, then their worth is devalued' (Howard *et al.*, 1997, p. 8). It has been argued that the normalization principle should apply to all persons with special needs, regardless of their degree of disability. While normalization will not remove a person's disability or make him or her normal, 'it does make possible a more normal and nonstigmatized life style' (Peterson, 1987, p. 338).

Some would say that the practice of 'full inclusion' is not something that should have to be justified on any other premise than that it is the 'right thing to do'. As expressed by a father of a child with a disability, 'Why must children "prove" they are ready to be in regular classrooms? We do not ask that of any other members of our society' (Howard *et al.*, 1997, p. 9).

Research on the topic of full inclusion is complex and, at times, arrives at conflicting conclusions. Some research, for example, indicates that, while children who are higher performing do better in inclusive settings, lower performing students tend to perform better in more segregated settings (Howard *et al.*, 1997). And not all parents are in favour of inclusion. Some feel that separate schooling is necessary to protect children with disabilities from rejection by their typically developing peers.

Many agree that there is no one 'right answer' to the question of what constitutes the least restrictive environment for young children with special needs and argue for placement decisions to be made on a case-by-case basis. Peterson (1987) proposed taking into account the following three important considerations when making such decisions:

1. the extent to which the 'intervention' increases the chances that the child will be developmentally more capable of functioning later in a less restrictive environment;
2. the extent to which the setting is culturally compatible with the values and practices of the community or subculture of which the family is a part;
3. the extent to which the setting is equipped to provide the forms of stimulation and care that are age appropriate for the child and consistent with the child's special needs.

It should also be noted that normalized experiences can be provided even in a segregated setting. The physical setting is only one aspect of an intervention programme. Other aspects include materials, staffing, schedule and activities. Each of these aspects should be evaluated in relation to the principle of normalization. The following questions may be helpful in conducting such an evaluation (either for a segregated or inclusive setting):

- To what extent does the physical environment appear and function like the environments serving typically developing children? Considerations related to this question include physical appearance, programme location and name of programme. The physical environment should reflect a child-centred versus clinical orientation. As such, it should feature age-appropriate decorations and furnishings and should include a display of children's creations. Intervention services (e.g. therapy sessions) should share the same space or be located in close proximity to the regular education programme. Adaptive equipment should be used and stored in ways that do not call attention to its presence, and children's privacy should be respected. Privacy is violated through such practices as posting individual child goals, data charts and behaviour plans. Privacy is also violated when there are no separate areas of the room for assisting individual children who may need to be diapered and dressed.

- To what extent do materials and activities match those provided for typically developing children? A normalized programme would offer activity centres (e.g. dramatic play area, art centre, water and sand play, block area), a book area, an outdoor play area, and displays of children's work versus focusing primarily on therapeutic equipment and activities.
- To what extent do staffing roles and responsibilities reflect staffing patterns in programmes serving typically developing children? While additional staff are often required to meet the needs of young children with disabilities, staff should not be assigned to work exclusively with an individual child. As one-on-one instruction is not the norm in regular education programmes, it should not be the norm in programmes serving children with disabilities. 'Extra assistance should be used in a manner that is nonintrusive and normalized' (Noonan and McCormick, 1993, p. 340). If a child with SEN needs assistance in an activity (such as working at the computer), a staff member may be assigned to monitor and assist all the children involved in that activity. This staff member can provide special assistance to the child with SEN nonintrusively in several different ways: she can reinforce children who are using the computer correctly, call attention to the different ways children are using the computer, encourage children to watch and imitate more competent peers, and suggest co-operative learning activities.

Specialized staff (i.e. speech/language therapists, physiotherapists) should also provide services in a nonintrusive and normalized way. Therapy sessions should be scheduled so as to interfere as little as possible with the typical schedule and activities of the classroom. In fact, recommended practices call for incorporating specialized therapies into the natural activities of the regular education programme (Noonan and McCormick, 1993). This approach to therapy is sometimes referred to as 'integrated therapy' and contrasts with the 'pull-out' model in which children are removed from the classroom for their individual therapy sessions. The integrated therapy model has several major advantages. 'In addition to being nonintrusive and normalizing, the integrated therapy approach ensures that specialized interventions are designed to be practical and immediately useful in natural settings' (Noonan and McCormick, 1993, p. 340).

Concerns relating to inclusion

While the controversy about full inclusion continues, many young children with disabilities are being served in the regular classroom setting. It is therefore necessary for early childhood teachers to learn how to meet the needs of children with special educational needs within the context of the daily routine. They should see to it that the child with SEN is integrated not only into the physical dimensions of an early childhood programme, but the instructional and social dimensions as well. Instructional inclusion means that, as far as possible, the activities in which the child with SEN participates should be the same as the activities in which the other children are participating. To make this a successful experience, the child with SEN will often require some special assistance and/or encouragement both from the classroom teacher and other members of the intervention team. It should be understood that unless an early childhood classroom can provide the appropriate services and support for children with SEN, it cannot serve effectively as the least restrictive environment for them.

As the literature indicates, many of the proposed benefits of inclusion do not occur without purposeful and careful support to promote them. Wolery and Wilbers (1994) offer the following examples:

- Many children with disabilities do not imitate their peers unless taught to do so.
- Many children with and without disabilities do not interact frequently unless support is provided to encourage such exchanges.
- Acceptance and positive attitudes about children with disabilities do not necessarily result simply from integration. Adults' behaviour can substantially influence the way children think and feel.

Physical inclusion alone, then, does not guarantee that the proposed benefits will occur. While more specific information and ideas on how to foster inclusion within the classroom will be presented in Chapter 11, the following discussion addresses several barriers to successful inclusion that exist at the community level, as well as some suggestions for dealing with these barriers.

- *Barrier 1*: Lack of adequate training in general and special early education. General early education teachers often feel that they do not have the knowledge and skills necessary for working with children with special educational needs. Special early education teachers, on the other hand, often cite the lack of adequate preparation in early childhood development and consultation as barriers for them in effectively serving young children with SEN within the context of the regular classroom. The idea of joint training programmes (i.e. for general and special early education teachers) has been suggested at both the preservice and inservice level of professional development as a positive step towards addressing this barrier. To make this happen, co-operation and collaboration are required, not only between training programmes at universities, but also among different community agencies involved in providing direct and indirect services to young children with disabilities and their families.

- *Barrier 2*: Lack of 'related services' in many programmes. As discussed in previous chapters, young children with SEN and their families are often in need of services from a variety of disciplines and agencies. Many early education programmes which include children with SEN do not employ – even on a part-time or consultant basis – members from disciplines directly related to the children's disability (such as physiotherapy, speech/language therapy and occupational therapy). In addition, many early childhood programmes are not in a position to address critical family information and support needs. Gaining access to and co-ordinating social services often becomes a major concern for families of young children with SEN. One positive step towards addressing this concern is the development of early childhood centres, which bring together a variety of services within one location. Both regular education and special education programmes can be housed in these centres, along with therapists, social workers and health-related programmes. Parent education and support, and even staff development activities, are often offered as part of the programming of early childhood centres as well.

Working together during transitions

Children with disabilities are often faced with transitions from one setting, class or programme to another. Such transitions usually involve stress and anxiety both for the child and his or her family. Getting used to something new, leaving something familiar, not knowing what new expectations and challenges must be faced – these are some of the factors contributing to stress and anxiety during times of transitions.

While everyone must face transitions in their lives, for young children with disabilities and their families these transitions tend to be more frequent and more demanding. This is due in part to the fact that children with disabilities often require individualized services involving multiple disciplines and a variety of agencies. A child's need for these services and his or her eligibility to receive such services tend to fluctuate over time. Eligibility is sometimes determined by age; sometimes by type and extent of need. Such conditions vary over time, resulting in a need for a change in services.

For many children and their families, the first major transition is from home to school. In the UK, children are required to attend school between the ages of 5 and 16. They may start earlier or leave later, but this is optional.

A child's transition from home to school and from one programme to another often generates some frustration, confusion, anxiety and surprises. For children and families – and, to a certain extent, staff – transitions represent times of vulnerability and the potential for problems. While all the stress associated with transitions may not be avoidable, it can be minimized. Careful planning plays an important part in reducing problems during times of transitions. Planning can remove the arbitrary boundaries among agencies and programmes and minimize the differences between settings and expectations (Noonan and McCormick, 1993).

Because transitions often involve the movement from one agency to another, interagency co-operation and co-ordination become crucial to smooth transitions. Lack of co-ordination between agencies may place children and their families at risk of the loss of appropriate services. In some instances, lack of co-ordination between agencies results in delaying a child's placement. In other instances, differences in eligibility requirements between agencies leave some children and families unserved. In addition, differences in curriculum and teaching style can negatively affect children's adjustment to a new programme and their acquisition of new skills.

To minimize these risks, careful planning is required at the agency, direct service and family levels. The following are some suggestions for each of these three levels.

1 *Interagency planning (agency level)*: Each agency serving young children and their families should develop a written transition plan outlining the activities involved in changing placement of a child and his or her family. These transition plans should be shared and compatible with those of other agencies. Some communities develop written agreements that identify shared philosophy, responsibilities and resources.
2 *Programme planning (direct service level)*: The direct service providers at the time of transition include (1) the sending programme (i.e. the child's current placement), and (2) the receiving programme (i.e. the child's next placement). The sending programme staff should obtain basic information regarding the next placement in order to prepare the child and family for the new programme. Such information might include the programme's philosophy, curriculum, schedule and skills expectations. Exchanging visits between programmes is one suggested way of obtaining some of this information. When possible, the sending programme should introduce the child to the skills that will be expected in the next environment and to the routine that will be experienced there. The sending programme should

also inform the family of differences in the level and type of family contact and support.

3 *Family planning (family level)*: Families should be given the opportunity to participate in all aspects of the transition process. They should be fully informed as to the anticipated sequence of activities and given a timeline for completing the transition. They should be encouraged to visit the new placement option and meet the new staff. Families can help prepare the child for the transition by taking the child for a visit to the new programme, discussing the change, and fostering the development of skills that will be expected in the new setting.

Planning for transitions can provide the necessary 'safety net' often needed as children and families take their first steps into new situations. Ideally, this safety net (i.e. assistance) should be there for the child and family as long as it is needed. This means that there should be overlap between the sending programme and the receiving programme and that the extent of this overlap should be determined on an individual basis. While a month of overlap or less may be sufficient for some families, others may require up to six months.

In addition to being flexible and responsive to individual families, transition should also include the following steps: (1) the completion of an evaluation of the child to determine current levels of performance and to identify special strengths and needs; (2) a discussion about future programme possibilities (i.e. potential settings where the child might receive services); (3) visits to potential programmes; (4) the selection of a programme and a verification of eligibility; (5) the completion of an application for enrolment; (6) preparation of the child and the receiving programme; and (7) monitoring of the child and family adjustment to the new programme.

There follows a discussion that addresses several related concerns and offers some suggestions on how to prepare the setting (i.e. the receiving programme) and the child for transitions and how to involve families in a meaningful way.

Preparing the setting

As discussed above, inclusion means more than 'allowing the child in' if he or she has the necessary skills. The message of inclusion is that 'all children belong' and that the programme will adjust to the child versus placing the demand on the child that he or she adjusts to the programme. Adjustment, or preparation, on the part of the receiving programme may include any or all of the following activities:

- identifying and removing barriers to physical access (e.g. making the school, classroom and learning centres wheelchair accessible);

- identifying and obtaining inservice training and technical assistance for the staff;
- identifying and obtaining special materials and equipment (e.g. communication boards, amplification devices);
- sharing of accurate information (e.g. information about the child, about programme goals and procedures).

Preparing the child

Skills needed for success in a programme are sometimes referred to as 'survival skills'. Such skills are related closely to teacher expectations, especially in terms of independent work and social behaviour. To prepare a child for the next environment, it is important to have some understanding of what these survival skills are. Some interesting work has been done in the USA to identify survival skills for children in preschool (ages 3 to 5) and kindergarten (ages 5 to 6) classrooms. Such studies have looked at programmes in different geographical locations and serving children from different ethnic and cultural backgrounds. In spite of these differences, skills identified as crucial to success tended to be similar across programmes. They also represent primarily social/communication and adaptive skills. The following is a list of skills that have been identified through various studies as survival skills at the preschool and kindergarten level (Noonan and McCormick, 1993):

- follows general rules and routines
- expresses wants and needs
- co-operates with/helps others
- complies with directions given by adults
- shares materials/toys with peers
- socializes with peers
- takes turns
- interacts verbally with adults
- interacts verbally with peers
- focuses attention on speaker
- makes own decisions.

It is important to understand that survival skills should not be considered as behavioural prerequisites for participating in an inclusive programme. They should instead be viewed as optimum goals. 'A child's failure to demonstrate any one or all of the skills on a survival skills checklist should not prevent the child's transition to, and placement in, mainstream early childhood settings' (Noonan and McCormick, 1993, p. 361).

Another concern related to transition and survival skills is the fact that children who may have developed and demonstrated certain skills in one setting do not always use them in other, different settings – that is, they do not transfer the skills from one environment to another. For example, a child with communication problems may use signs and gestures to express needs and wants at home, but may not use these same skills at school. Another example would be a child with attention deficit disorder (ADD) who has learned to block out 'distractions' at home (e.g. street noise, movement of family members around the house, TV) but cannot attend to a task at school due to distracting sounds and movement around the classroom. Close observation and dialogue between sending and receiving programmes and parents can lead to early identification of this lack of transfer. Strategies may then be developed to address this concern before additional problems (e.g. secondary handicaps, poor self-concept, low expectations) develop.

Another major concern sometimes centres on differing expectations. Even though the survival skills presented above tend to be common across programmes, it sometimes happens that a skill that is considered crucial in one setting may not be so valued in another. This 'mismatch' can lead to anxiety and stress for all involved – the child, parents and staff. Johnson and Mandell (1988) addressed this concern in the area of social skills and related expectations. They developed and field-tested an observational tool that can be used to identify and address a mismatch in expectations and skills as a child moves from one programme to another. A copy of this instrument (i.e. the SOME scale – Social Observation for Mainstreamed Environments) is presented in Figure 10.1.

The SOME scale may be used to facilitate discussion between the sending and receiving programmes and for identifying potential areas of concern. It may also be used to identify a child's strengths and to plan instructional strategies around both strengths and concerns. For example, the first item on the SOME scale refers to the child's ability to ask for help when needed. If the child does not demonstrate this skill, a minus (–) is recorded in the 'Child's performance' column. If this skill reflects a skill considered essential by the teacher in the receiving programme, a plus (+) is recorded in the 'Classroom expectations' column. A minus paired with a plus reflects a mismatch. If this mismatch is not addressed prior to the child entering the programme, related problems are likely to occur. Options for addressing this mismatch include (1) helping the child develop the desired skill and (2) working with the teacher to modify his or her expectations and procedures.

A mismatch, however, can also occur in the opposite direction, i.e. the child may have a skill that the teacher does not necessarily consider to be essential. In this case, a plus is recorded in the 'Child's performance' column and a minus in the 'Classroom expectations' column. This mismatch can be used to highlight a child's strength. If the skill is 'plays well with others', the teacher can use this information to enhance the child's

Child's Name: ____________________ Date: ____________

Individual(s) observing the child: ____________________

Individual observing the classroom: ____________________

Other settings in which child was observed: ____________________

Directions: In the first column, mark a plus (+) if the child usually exhibits the behaviour, a minus (–) if the child tends not to exhibit the behaviour. In the second column, mark a plus if the classroom teacher expects the children to exhibit the behaviour, a minus if the behaviour is not one of the classroom expectations. Use the third column for noting any related observations or concerns. In the fourth column, write in proposed resolutions to areas of concern; that is, in areas where the behaviours are expected but are not exhibited by the child.

Behaviour	*Child's performance*	*Classroom expectations*	*Comments*	*Resolution*
1. Asks for help when needed				
2. Plays well with others				
3. Obeys class rules				
4. Attends to task for short periods of time				
5. Completes tasks with minimum adult assistance				
6. Initiates interactions with peers				
7. Initiates interactions with adults				
8. Observes other children				

9. Imitates other children				
10. Makes simple decisions				
11. Practices turn taking				
12. Respects others' belongings				
13. Respects others' feelings				
14. Follows simple directions				
15. Uses verbal vs. nonverbal means to express feelings				
Other				
Other				

Recommendations: ____________________

Signatures: ____________________

Figure 10.1 SOME Scale (Social Observation for Mainstreamed Environments)
Source: Johnson & Mandell (1988, p. 21), with kind permission.

status with his or her peers (i.e. by arranging time and place opportunities to demonstrate this skill, by calling attention to the child's performance and so on).

To ease the transition of the child from one programme to another, steps should be taken to lessen differences between the sending and receiving settings. If possible, it is also helpful to extend the transition gradually over time. This can happen more easily if both programmes (e.g. Reception year and Year 1) are housed within the same building. This arrangement would allow for periodic visits of the Reception year class to the Year 1 class. Children would then have the opportunity to familiarize themselves gradually with the following year's classroom and teacher.

If the sending and receiving programmes are not housed in the same building, field trips to the new school could still be arranged. To make the visit to the school as friendly as possible, the visit might include lunch or a snack, time for play outdoors, and participation in some fun group activities. After the visit, children should be engaged in a conversation about the experience and encouraged to role play the process of going to a new school.

Working with the family

Parents have much to offer as well as much to gain by being involved in the transition process (Noonan and McCormick, 1993). The following are some of the ways in which parents can be involved:

- providing valuable information about their child, their goals and vision for their child, and ways in which they wish to be involved;
- teaching their child skills at home that will help their child to be successful in the new programme (e.g. asking for help when needed, attending to a speaker, interacting with peers);
- providing emotional support for their child throughout the transition process.

Parents have identified some of the ways professionals can help them during the process of transition. The following are some of their suggestions:

- provide information about community services and parents' legal rights;
- provide information about what to look for in evaluating potential future placements (e.g. child–staff ratio, daily routine);
- identify 'crucial skills' their child will need to be successful in the next environment (i.e. new setting);
- reassure them that they (i.e. the professionals) will monitor the success of the child's transition and provide support as needed.

The role of the teacher

The transition process places new demands on the teacher as well. While facilitating transition from one programme to another can be quite interesting and rewarding, it can also be frustrating. The transition process often involves additional tasks for the teacher. For the sending teacher, such tasks may include the following:

- meeting with families to discuss and make plans for the transition process;
- visiting programme sites with or without the families;
- sharing information with the receiving teachers;
- collecting information concerning teacher expectations;
- preparing the child for a successful transition (emotionally and through skill development);
- monitoring the child's adjustment to the new placement;
- serving as an ongoing resource to the family and receiving programme.

The receiving teacher, too, has a special role to play in the transition process. Tasks associated with this role include:

- learning about the child's strengths, needs, special interests and individual background;
- modifying the physical aspects of the classroom as needed;
- adjusting the routine, instructional strategies and expectations as appropriate;
- establishing a relationship and communication pattern with the parents;
- providing feedback to the sending programme.

Indicators of a successful transition

The following statements summarize many of the recommended practices developed for smooth transitions. These statements may be used as indicators to evaluate the success of a child's and family's transition from one programme to another.

- Interruption of needed services is avoided.
- The child, family and service providers are given opportunities to prepare for changes that will occur.
- The child's strengths as well as needs are used as a basis from which planning occurs.
- Families are given information about their rights and the range of options available to them and their child.

- Families are enabled to provide input into their child's educational programme.
- The most appropriate and most supportive environment is identified.
- The child is prepared (emotionally and through skill development) for the new environment.
- Continuity of curriculum and routine is facilitated from one setting to the next.
- The child receives support in the new setting.
- Families are offered support and opportunities for involvement throughout the transition process.
- The child's adjustment to the new setting is evaluated and changes are made as necessary.
- There is ongoing communication and collaboration among professionals providing services to the child and family.

Case study – Roy and Janis

Background information

Roy is a Year 1 teacher in an inclusive education programme. This is his second year of teaching. Janis is a learning support assistant (LSA) assigned to Roy's classroom. She has worked as an LSA for twelve years, the past five years in an early childhood classroom. Roy is firmly committed to a developmentally appropriate intervention model and looks for ways to foster individual child goals and activities through the naturally occurring events of the day. Janis, on the other hand, feels that children with special needs would learn more efficiently through a direct instruction approach. She therefore gives frequent directives to children on what they should and should not do and constantly corrects them for 'errors' in performance. For example, if a child says, 'She taked it from me', Janis responds by telling him to say 'She took it from me'. Only after the child has repeated the 'correct way' of expressing his message will Janis attend to the content of the message. If a child's goal is learning to write his or her own name, Janis will sometimes pull that child from another activity (such as painting or looking at books) to work on paper and pencil tasks.

Roy is not pleased with what Janis does in the classroom. He has tried to explain the philosophy and guidelines of the developmentally appropriate intervention approach, but Janis remains unconvinced. She views Roy as being young and inexperienced. She also believes that what is currently being taught at the university in the teacher education programme is just a trend that will soon be replaced with something else. She therefore continues to use the direct instruction approach. She often keeps records relating to the child's performance (e.g. 'Jimmy wrote his name today with some hand-over-hand support') and will sometimes share her observations with the parents. Some of the parents think that Janis is wonderful because she works so hard on the children's instructional goals.

Discussion

The 'teaming' between Roy and Janis is dysfunctional. They do not share a common philosophy, their instructional strategies conflict, and the information they provide to parents often results in confusion and frustration. Both Roy and Janis are convinced that their way is the right way. Both want what is best for the children but fail to see that their lack of teaming is one of the major obstacles to an optimal learning environment.

Mrs Lane, the headteacher, begins to sense the nature of the problem when she asks for Roy's opinion about an appropriate placement for Emily for the following year. Emily, a child with Down syndrome, is currently in Roy's class. Her developmental status is approximately two years below age expectations. Roy indicates that he feels Emily can go on to a Year 2 class in the same building, as long as the teacher understands the nature and extent of Emily's special needs and is provided with some assistance in making appropriate curriculum adaptations for her. Janis overhears this conversation and stops by the school office later in the afternoon to express her concern. Janis has been a friend of Emily's family since Emily was born and feels some ownership regarding her intervention programme. Janis believes that Emily must first accomplish some of her current goals before she will be ready for Year 2. She suggests that progress towards these goals has been slow, due in part to the many 'unrelated' activities she does in class.

Mrs Lane asks Roy and Janis to meet with her the next day. She tells them that she is concerned about the lack of consistency in their approach to working with children with SEN. After some discussion about the issue, she asks each of them to review the school's philosophy and to relate their instructional strategies to this written statement. The school's philosophy statement starts with the following sentence: 'All children have the right to an educational environment that recognizes and respects them as active learners and provides them with the opportunity to construct their own understandings about the world around them.' Roy feels comfortable with this statement; Janis does not. Janis believes that not all children are capable of being active learners and constructing their own knowledge. It soon becomes evident that one of the major barriers to effective teaming for Roy and Janis resides in their differing philosophies of how young children learn. Mrs Lane was wise to use the school's written philosophy as a source of comparison.

Mrs Lane makes arrangements for Janis to spend a day in another classroom with an experienced teacher who can explain and demonstrate how the school's philosophy is reflected in individually appropriate instructional goals and strategies. Mrs Lane then works with Roy to identify ways of making his approach more explicit. For example, she suggests that Roy display posters around the classroom to illustrate the learning potential of the different activity centres. She also asks Roy to devise a way of documenting progress towards individual child goals and objectives. Her third suggestion is that Roy develop a parent newsletter and use it to describe different aspects of the curriculum, including the value of play and child-initiated activities.

After six weeks, Mrs Lane meets with Roy and Janis again. This time, the conversation focuses on self-identified professional development needs. Roy is interested in inservice opportunities that address in more detail the activity-based intervention approach and how to evaluate the effectiveness of this approach. Janis wants to learn more about ways to extend children's play in non-directive ways – that is, she wants to know how to challenge children's thinking and skill development through a more discovery-based approach. Once Roy and Janis became aware of the professional–development interests of each other, they began to share information and ideas about related resources. They also decided to use the classroom as a 'bulletin board' to make a statement about the curriculum. One statement that is now displayed in large letters across the front of the room reads, 'Young children learn through discovery'. Photographs and children's artwork posted around the room reflect children in the process of making their own discoveries.

Part IV

MEETING THE NEEDS OF THE INDIVIDUAL CHILD

Part IV presents information and ideas on how to make the learning environment and exploration opportunities accessible to all young children in the early years classroom. The primary focus is on the individual child with special educational needs and his or her unique strengths, needs, interests, learning style, and ways of interacting with other people and the physical environment. The discussion throughout this section is based on the understanding that curriculum for young children consists primarily of the physical and social environment as they experience it. It is also based on the understanding that for practices to be developmentally appropriate they must also be individually appropriate (Bredekamp and Copple, 1997).

Children with special educational needs are, at least in some ways, at a different stage developmentally than many of their classmates. The inclusive early years classroom must therefore provide learning opportunities that reflect a range of abilities. The material presented in Chapters 11 and 12 is designed to provide some specific guidance on how this might be done.

11

A CURRICULUM FOR EVERY CHILD

The environment as curriculum

Curriculum might be defined in various ways. To some, curriculum refers to what is taught. This concept of curriculum focuses on 'what is offered' versus 'what is experienced'. While 'what is offered' (i.e. 'a range of studies') may be an appropriate way to define curriculum for older students, it does not reflect the nature of young children and the ways in which they learn. For young children, defining curriculum in terms of the environment as they experience it would be more appropriate. This definition is consistent with the early childhood special education literature, where curriculum has been described as 'the sum of that child's interactions (experiences) with the environment' (Wolery and Sainato, 1996, p. 132). It has also been referred to as 'curriculum-is-what-happens' (McCracken, 1993).

For young children with special educational needs, it is crucial to consider that the nature of a disability can interfere with their experience of the environment as it is presented or arranged by the classroom teacher. This interference tends to diminish children's learning opportunities in the classroom. Educators therefore cannot assume that the needs of every child can be met by creating a stimulating classroom environment and encouraging children to learn on their own. No matter how enriching the environment appears to be, it is not enriching for the child who cannot access it for one reason or another. This is easy to understand in terms of a hearing or vision problem. If some children cannot hear the voices of their classmates and the teacher, the verbal environment will not be stimulating to them. Similarly, if some children cannot see the variety of materials available in the classroom, the visual environment will neither motivate them to access the materials nor stimulate their thinking about how to use what is available to them.

Other disabilities, too, can interfere with a child's access to an environment, often in less obvious ways than deafness or blindness. An attention deficit disorder (ADD), for example, can prevent a child from attending to specific stimuli in the environment. The child with ADD may find it difficult to focus on such aspects of the environment as the teacher's voice, the details of a puzzle, the intricacies of dramatic play and so on. This child's difficulty in focusing or attending becomes a barrier to engagement with materials and people in the classroom, and thus limits his or her learning opportunities.

Recommended practices in early childhood special education call for both (1) the improvement of the child's skills to access the environment, and (2) environmental accommodations. At times, the pressure to 'fix' the child (i.e. to improve the child's skills) overshadows the importance of making environmental accommodations. This is unfortunate, since the pressure on the child can lead to frustration on the part of the child, the parents and the staff. Without appropriate environmental accommodations, the child's motivation and opportunities to become engaged with his or her environment will also be diminished.

Environmental accommodations for children with special education needs can address all or some of the following: the physical structure, the visual system, the schedule, the position of the teacher, and the use of adaptive equipment and materials. There follows a brief discussion of the first four of these factors.

The physical structure

The physical structure refers to the way space is organized, the furniture placed and the materials arranged. Generally, physical arrangements and facilities that are effective for typical young children will be suitable for children with SEN. For the benefit of all children, the physical structure of a classroom should be consistent with the desired learning activities and curricular goals. The physical structure should also serve as an easily read guide that helps the children to become or stay engaged in meaningful learning activities. While all children benefit from a well-organized physical environment, children with SEN can receive additional assistance by highlighting certain aspects of the organizational structure. Using tape to clearly define a circle on the floor is a type of organizational structure that can help children position themselves for such group activities as story time. The tape serves as a visual cue as to what it means to sit in a circle. An environmental accommodation that may be helpful to many children with SEN would be to use individual carpet squares as 'position markers'. While the tape alone defines the circle, it does not establish individual markers or boundaries. Use of the carpet squares, along with the tape, provides more definitive guidance. This may be especially helpful for young children with attention deficits, behaviour problems and visual impairments.

The following are some additional examples of how to highlight the organizational structure of the physical environment. These examples illustrate how the environment can be used as an instructional tool.

- Use pictures of items to label containers and shelves for the storage of materials. The shelves where blocks are to be stored, for example, could be marked with pictures of blocks.
- Use photographs of individual children to mark their personal 'cubby-holes' or storage areas. These photographs could also be used on individual work folders and/or book bags.
- Colour code items and learning centres to correspond to appropriate use of materials. The writing corner, for example, may be designated as the 'blue area'. A large blue banner might be used to label the area. Blue markings on items belonging to this area could help children to keep materials organized and provide guidance as to their appropriate use. A blue dot on such items as pencils, rulers, staplers, paper punch, typewriter, stencils and so on would suggest to the children that these materials all relate to the process of writing or working in an office.

Additional accommodations to the physical structure that may be helpful for children with SEN include greater space within the classroom. More space may be required to accommodate special equipment (e.g. wheelchairs, walkers, standing boards) and a larger number of adults (e.g. therapists, teacher's assistants). Special attention should also be given to the sturdiness of equipment and materials. Shelves and tables, for example, must be strong enough to support children who have difficulty standing and maintaining balance. It is also important that clutter be minimized. Clutter can interfere with mobility, safety and the engagement of children with SEN. Routes from one area of the room to another should be direct, should minimize cross traffic, and should be free of obstacles. For safety and easier access, doors should remain fully open. Sharp edges on furniture should be padded and broken materials repaired or replaced.

The outdoor environment must also be considered carefully. See Chapter 12 for a discussion of this important topic.

The visual system

The visual system is related closely to and overlaps with the physical structure. It includes direction or guidance for the student as to what to do and when to do it. This can be especially helpful to children with SEN who have difficulty processing and/or following verbal directions. A visual system could be used for grouping children for co-operative activities, for specifying steps to be taken to complete an activity, and for providing guidance on how to move from one area to another. The following are examples of each:

- Children are often expected to work together with a partner or in a small group. Visual cues can be used to help keep children with their partner or group. Such visual cues might be symbols or pictures that they wear during the group activity.

- Many young children with SEN find it difficult to complete successfully activities that involve a series of steps, especially if these steps need to be followed in a specified order. Such activities may vary from how to make a peanut butter sandwich for lunch to how to operate a program on a computer. Visual cues in the form of simple drawings or pictures can be used to illustrate the steps to be taken.
- Cut-outs of footprints could serve as a visual system to guide children on how to move from one area to another. Such footprints might be used on stairways and in hallways, for example, to show children how to 'keep to the right' when using the stairs or moving through the halls.

The schedule

The intent of inclusion is to integrate the child with SEN into the daily routine of the regular education classroom. This is in contrast to providing a special schedule for the child with a disability. However, to maximize that child's chances of success, some accommodations to the schedule may be necessary. These accommodations should be as nonintrusive and inconspicuous as possible. Some children with SEN need more time to complete a task than their classmates. Rather than rushing the child or doing the task for him or her, accommodations to the schedule should allow the additional time. For example, a child with a physical disability may be able to use the toilet on his or her own if given enough time. One accommodation to the schedule would be to allow the child to start to walk down the hall to the toilets while the other children are still engaged in independent work in the classroom. It would be a mistake, however, to make a practice of always excusing the child from 'clean-up' activities or pulling him or her from a co-operative learning activity to accommodate the need for extra time to use the toilet. The extra time should not be viewed as a privilege or punishment, nor should it be the prerogative of only children with SEN. Most children can benefit from individual accommodations to the schedule at times. These accommodations should be based on individual circumstances and needs and not on the designation of SEN.

The position of the teacher

Where the teacher is in relation to the child with SEN and the way the teacher uses him- or herself to support or provide direction to the child is also an area that allows for environmental accommodation. If the goal is to enhance independent work, the teacher should provide greater distance between him- or herself and the child. If, however, the child needs extra support and/or guidance, closer proximity would be appropriate.

Individualized objectives

When working with children with SEN, teachers will need to identify individual objectives in addition to working from the early learning goals established for the entire group. Individualized objectives specify crucial developmental skills to be taught. For young children with SEN, it is not an appropriate practice to simply wait for such skills to emerge (Peterson, 1987). Individualized objectives are determined in part by assessment results. The focus of assessment data, however, should not be on scores or the child's developmental age, but rather on what the child can do and how the child learns best.

Questions that may be helpful in setting individualized objectives include the following:

- What can this child do independently? (i.e. What is the child's current level of functioning in each developmental domain?)
- What skills are in the process of being acquired? (i.e. What does the child do with support and assistance?)
- What critical developmental skills must the child attain? (i.e. What does the child need to learn to be more independent?)
- What seems to work with this child? (i.e. How does he or she learn best?)

The answers to these questions and other information obtained throughout the assessment process (including parental priorities) provide the necessary information for developing individualized objectives. These objectives should then be integrated into the instructional programme. An important point to be kept in mind, however, is that while the objectives are individualized, the instructional programme should be implemented in an integrated fashion. This means that the child with SEN is not pulled away from the regular routine of the classroom to work on his or her objectives. With an integrated approach, individualized objectives are embedded within the context of the broader classroom activities and with consideration to the development of the whole child in relationship to his or her environments (Horn *et al.*, 2000).

Developmental framework

At one time, individualized objectives for children with SEN reflected a behavioural and clinical approach to intervention. With this approach, objectives focused almost exclusively on the child's weaknesses or areas of deficit. Direct teaching methods were then used to remediate these areas of weakness. Such methods were designed to push or pull the child up to the next developmental level. The following example illustrates this approach.

Through the assessment process, one of Tim's deficits was identified as the failure to use language to express needs or wants. A related objective was then developed – 'At snack time, Tim will use words to ask for juice and a snack.' To get Tim to perform this targeted behaviour, the teacher decided to withhold refreshments at snack time until children requested them. If individual children did not request refreshments, she would prompt them to do so. After introducing this new routine to the children, most of them had no trouble in requesting juice and a snack ('May I have juice and a biscuit, please?'). Tim, however, did not make such a request. The teacher therefore told him to say, 'Juice, please' and 'Biscuit, please'. After several prompts, Tim repeated what the teacher modelled.

Some serious concerns relating to this approach soon surfaced. Waiting for individual children to request refreshments diminished the social interaction and related discussion that had been occurring previously during snack time. Prior to this new intervention technique, spontaneous conversations at snack time often focused on what the children had been doing earlier in the morning or what one of them had done the night before. In addition, this intervention technique was drawing attention to Tim's deficit. Most of the other children requested their refreshments without prompting and often with a complete sentence. Some of them, however, were beginning to say only what Tim said (i.e. 'Juice, please'). The teacher also noticed that Tim did not use language to express needs or wants during other situations that came up during the day. In other words, what Tim was doing at snack time did not carry over to other situations.

An alternative approach is to develop individualized objectives around broad competencies versus isolated behaviours. Instructional strategies to foster these competencies are then embedded within the daily routine with special attention to child-initiated activities. With this approach, the situation for Tim might have been different, as follows:

An individualized objective states that 'Tim will use words and gestures to express needs and wants'. Rather than 'staging' times when Tim must demonstrate this skill, the teacher observes closely for naturally occurring situations when she can prompt, model and call attention to the targeted behaviour. She notices, for example, that at one point during the day Tim tries to put an audiotape in the tape player, but is having difficulty doing so. The teacher intervenes by saying, 'Tim, do you need some help?' Tim nods his head to indicate 'Yes'. The teacher then prompts Tim to say, 'Please help me'. Later, the teacher models the desired behaviour. She walks over to Tim and says, 'I need help hanging up this paper. Hold one side for me, please.' She also uses a naturally occurring event to call attention to the targeted behaviour. When Sandra asks for help in getting a lid off a paste bottle, the teacher refers her to Tim by saying, 'My hands are wet right now. Could you ask Tim to help you?' After using these child-initiated or more naturally occurring strategies over a period of several weeks, the teacher notices that Tim is beginning to use words to express his needs and wants. She first notices this when Tim approaches her with a paper he had been working on. In trying to fold the paper, Tim accidentally tore it. Tim shows the teacher his paper and says, 'Tape, please'.

These two approaches to developing and fostering individualized objectives differ in a number of ways. The first represents a more deficit-oriented approach. It is based on specific skills and isolated behaviours. Related instructional techniques involve direct instruction and adult-initiated activities. The second approach represents a more developmental approach. It is based on broad competencies and context-oriented behaviours. Related instructional techniques include modelling, responsivity and child-initiated activities. The first approach relies more on extrinsic rewards (e.g. a snack) versus intrinsic motivation (e.g. the ability to ask for and receive help when needed).

Individualized objectives should always be consistent with developmentally appropriate practices (DAP). The following criteria may be helpful in deciding which objectives reflect DAP. They:

- are written broadly to allow for flexibility;
- allow implementation within the context of the daily routine;
- include skills that will increase opportunities for positive interactions with typically developing peers;
- represent child-initiated versus teacher-directed behaviours;
- are appropriate to the child's developmental level;
- allow for generalization across settings and activities;
- reflect current competencies as well as areas of concern;
- serve a functional purpose in the variety of contexts in which the child participates;
- include skills that will increase options for successful participation in future inclusive environments;
- meet the unique needs, strengths and interests of the child.

The objectives presented in Box 11.1 have been developed with the above criteria in mind. They have also been developed around the understanding that the young child is an active participant and interactor in the learning process and that he or she is always growing towards more independent functioning. While these objectives are categorized under the areas of language development, social development, emotional development, physical development and cognitive development, they are all designed to

Box 11.1 Objectives reflecting a developmental framework

Language development
- Uses words and/or gestures to express needs and wants
- Uses descriptive words to add specificity to statements (soft, happy, etc.)
- Uses location words appropriately (in, on, under)
- Initiates verbal interaction with adults
- Initiates verbal interaction with peers
- Uses questions to obtain needed information
- Describes activities of self and others
- Participates in short conversations
- Follows simple directions
- Responds to simple questions

Social development
- Responds to invitation to play with another child
- Interacts with adults
- Interacts with peers
- Plays in pairs or small groups
- Understands and follows rules of fair play

Emotional development
- Responds to verbal redirection when frustrated
- Expresses pride in accomplishments
- Shows concern for others in a group

Physical development
- Runs around obstacles and turns corners
- Throws a ball with ability to direct
- Manipulates simple writing and art tools (pencils, pens, paintbrushes)
- Performs basic dressing tasks (buttons, zips)

Cognitive development
- Makes simple choices
- Attends to simple tasks for a reasonable length of time
- Explores multiple use of objects
- Predicts/anticipates probable outcomes and consequences
- Draws simple figures (stick figures, circles, letters)
- Matches pictures to simple objects

support development as a whole. This list is by no means meant to be inclusive of all the skills or areas needed for healthy child development. Its purpose is to provide examples of objectives written from a developmental framework for intervention.

Embedding objectives in the daily routine

Several planning strategies have been developed for incorporating individualized objectives within the routine of daily activities in an early education setting. Figure 11.1 represents one such planning tool. The

Child's name: ____________________

Individualized objectives	Motor	Communication	Cognitive	Social	Self-help
Daily routines					
Arrival		X		X	X
Bathroom					X
Large group	X		X		
Learning centres		X	X	X	
Clean-up		X			
Bathroom					X
Snack		X			X
Outdoor activities	X			X	
Bathroom					X
Story time		X			
Dismissal				X	X

Figure 11.1 Embedding individualized objectives in the daily routine

idea of this matrix is to identify the daily routines and then to match individualized objectives to the kinds of skills that can be learned or practised during those times.

Another planning tool that may be helpful in fostering the development of individualized objectives is presented in Figure 11.2. This matrix is designed to help teachers focus on individual children during different times of the day – that is, times of the day that may be most conducive to learning or practising targeted skills.

The matrix presented in Figure 11.2 suggests that Bill may need special help or support during clean-up times. Bill may have difficulty staying on task or following directions. Clean-up times usually offer opportunities to practise such skills. This same matrix indicates that centre time is a good time to foster some of Joe's individualized objectives. Such objectives might relate to cognitive development and involve the development of such skills as problem solving, discriminating between similar objects and seriation.

Children's names	Bill	Joe	Kayla	Levi	Ann	George	Megan
Daily routines							
Arrival					X		
Bathroom							X
Large group							X
Learning centres	X	X	X	X		X	
Clean-up	X						X
Bathroom							X
Snack			X	X	X		
Outdoor activities		X					
Bathroom							X
Story time					X	X	
Dismissal	X						

Objectives:
Bill – Follow simple directions; use location words appropriately
Joe – Explore multiple use of objects; initiate verbal interaction with peers
Kayla – Use spoon independently; use words to express needs and wants
Levi – Match pictures to simple objects; use descriptive words
Ann – Participate in short conversations; respond to simple questions
George – Respond to simple questions; show concern for others in a group
Megan – Perform basic dressing tasks; follow simple directions

Figure 11.2 Individualized supports

After individualized objectives have been developed and some thought has been given to how to foster the acquisition of the targeted skills, another important consideration relates to the level of intervention and/or support needed by the child. Determining when and how to intervene requires careful observation of the child. It also requires observation over time. One major focus of the observation should be on how the child plays. If the child plays with active exploration and experimentation, the level of direct adult involvement should be considerably different from that required for a child who exhibits only low levels of play or repeats the same play behaviours steadily over time. For the child with poor play skills, the teacher may need to model new behaviours, introduce new materials, or demonstrate an extension of the child's activity.

For children with SEN, it is important for the teacher to provide opportunities for them to develop and practise skills related to their individualized objectives. Many such opportunities tend to occur during the regularly scheduled activities of the day – story time, self-help tasks, social interactions and so on. At times, individual children may need prompting or direction to encourage them to use materials or engage in activities directly related to their individualized objectives. For example, one of Carl's objectives may be to manipulate simple writing and art tools. Carl, however, rarely chooses to work at either the writing centre or the art centre. He spends most of his free-choice time using building materials or engaging in 'car and truck' play. In this case, the teacher will need to be more directive at times in order to foster the development of the targeted skills. She can still do this, however, within the context of car and truck play. She might, for example, ask children to write their names on a 'sign-up sheet' next to the learning centre of their choice. She might also ask them to 'check out' materials they want to use. This strategy could assist all the children with organizational skills, while helping Carl with his writing skills.

Individualized objectives and related instructional practices should reflect a child's preferences for and interests in various toys, materials and activities. In addition to closely observing children for information about their preferences and interests, parents and other family members should also be consulted. Activities and materials related to a child's preferences and interests generally motivate the child to become engaged in meaningful ways and serve as effective vehicles for accomplishing individualized objectives.

Individualized objectives and related instructional practices should also reflect an understanding of how the child responds to adults and peers. Through direct observation, teachers can identify the types of adult and peer behaviour which usually result in sustained interaction and positive reactions from the child. Teachers should also determine whether or not – or in what way – the child complies with adult requests. Does the child follow group instructions or only instructions that are given individually? Such information can help the teacher determine the kind and extent of support a child needs to participate in classroom activities. Another area of concern is whether the child imitates adults and other children. If the child does not imitate others, he or she may need to be taught to do so. Techniques that might be used to teach imitation include the following:

- Imitate the child and then wait for him or her to repeat your action: position yourself very near and in front of the child. Wait for the child to perform an action. Imitate the child's action. Look expectantly at the child, waiting for him or her to repeat your action. If the child does not, imitate the action again and then wait once more to see if he or she will repeat the action. After the child repeats the action, add something slightly new. Wait for the child to repeat this new version. For example, if Jerry pushes his hand down into the sand, you do the same. If he repeats this action, add a variation to it. You might do this by turning your hand over while it is under the sand and bringing it up with some sand cupped in your hand. Continue this back-and-forth game, where imitation is one of the elements that makes it fun.

- Prompt the child to imitate: a child can be prompted to imitate through verbal suggestions – 'See what Janie is doing. Can you do what she's doing?' or 'Jerry, it's your turn. Step up on the stage like Janie did.'

Implementation of individualized objectives should always occur within the context of existing classroom activities and routines. It should 'neither supplant the classroom curriculum nor restrict the child's participation in classroom activities' (Horn *et al.*, 2000, p. 208).

Promoting social interaction

As learning during the early childhood years is related so closely to interactions with others, promoting social interaction should be a crucial component of an early childhood programme. As mentioned in Chapter 5, children with special educational needs (SEN) tend to be less socially competent than their typically developing peers. As a result, they tend to be socially isolated. In planning an individualized plan for young children with disabilities, attention to social interaction concerns should be considered carefully. The following discussion on co-operative learning activities relates to this concern.

Co-operative learning, one strategy that can be used to foster social interaction, is a non-competitive approach to group learning focusing on co-operative goals. This strategy involves structuring activities that teach children to encourage one another, celebrate each other's successes and work towards common goals (Johnson and Johnson, 1986; Noonan and McCormick, 1993). A primary purpose of co-operative learning is to foster co-operative interactions between children and to teach them the skills involved. It also tends to promote child engagement. For preschoolers, co-operative learning activities may be especially helpful in promoting social and communication skills of children with disabilities served in a typical early childhood setting.

Co-operative learning activities need to be planned carefully and teacher supported. If not, such activities can easily become situations of conflict, frustration and confusion. To be educationally useful, a co-operative learning activity should involve children in something interesting and challenging. Children should be given the opportunity to make some decisions about how they perform group tasks. They should also be given the opportunity to judge their own success. Finally, co-operative learning activities should permit all members of the group to participate actively and successfully throughout the process.

Each child in a co-operative learning group has a clearly defined role, and each role is equally valued. For example, one child might serve as the leader of the group, while another child serves as the manager (in charge of getting supplies). Such an arrangement allows for active participation by children with varying abilities.

The teacher's role in co-operative learning activities is to teach co-operative skills so that the group can function effectively. Such skills include (1) asking for/offering help, (2) listening to others, (3) sharing materials and ideas, (4) taking turns, and (5) showing someone how to do something or helping them to accomplish a task. The teacher may also have to remind the children to stay near one another and to help each other. In addition, the teacher should monitor the group carefully to see where assistance is needed. Finally, it is important for the teacher to provide positive feedback (e.g. 'You really worked well together. I like the way you listened to each other'). Of course, it is also important for the teacher to carefully select the lessons and activities with which the children will be involved during the co-operative learning process. The lessons and activities must lend themselves to positive peer interactions and be appropriate for the children's age and ability.

Fostering social inclusion[1]

Strategies that might be used to foster the social inclusion of children with special needs should include attention to factors within the child and in the environment. Unfortunately, changes within the child tend to receive almost all our attention, usually in the form of training of social skills (Meyer, 2001). One breakdown of strategies fostering social inclusion include the following three areas: (1) supporting children's participation in interactive play with peers, (2) fostering the acquisition of specific social skills, and (3) fostering the development of friendships with peers (Meyer, 2001).

1 An earlier version of this section was published in Early Childhood News (March/April, 2002) and is referenced.

Supporting children's participation in interactive play with peers

Meyer (2001) identified several categories of adult behaviour related directly to peer social interactions. She refers to them as 'just right', 'blocked' and 'missed opportunities'. The behaviour is 'just right' if it facilitates a social interaction between children. Such facilitation may come in the form of 'play tutoring' (Johnson *et al.*, 1987). With play tutoring, the adult makes comments and suggestions that lead children to play together. This should be done without the adult 'taking over' the play situation. For example, if two children are engaged in parallel play in the 'kitchen corner', the adult might suggest that one child serve his 'soup' to the other child. In this situation, the child has been making 'soup' with another child nearby. The teacher's suggestion fits the play episode already in place. If suggestions are not sufficient in stimulating social play of any enduring length, the adult can also help by actually entering the play situation. This step is 'more intrusive' and should be used only if the suggestions were not successful.

Facilitation is not always necessary, however. Some well-intentioned adult behaviours actually 'block' peer social interaction. This occurs when an adult steps in and interrupts an interaction in progress. While the intent may be to solve a problem, the outcome may be a 'blocked' interaction between peers. There are other times, however, when adults would do well to 'seize the moment' to foster peer interaction. Such moments are often unplanned. This occurs when situations conducive to rich social interaction simply emerge. Such situations are sometimes referred to as 'teachable moments'. According to Meyer (2001), 'missed opportunities' occur when adults fail to recognize and capitalize on these moments.

Missed opportunities can occur when adults assume that social inclusion will take care of itself; they fail to look for 'teachable moments'. Missed opportunities can also occur when adults monopolize a child's time and agenda and when they have very specific expectations about what should occur. For example, someone decides that Jeff, a child with a disability, should say 'hullo' to peers as he enters the classroom. Jeff is positioned and instructed to do just that. In the meantime, other children are choosing learning centers and talking with their friends as they enter the room. A peer asks Jeff if he would like to help make a road in the block area. Jeff, however, is expected to stay engaged in 'greeting' for a period of time before choosing a centre activity. In this case, the expectation is not consistent with the ongoing flow of activities, and the child with special needs becomes an island in the mainstream (Meyer, 2001).

In addition to play tutoring, there are several other strategies which adults can use to support children's participation in interactive play with peers. One such strategy involves 'setting the stage' for interaction to occur. With this strategy, adults provide or 'stage' opportunities which invite social interaction. In setting the stage, elements of both the physical and emotional domains of the classroom are critiqued and structured in relation to the goal of enhancing interactive play. Materials and activities are evaluated, since certain types of play materials and classroom activities are more likely to enhance peer–peer interaction than other types (Kemple and Hartle, 1997). Some of the social toys that tend to foster interactive play include balls, wagons, housekeeping props, cars and other vehicles. Play activities that encourage social interactions include sociodramatic theme play – camping, travelling, housekeeping – and group play involving partners or friends. Certain songs and rhymes, for example, encourage children to engage in such partner activities as shaking hands or smiling at each other.

The emotional climate of the classroom also influences peer–peer social interaction. A democratic style of discipline is more conducive than other styles of discipline to helping children interact positively and peacefully with one another (Kemple and Hartle, 1997). Adults working within a democratic style of discipline set firm limits on inappropriate behaviour and rely largely on explanations to help children learn appropriate behaviour. The democratic style of discipline falls between a laissez-faire, or highly permissive, approach and an authoritarian approach that relies on harsh, punitive practices. A democratic style of discipline allows children 'to feel listened to, to understand the rules and the reasons behind the rules, and to feel confident that they will be protected' (Kemple and Hartle, 1997, p. 140). Directive and coercive interactions, on the other hand, tend to impede both the social/emotional development of young children and interactive play between peers.

Fostering the acquisition of specific social skills

The competencies and behaviours of a child with special needs exert a major influence on the nature and quality of the social interactions that occur between the child and his or her social partners. If the child is unable to receive or interpret the partner's social initiatives or responses, the interaction is thwarted. Without help, young children with disabilities are often unable to provide the same kind of positive feedback to their social partners (adults or peers) as children without disabilities. A child with delayed cognitive development, for example, may be unable to see the same possibilities for pretend play as his or her typically developing peers and thus not grasp the nature of a role-play situation. The child's comments and actions may then be out of tune with what the other children are doing. In the other children's eyes, this may make the child with special needs less desirable as a play partner or friend. Adults need to intervene in these situations to help the child with special needs acquire specific social skills. Such help can come in the form of prompts.

Some children with disabilities need direct prompts on how and when to interact with other children. Prompts may focus on such specific social interactions skills as making eye contact, looking at the person speaking, making and responding to requests and so on. Research indicates that prompts from both adults and peers can be effective in helping children with disabilities interact successfully with their typical peers (McEvoy and Odom, 1996).

Prompts can involve intense adult involvement or less intense involvement. The extent of involvement should always be determined by the individual needs of the child, with little or no intervention the ultimate goal.

Another important consideration in helping children develop new social skills is to choose the 'target behaviours' carefully. Not all social skills are of equal value in developing and maintaining friends. Teachers need to make the right decisions about changes in children's repertoires rather than teaching children behaviours that make little difference in social interactions (Meyer, 2001). It is also important to focus on goals that are valued by the child's family and cultural context. Unless the educational goals are valued by the child's family and are consistent with their culture, the skills mastered will not be maintained or useful in the child's daily life outside the classroom (Meyer, 2001). Increasing the child's repertoire of interactive skills is more complex than simply working from a generic list of social interaction goals.

Fostering the development of friendships with peers

Since many young children with disabilities are not readily accepted as friends by their peers, it becomes incumbent upon adults to foster such acceptance. Adults can do this by helping the child with special needs learn specific social competencies associated with being liked by peers. One such competency is the ability to 'read' other children's emotional responses (Kemple and Hartle, 1997). Adults can foster this skill by calling attention to the emotional aspects of social interactions and helping children state their feelings, ideas and desires clearly. For example, if a child with special needs pushes another child, the adult might intervene by saying, 'Jesse, look at Tonya. Her face is sad because you pushed her.' The adult can also help children use appropriate words to express their needs and wants versus resorting to physical action for such expressions. For example, the adult might say, 'Jesse, don't push Tonya. Ask her if you can work at the table with her.' Other ways in which adults can guide children through the process of resolving differences and solving problems include:

- paraphrasing each child's view to the other;
- clearly defining the problem in terms that are understood by both parties;

- helping children develop their own alternative solutions;
- offering new ideas when needed;
- facilitating discussion of the merits of suggested solutions;
- acknowledging the effort and emotional investment each child contributes to the situation.

(Kemple and Hartle, 1997)

By observing children closely and identifying moments when they need support in interacting with others, adults can help children with disabilities experience success and satisfaction in social situations. Not only will children then be more likely to engage in similar interactions in the future, they will also feel good about having friends and knowing how to be a friend to others. Peer involvement in fostering social inclusion should always be based on interest in an equal-status relationship – that is, peers should view the child with special needs as 'just another child' and as a potential 'regular friend' or 'best friend'. Without such expectations, the social relationships that develop will continue to be restricted to just a few – and less satisfying – frames of friendship.

Behavioural guidance

Behaviour problems in children are associated with poor academic achievement, poor interpersonal skills and increased risk of mental health problems (Hemphill, 1996; Rowe and Rowe, 1992). We also know that 'the problem behaviour of older students and adults is likely to have had its roots in difficult behaviour at a young age' (Stephenson *et al.*, 2000, p. 225). Thus it is important to learn about the nature of behaviour problems in young children and ways to address this concern.

Some research suggests that teachers believe that 16 per cent of 4- to 7-year-old children have 'definite' behavioural problems and that a further 17 per cent have 'mild problems' (Roffey and O'Reirdan, 2001). Research also suggests that behaviours of greatest concern to teachers in the early years of school are distractibility, aggression and disobedience (Stephenson *et al.*, 2000). These behaviours are often learned and/or exhibited early in life.

Bullying

'Bullying', one type of aggressive behaviour, is especially troubling. Bullying, as defined in the literature, 'occurs when another child or children are deliberately mean to someone else several times, weeks, or months at a time' (Drecktrah and Blaskowski, 2000, p. 40). Bullying also includes 'a deliberate use of power and threat to intimidate and undermine another child (Roffey and O'Reirdan, 2001, p. 108).

Bullying can be verbal, physical or indirect. An example of indirect bullying is the deliberate exclusion of someone from social groups. Bullying is usually unprovoked and initiated by someone who is stronger than the victim. Some evidence suggests that when bullying behaviour is not addressed at an early stage, it tends to continue and escalate as the child gets older (Roffey and O'Reirdan, 2001).

'Statistics from England, Scandinavia, Australia, and the U.S. indicate that bullying is a major social problem' (Drecktrah and Blaskowski, 2000, p. 40). Some work has been done to identify the reasons for bullying. Barone (1997) cites four such reasons: (1) adults often view bullying as a normal part of growing up; (2) adults have become desensitized to bullying and tend not to notice it; (3) educators are often overwhelmed by other problems: and (4) schools may be reluctant to identify bullying, as they feel they do not have the resources to address it. According to Roffey and O'Reirdan (2001), 'much bullying behavior is a result of poor social skills or low self-esteem' (p. 108).

Teachers and children who are the victims of bullying tend to view a bullying problem quite differently, with the extent of the problem representing one area of considerable difference. In one study (Drecktrah and Blaskowski, 2000), elementary school staff estimated that 7.1 per cent of students were bullied. Over 69 per cent of the students in this school, however, reported that they had been bullied. 'This suggests that the staff does not recognize the extent of the bullying problem that students in their school face' (Drecktrah and Blaskowski, 2000, p. 42). Some studies suggest that one in five children attending school are afraid through much of their school day (Drecktrah and Blaskowski, 2000).

There are some specific signs of aggression in young children which may later take the form of overt violent behaviour. Warning signs published by the American Psychological Association and the American Academy of Pediatrics (1999) include the following:

- Has many temper tantrums in a single day or several lasting more than fifteen minutes and often cannot be calmed down by parents, family members or other caregivers.
- Has many aggressive outbursts, often for no reason.
- Is overly active, impulsive and fearless.
- Consistently refuses to follow directions and listen to adults.
- Does not seem attached to parents; for example, does not touch, look for or return to parents in strange places.
- Frequently watches violence on television, engages in play that has violent themes, or is cruel towards other children.

Some research suggests that bullying and other forms of aggressive behaviour can be decreased by (1) helping children develop confidence in knowing how to solve problems, (2) teaching them how to seek help from adults, (3) teaching them how to exercise self-control over their actions, and (4) improving their ability to communicate with others (Drecktrah and Blaskowski, 2000; Goleman, 1995). Roffey and O'Reirdan (2001) suggest that bullying behaviour can also be reduced by teaching all children how to resist bullying behaviour. They recommend teaching children how to use simple assertiveness strategies. The simplest one, they say, 'is to teach them to say clearly and directly: "Stop it, I don't like it" and then move away' (p. 108).

The development of empathy is also considered important to combating bullying behaviour (Drecktrah and Blaskowski, 2000). Empathy – understanding and caring about another's feelings – is difficult, especially for young children who are egocentric. While we know that empathy develops sequentially and over time, there are some indications that even young children exhibit some forms of empathy. For example, when hearing the cry of another baby, an infant will often respond by crying. As the child grows older (during the preschool years), children will often show signs of concern when they see another child in distress (Krull, 2000).

Several ways in which adults can support the development of empathy include encouraging children to talk about their own feelings and modelling empathy by talking about how others might be feeling (Krull, 2000).

Prevention approach

The best approach to behavioural guidance focuses on prevention versus intervention. Prevention deals with the promotion of positive behaviour and recognizes the fact that there is a learning component to all behaviours with which teachers can work (Roffey and O'Reirdan, 2001). This does not suggest, however, that all behaviours of concern are within the control of the teacher. Some are not; and teachers need to focus their efforts on what is within their power to change (Roffey and O'Reirdan, 2001).

In taking a preventive approach to behaviour guidance, teachers need to be aware of specific skills and attributes associated with positive behaviour or successful behavioural self-management. Items from the following list are based on work by Roffey and O'Reirdan (2001). They indicate that skills and attributes needed for appropriate behaviour management include:

- self-awareness
- self-confidence and self-esteem
- an understanding about feelings and ways of expressing these feelings
- empathy and an appreciation that people have different perspectives
- decision-making abilities
- effective communication skills.

In taking a preventive approach, teachers also need to be aware of the categories of behaviour which may be cause for concern so that they may be addressed as early as possible. Roffey and O'Reirdan (2001) have identified the following six categories:

1 Behaviour as part of a learning or language difficulty (e.g. having trouble understanding and following directions).
2 Behaviour that stems from poor social interactions (e.g. does not know how to play and work co-operatively with others).
3 Disruptive behaviour (e.g. difficulty with behavioural boundaries; uses such behaviour to get attention).
4 Behaviour that is the result of an inability to settle to work or respond to direction (e.g. finds concentration difficult; may be poorly motivated).
5 Behaviour that is extreme and accompanied either by a high level of emotion or by worrying 'blankness' (e.g. something has happened, or is happening, to the child which is making him or her distressed, angry, withdrawn or demanding).
6 Behaviour that is particularly unusual (e.g. repetitive, bizarre or socially inappropriate behaviour).

The 'Quiet Place'

Behavioural guidance initiatives often focus on extrinsic approaches and include delivering training to the significant people in the child's life: parents, peers, and teachers. The 'Quiet Place' project uses a different approach. Its primary focus is on healthy emotional development and takes into account the child's inner world (Spalding, 2000). Through this project, children who are experiencing emotional and behavioural difficulties are provided with a variety of therapeutic interventions in an environment conducive to a sense of well-being and relaxation. As such, the 'Quiet Place' works from a positive model of health founded upon a holistic approach to personal development (Spalding, 2000). Examples of therapeutic interventions available to the children in the programme include neurolinguistic programming, sand play, story telling and metaphor work, head and face massage, systematic relaxation and reflexology. Computer software based on biofeedback techniques designed to promote relaxation is also available. Finally, 'the provision of an appropriate and nurturing environment complements the range of therapeutic approaches on offer' (Spalding, 2000, p. 130).

The furnishings of a 'Quiet Place' room are designed to promote a sense of peace and relaxation. Such rooms often contain soft furnishings, including beanbags and a variety of soft toys, such as teddy bears and puppets. They also feature 'mini-environments' such as tent-like areas and cozy corners. Some rooms have water cascades, plants, and musical instruments. A number of therapists work with the children in the 'Quiet Place'. Children usually attend several sessions per week over a period of about six weeks. Parents are also invited into the room.

'Quiet Place' rooms are currently housed in several mainstream primary schools. The first 'Quiet Place' room was established in 1998 in Millwood School in the Speke area of Liverpool. Since then, further rooms have been established in the Liverpool area, including Stockton Wood Infants School and Hope Valley School.

The 'Quiet Place' project was established in response to 'the poor levels of support available for an estimated 10% to 12% of children who experience mental health problems' (Spalding, 2000, p. 129). The project was also designed as a way to wrap multidisciplinary services 'around the school as the location most frequented by families, and often their first "port of call" when under stress (DfEE, 1999)' (Spalding, 2000, p. 129).

While the 'Quiet Place' approach focuses primarily on the child, in the majority of cases it also involves the family. In fact, the 'Quiet Place' initiative has been designed particularly to work with high-risk families who have been identified as having children already presenting serious behavioural concerns. 'The prime outcome is realised by an increase in parental empowerment and confidence in handling children within their own family, as well as within the school and the general community' (Spalding, 2000, p. 129). Another desired outcome is the long-term inclusion of children in regular classes.

As reported by Spalding (2000), research findings from a systematic evaluation of the 'Quiet Place' project indicate that the programme has been effective in the following ways:

- having a calming influence on the children
- marked improvement in self-confidence
- increased ability to reflect and talk things through
- improved anger management
- reduction in parental stress.

Spalding (2000) reports that, while these results failed to reach levels of statistical significance compared with the control group, 'there is little doubt . . . that the "Quiet Place" intervention has a positive effect overall on emotional development' (pp. 133–134).

Cultural diversity

Many reasons may be given as to why we should value diversity and teach our young children to do so. One reason is that children have a right to value diversity (Gardner, 2001; Lane, 1984). They also have a right to know that their personal race, ethnicity and culture are valued by others. What children experience at school (through both formal instruction and all other aspects of the school experience) gives them messages about whether or not their culture is understood and valued.

Too often, there are considerable differences between what children experience at home and what they experience at school. Such differences can greatly affect their performance and feelings of self-worth. As McCracken (1993, pp. 10–11) notes, 'Most young children function quite well at home and in their own neighborhoods. They are relaxed, have friends, and feel as though they have some control over their lives.' Once they enter the unfamiliar environment of the school, their performance and self-esteem may drop considerably.

Teachers need to realize that differences between what children experience at home and at school can cause anxiety and negatively affect performance. 'The greater disparity between home and school, the greater the anxiety for children' (McCracken, 1993, p. 10). To reduce this anxiety and maximize the child's chances of success, home and school environments should be fairly congruent. In order for this to happen, teachers must become 'well-informed about, sensitive to, and responsive to cultural differences' (McCracken, 1993, p. 11).

Through a careful selection of classroom resources and teaching strategies, teachers can introduce familiar aspects of the child's community into the classroom. By merging school experiences with what the child experiences in his or her community, children become empowered as learners. 'One of the principal aspects of empowerment is respect. Students are empowered when information is presented in such a way that they can walk out of the classroom feeling that they are a part of the information' (Hilliard, 1991/1992, p. 29). If cultural differences are ignored – or worse – treated as deficits, the child and his or her family are likely to feel estranged from the programme and less likely to benefit from it.

Culture is like a framework that 'guides and bounds life practices' (Hanson, 1992, p. 3). Cultural diversity, then, refers to more than diversity in relation to race and ethnicity. It encompasses values, customs and other dimensions of one's lifestyle, including family composition. Due to the great variability in family characteristics, it is important for early childhood professionals to acknowledge a broad, inclusive definition of family (Howard *et al.*, 1997). A broad definition recognizes that many families differ from the traditional nuclear family consisting of a father, mother, and their biological sons and daughters. Many children live in single-parent homes, in homes with blended families (i.e. with step-parents), in foster homes, in homes with adoptive parents, and in homes with extended family. Some live with gay or lesbian parents, some with grandparents, and some with parents who are teenagers. Thus 'terms such as "traditional" and "nuclear" are no longer meaningful for describing families' (Hanson and Lynch, 1995, p. 46).

It is not unusual for a child's family make-up to change several times over his or her growing-up years. The family's socio-economic status may change as well. Many children will live in poverty for all or part of their early childhood years. Some live with abuse and neglect. In light of these many differences, teachers should use instructional activities that reflect an understanding of and sensitivity to such differences.

Professionals who work with young children with disabilities tend to be in close contact with families at a sensitive time – that is, at the time of, or soon after, the family becomes aware of their child's special needs. Thus, while all professionals should work in a culturally competent manner, this becomes particularly important for professionals working with young children with special needs. Cultural competence refers to the ability to honour and respect those beliefs, interpersonal styles, attitudes and behaviours both of families who are receiving services and the multicultural staff who are providing services. Work by Cross and colleagues (1989) indicates that cultural competence is demonstrated in the following ways:

- *Acknowledging and valuing differences*: This includes not only respecting the uniqueness of individuals, but also developing an understanding of how race, culture and ethnicity influence families and children.
- *Conducting a cultural self-assessment*: This involves becoming aware of one's own culture and the way in which related cultural perspectives shape personal and professional behaviour.
- *Recognizing and understanding the dynamics of difference*: This means understanding that factors such as racism, social status, and history influence the way individuals of different cultures interact with each other.
- *Acquiring cultural knowledge*: This involves becoming informed about different cultures, but also being aware of variations within groups.
- *Adapting to diversity*: This means matching practices to the needs and styles of family cultures. Identifying and using culturally unbiased assessment procedures is one example of adapting to diversity.

If professionals do not have knowledge of and respect for the language, lifestyle, beliefs and values of the families they serve, they run the risk of being offensive or ineffective in their role as members of an early intervention team. Professionals must take care, however, not to assign certain characteristics to an individual just because he or she is a member of a certain ethnic group. Members of any cultural group will differ in how they reflect or identify with that group's cultural beliefs and practices. While some individuals hold a primary identification with one particular group, others do not. Some may identify primarily with one cultural orientation at work and another at home. Cultural identity, then, should be viewed as one of several factors contributing to an individual's practices and beliefs. Other factors certainly include age, gender, socio-economic status, level of education and extent of family support. Thus, while early childhood professionals should be aware of and responsive to general cultural practices and preferences, they should also recognize that 'as many differences exist within groups as across groups' (Hanson and Lynch, 1995, p. 54).

Professionals working with young children and their families should have not only an understanding and appreciation of cultural diversity, but should also share this appreciation through their teaching. In the classroom, this is often referred to as multicultural education. To avoid the mistakes often associated with the various approaches to multicultural education outlined above, the following guidelines are offered.

- Use only accurate and fair portrayals of different cultures and individuals. Stereotypes should definitely be avoided. If historical presentations are used, they should be paired with contemporary presentations.
- Focus more on the everyday lives of people from different cultures versus their festivals and other special occasions.
- Use materials that are written and illustrated by people of the culture being described as much as possible.
- Use only terminology that is current and positive. Avoid all forms of condescending, patronizing, or dehumanizing terminology (e.g. savage, wild).
- Present people as unique individuals within a culture, rather than as the embodiment of a culture.
- Strive to diversify the staff. A programme should include staff members who represent the ethnic, cultural and language diversity of the children and families being served.
- Involve families in the programme. 'Programmes that value children value their families' (McCracken, 1993, p. 65). Schools should invite families to share information and ideas regarding educational goals, learning activities and community resources.
- Foster pride in each child's cultural heritage. Respect for each family's culture is essential for children to feel pride in themselves and in their heritage.

To implement the above suggestions, teachers should start by collecting information on the developmental characteristics and cultural experiences of all the children in the classroom. They should then select and arrange materials in their learning spaces that reflect the cultures of individual children and/or the neighbourhood where they live. Once this is in place, teachers should observe closely the children's use of the materials and note related interests and questions that emerge. These observations should be used to plan new learning activities for the children. Such activities should link new concepts with those the children have already acquired. Thus new learning will be related to what is already familiar to the child.

Gardner (2001), in outlining key points of multicultural education, stresses the importance of including knowledge and understanding which:

- reflect the cultural, ethnic and religious diversity of the world in which we live;
- recognize that human beings share common values, aspirations and needs;
- provide examples of excellence from all cultures.

While Gardner outlines additional key points in his work, these three seem most applicable to the education of young children.

Multiple intelligences

Intelligence is sometimes defined as the ability to learn and to know. One's intelligence is often measured or quantified in terms of performance on logical and linguistic tasks. This approach to defining and measuring intelligence suggests that it is a single entity. Recent research, however, suggests that there are multiple intelligences or ways of knowing. The following seven intelligences were articulated by Gardner (1983):

- linguistic (having to do with language)
- logical-mathematical (most closely related to science and maths)
- musical
- spatial
- bodily kinaesthetic (having to do with bodily movement)
- interpersonal (having to do with relationships between and among people)
- intrapersonal (related to self-knowledge).

Gardner (1997) has suggested an eighth type of intelligence – that of 'naturalist intelligence'. This intelligence is described as the ability to recognize important distinctions in the natural world.

Gardner's work has led to an increased understanding of the fact that all children are intelligent. A question that should guide educational programming for an individual child is not whether that child can learn, but how he or she learns best. To do justice to the different ways in which children learn, frequent opportunities relating to the development of each type of intelligence must be provided. This can be particularly important for children with special educational needs. Just as their disability will tend to impede learning in some area(s) of development, their individual intelligence will enhance learning if appropriate opportunities are provided. As mentioned frequently throughout this book, to individualize a programme means more than accommodating for areas of weakness. It also means providing opportunities for areas of strength.

The theory of multiple intelligences raises several significant issues related to special education. The following are five such issues that have been identified by Goldman and Gardner (1989).

1 One issue emanating from the theory of multiple intelligences relates to the concept of being 'learning disabled'. To refer to a child as being learning disabled or as having a learning disability suggests there is only one kind of intelligence – that based on language and logic. The child's other potential areas of intelligence are not considered.
2 The theory of multiple intelligences also reduces the impact of a child's deficit area, or area of disability, by focusing on other areas (intelligences) where the child does not have deficits. This theory suggests further that strength in one area can compensate for and even be used to teach effectively in an area of apparent weakness. For example, a child with difficulties in linguistics may be able to use some of his or her spatial skills to accomplish certain tasks usually associated with verbal ability. Such a child might draw a map instead of giving someone verbal directions.
3 A third issue relates to assessment. Traditional assessment procedures emphasize linguistic and logical skills. Children whose skills lie primarily in other intelligences are thus short-changed. Goldman and Gardner (1989) thus suggest that a new system of assessment should be developed and used so that individual abilities may be identified as fully as possible early in the child's academic career. Assessment based on the theory of multiple intelligences would seek to capture the expanse of human potential in all intelligences and identify each child's unique intellectual propensities.
4 A fourth issue relates to school outcomes. An understanding of multiple intelligences suggests that the traditional idea of desirable school outcomes would have to be expanded to encompass a wider range of vocational and avocational roles. Achievement in standard academic areas would be only one of a number of goals. With this approach, the school could become a place where students can follow their own intellectual abilities and interests and be rewarded for doing so.
5 Another issue relates to curriculum and instruction. The theory of multiple intelligences suggests that curriculum and instruction should be tailored as much as possible to the inclinations, working styles and

profiles of intelligence for each individual student. The theory also suggests that instructional programmes should provide students with a wide range of materials and activities (i.e. a variety that fosters development across multiple intelligences versus the development of intelligence as a single entity). A classroom reflecting the theory of multiple intelligences would be furnished with engaging materials and activities that span the many realms of intelligence. Such materials would be open-ended in design so that children have the opportunity to express themselves in their preferred form of expression. A classroom so equipped would maximize the chance of eliciting and fostering children's special abilities. It would expand and individualize the curriculum and thus create an environment that welcomes children with special needs. In summary, it would give all children the opportunity to develop and be recognized for their special abilities.

12

EXPLORATIONS AND EXPERIENCES

Young children with disabilities have needs that are both similar to and unique from their typically developing peers. Because of the similarities, many of the teaching strategies used with typically developing children may also be used effectively with children with special educational needs. However, due to the unique needs of young children with SEN, adaptations may also be required. Without these adaptations, some children with SEN will be faced with serious barriers to experiencing and exploring the learning environment.

Guidelines for adaptations

Generally, adaptations to accommodate a child with SEN should be kept to a minimum. To be consistent with the principles of normalization and the least restrictive environment, any adaptations that are made should be as unobtrusive as possible (Wilson, 2000b). Other values and considerations to bear in mind regarding adaptations relate to 'meaningful participation, relationships, membership, positive outcomes, and honoring the culture within an environment' (Erwin and Schreiber, 1999, p. 168). Some of the related criteria for determining the appropriateness of adaptations, as outlined by Erwin and Schreiber (1999), are as follows:

- The adaptation or support ensures that the child can participate in an active and meaningful way in an experience or activity.
- The adaptation or support strongly promotes peer relationships and membership of the group.
- The adaptation or support produces outcomes for the child that are healthy, meaningful and individualized.
- The adaptation or support is consistent with the climate and culture of the natural setting.

Finally, Erwin and Schreiber (1999) offer six guiding principles for developing supports for young children with special needs. These guiding principles are consistent with the values and criteria outlined above. They are as follows.

1 Adaptations or supports should be as ordinary, nonstigmatizing, and unobtrusive as possible.
2 Supports provided by peers should always be considered.
3 Adaptations or supports must reflect children's rights to exercise control over the environment and their own lives.
4 Families should be involved in identifying supports.
5 The effectiveness of adaptations or supports must be closely monitored.
6 Adaptations or supports must be consistent with a climate that promotes membership and community spirit.

Positive learning environments

According to Dunst (2000), 'Development-enhancing child learning opportunities are ones that are interesting, engaging, and competency producing and result in a child's sense of mastery about his or her capabilities' (p. 101). While these criteria for learning opportunities are important for all children, they are even more crucial for children with special needs. If environments are not interesting and engaging, children will not be motivated to spend time manipulating and exploring, especially if a handicapping condition makes it difficult to do so. Environments, however, should be planned with more than 'fun' in mind. As Dunst indicates, learning opportunities must also be competency producing. A related challenge for teachers is to determine what competencies to target for individual children and then to plan environments and activities which promote the development of such competencies.

Some interesting work relating to quality and quality enhancement in early childhood education indicates that the teacher's ability to adopt a child's perspective plays an important role in creating an environment that promotes learning (Sheridan, 2001). In fact, some research indicates that the interaction between teacher and child is 'the most important factor for quality and quality enhancement' (Sheridan, 2001, p. 9). Taking a child's perspective involves being aware that 'even very young children have their own goals, interests and intentions about what they wish to explore and learn about' (Sheridan, 2001, p. 9). To create a positive learning environment, teachers need to keep the children's interests and abilities in mind. As indicated in Chapter 2, many young children are able to articulate what is important to them.

Promoting engagement

Positive learning environments promote engagement; that is, 'the amount of time a child spends in developmentally and contextually appropriate behaviours' (McWilliam, 1991, p. 42). The term 'on-task' is sometimes used to describe children's behaviours when they are engaged in instructional tasks. For an individual child, being engaged means being involved with the environment in a way that matches the expectations for a child of that developmental status and for that situation (McWilliam, 1991). Thus engagement is exhibited in different ways by different children and in different circumstances.

A high level of engagement promotes learning and prevents or reduces behaviour problems. Researchers have found, for example, that the longer a child is on-task the higher he or she scores in tests of achievement (McWilliam, 1991). As many children with SEN have difficulty establishing and maintaining engagement with their environment, an important goal of early intervention is to promote children's engagement in increasingly more complex and challenging ways.

The nature and quality of the environment has a lot to do with how engaged children will be in learning activities. Engaging environments tend to be high in responsivity. This means that the environment provides children with predictable and immediate feedback when they interact with their environment. Many toys designed for infants have high responsiveness. Crib mobiles, for example, often provide a visual and auditory response for any action done to it (e.g. touching it, pulling it, striking it). The infant's facial expressions and verbal reactions to such immediate feedback speak to the strength of a responsive environment.

An environment that provides immediate and consistent feedback helps children acquire a sense of power and security in controlling their environment. Children who feel they cannot control their environment often develop 'learned helplessness'. This tends to happen more frequently for children with disabilities.

Teachers can increase the responsivity of the environment by choosing materials and planning activities that provide immediate positive reinforcement. They should also make sure that all materials and equipment are in good working order. If the battery in a flashlight is dead or the paint in a jar is dry, for example, children will experience frustration and disappointment when they try to use these materials. They will then be less inclined to try them again and possibly less inclined to try other materials as well.

Bailey and Wolery (1992) offer five suggestions for improving the initial attractiveness of activities and materials to facilitate engagement. They are as follows:

1 Provide appealing materials. The appeal of materials can be enhanced by colour (bright rather than drab), by size (extra large or extra small) and by sound. Three-dimensional objects are more appealing than two-dimensional ones. As mentioned above, materials that provide

immediate feedback are also motivating. Materials tend to be more appealing if they match children's interest and level of development. Certainly novelty is another important factor. Novelty in the art centre, for example, would be enhanced if the type of materials available were to vary periodically. One week, the children may have access to paint and large sheets of rectangular white paper. The next week, the art centre might feature blue construction paper cut in the shapes of oceans, rivers and lakes, along with a variety of 'cut-outs' representing plants and animals that live in the water. Children could then create their own seascapes with glue or paste.

One school developed a toy rotation plan to provide variety and enhance engagement (McGee *et al.*, 1991). They began by coding classroom materials according to dimensions of size, complexity, developmental level, category and sensory quality. The inventory of materials was then divided into twelve sets, each containing ten items. Each set includes a mix of materials representing each of the above dimensions (i.e. size, complexity, developmental level, category and sensory quality). Each completed set thus offers the following:

- a combination of items that vary in size and complexity;
- items that represent a range of developmental levels;
- items that address a variety of educational goals;
- items that include a full array of sensory qualities.

Two such sets are in the room at any one time. Of course, there are other materials that remain in the room all the time (e.g. dolls, books, blocks), as they can be used in conjunction with the rotation materials. The rotation schedule is arranged so that more developmentally challenging materials are made available as the year progresses.

2 Make participation a privilege rather than a duty. Engagement tends to be greatly enhanced when activities and materials are self-selected. Making an activity something the children have to do usually detracts considerably from their interest in it.

3 Give children immediate roles in activities. Children are not engaged when they are only passively involved in an activity (e.g. listening to a story, watching others perform, awaiting their turn). Engagement can be enhanced by finding ways to keep all children actively involved. During story time, for example, children could use puppets, stuffed animals and clothing props to take on roles of characters in the story. For other activities, children might be given roles as helpers, leaders, data collectors or cheering squad. For all children, but especially for children with disabilities, roles must be designed to suit their individual skill level.

4 Use instructions to initiate or prompt interactions when needed. Children who are not engaged with materials or in an activity may

need a specific command or prompt to get them started. For example, if Tonya is in the book corner with two or three other children, but is not looking at books or interacting with others, the teacher might say something like, 'Tonya, did you see the book about dinosaurs that Anna is using? Can you find a book about dinosaurs, too?'

5 Identify children's preference for materials. People tend to stay with materials and activities that are of interest to them. Some people like to play a musical instrument and may spend hours with that instrument. Others may enjoy tennis and spend as much of their free time as possible out on the courts. Activities that are not of interest, however, tend to get abandoned rather quickly. For some, this may be learning a second language or cooking gourmet meals. While the above examples relate primarily to adults, the same concept is applicable to young children. Young children are more likely to become engaged and to maintain engagement with materials and activities that are of interest to them.

Through close observation, teachers can identify the preferences of individual children. By then making the preferred materials and activities available, they can greatly enhance the child's engagement. The problem is that children with severe disabilities tend to have restricted preferences (McGee *et al.*, 1991). In such cases, identifying the sensory preferences versus specific toy preferences may be helpful. Some children respond better to items with strong visual characteristics, while others may prefer auditory toys. Dramatic reductions in maladaptive behaviours have been achieved by using potent reinforcers that have been carefully selected according to each child's preferences (McGee *et al.*, 1991).

One school developed 'hobby boxes' to hold individualized materials (i.e. materials selected specifically with regard to an individual child's strongest preferences, interests and abilities) (McGee *et al.*, 1991). Each hobby box is marked with the child's name, and items stored in the box are marked with the child's initials. The hobby boxes are then stored on high shelves, within the child's view but out of his or her reach. This arrangement promotes social interactions with adults and verbal requests for materials. Materials in the hobby boxes are used only if (1) the child requests them, or (2) the teacher presents the materials to the child when he or she is not engaged with other materials in the classroom. Non-engagement is not an option. Therefore, the collection of preferred materials in a child's hobby box makes it easier for the teacher to redirect the child who is not engaged.

Promoting independence

A challenge of programmes serving young children with special educational needs is establishing a balance between fostering independence (i.e. persuading children to do things on their own) and ensuring that they are not left out of some activities because of their lack of required skills. To promote participation, it is sometimes necessary to provide adult support and to make special accommodations for children with SEN. If a child's disability prevents him or her from participating in an activity if help were not provided, such help should be given. The extent of the help, however, should encourage the child with SEN to do as much as possible on his or her own.

It is not only physical constraints that tend to impede a child's exploration and sense of independence; social constraints can do so as well. Adults concerned with children's safety may restrict access unduly to certain experiences. They may do things for and to the children rather than allow them to explore, interact and problem solve on their own. They may make unnecessary adaptations to the physical and social environment. This practice places control and responsibility for accessing the environment outside the realm of the child with a disability and within the control of other people. 'This response runs counter to the most deeply held ideals of personal independence in our society' (Mettler, 1987, p. 478). It is therefore extremely important that adults avoid 'over-controlling' the environment for children with disabilities.

Aids to exploration

There are a number of aids to exploration that may be used to help a child with special needs interact with the environment. Assistive technology is one such aid. Assistive technology can make it possible for children with disabilities to accomplish tasks that would otherwise be difficult or impossible. For example, a child who is unable to walk may use a wheelchair to go to the dining-room. If the dining-room is a long way from the classroom, the child may need a powered wheelchair to get there on time (i.e. when his or her classmates get there). Another child who is unable to write with a pencil legibly or quickly enough to keep up with classroom work may have to use a computer for written assignments.

Assistive technology

In each of the above examples, there is a gap between the child's abilities and the skills needed to perform the required tasks or activities. Assistive technology provides the tools to bridge this gap, allowing many children with disabilities to participate meaningfully in regular education environments.

The term 'assistive technology' covers a wide range of devices and services. They may be 'low tech', such as handheld magnifiers and velcro strips, or more 'high-tech' devices, such as computerized augmentative communication systems. The following is a list of different types of assistive technology, along with examples of each.

- *Mobility devices* (e.g. canes, walkers, manual or powered wheelchairs, scooters, adapted bikes)
- *Positioning devices* (e.g. corner chairs or floor sitters, standing frames, chair inserts, wedges, pillows, straps)
- *Self-care devices* (e.g. adapted utensils, switch-operated electronic feeders, buttonhooks, velcro fasteners, toilet seats)
- *Computer access devices* (e.g. trackballs, touch windows, switches)
- *Sensory aids* (e.g. closed-captioned TV, text enlargers, speech output devices, magnifiers, tape recordings, Braille, large-print books)
- *Augmentative communication devices* (e.g. spelling or symbol boards, picture cards)
- *Recreational devices* (e.g. computer games, drawing and music software, beeping balls)
- *Architectural barrier removal* (e.g. ramps, powered door openers, special hinges)

Adapting toys and other learning materials

The selection of toys and other learning materials can enhance or hinder a child's success in a programme. This is especially true for children with disabilities. Their unique motor, sensory, developmental and normalization needs often put special limitations on the kinds of toys and other learning materials that will be useful to them. Since it is often difficult to find materials that are just right for a particular child with a disability, adaptations to what is available must sometimes be made. Mechanical adaptations are sometimes used to allow a child to have greater control and independent use of certain toys and learning materials. For example, adding a push switch to a wind-up toy makes it easier for the child to use the toy without assistance. Other materials may be modified by replacing buttons or ties on clothing with velcro and adding a 'grip' to a pencil or pen for easier handling.

Additional strategies for appropriately adapting toys and other learning materials for children with disabilities have been suggested by Musselwhite (1986) and include:

- *Stabilizing* (e.g. attaching play materials to a steady surface).
- *Enlarging* (e.g. enlarging materials or key parts of materials to enhance visual perception and/or item manipulation).

- *Prosthetizing* (e.g. attaching additional parts for easier access for persons who are physically disabled or visually impaired, such as adding 'grasp knobs' to wooden puzzle pieces).
- *Reducing required response* (e.g. minimizing distance, range of motion and/or complexity of response).
- *Making more concrete* (e.g. reducing the abstract quality of an item).
- *Removing extraneous cues* to focus the child's attention on one quality at a time (e.g. if the task is shape recognition, avoid using multiple colours).
- *Removing distracting stimuli* (e.g. keeping backgrounds in work areas simple).
- *Adding or enhancing cues* (e.g. increasing visual and tactile stimuli).
- *Improving safety and durability* (e.g. avoiding sharp objects and objects with sharp edges, protecting objects from drool and other sources of dampness, and increasing the strength of toys).

Adapting goals or outcomes

The goals or outcomes of an instructional activity may also be adapted so that children with differing levels of ability can participate actively at their own level and meet their individual objectives. For example, the goal of a science project for a student with developmental delays may be to stimulate and enhance language development. The goal of a typically developing peer working on the same project may be to learn a scientific principle. Another example might be for one child to use Cuisinnaire rods for sorting and learning colours, while other children use the same materials to learn maths concepts.

Adapting tasks

Tasks can also be adapted to help a child with special needs to be successful in classroom activities. Learning tasks may be adapted in a number of different ways, including the following:

- *Time designations* – adapt the time allotted for learning, task completion and testing.
- *Level of support* – increase the amount of personal support by using a peer partner or providing extra adult assistance.
- *Level of difficulty or complexity* – simplify a task or the way in which it must be accomplished (e.g. kick a ball from a stationary position versus while running; use a calculator to figure maths problems).
- *Size* – adapt the number of items that a child is expected to learn or complete (e.g. assign only five instead of ten spelling words).
- *Output or performance* – adapt how the student can respond to an

instructional task (e.g. instead of answering questions verbally, allow the child to point to the correct response).

- *Type of participation* – adapt the extent to which a child is actively involved in a task (e.g. ask one student to hold a map while others point out locations).

Attending to the outdoor environment

The outdoor environment has enormous potential for stimulating growth and development, yet this potential is often overlooked and underused. In fact, research indicates that the outdoor play space (or playground) is the most neglected component of preschool and school programmes (Taylor and Morris, 1996). While this situation represents a serious disservice to all young children, it is especially troublesome for young children with special needs.

Young children learn by using their senses and motor abilities to gather and interpret information about the world around them. They respond to stimulation in their surroundings, and use their senses to give them feedback and cues so that they can navigate, orient themselves and make meaning about their environment.

The quality of the environment – especially in terms of sensory stimulation and opportunities for motoric manipulation – is critical to how young children will develop and learn in any particular setting. Early childhood professionals understand the need for creating environments that stimulate the senses and offer physical, social, emotional, aesthetic and cognitive experiences. A well-planned outdoor environment can meet all the criteria for a stimulating learning environment. Outdoor environments also tend to be appealing to young children. Most youngsters love to go outdoors where, in many cases, they have richer opportunities for open-ended play, exploration and hands-on experimentation than what they have indoors. Outdoor environments can also put children in touch with other living things (i.e. animals and plants), and introduce them to the beauty and wonders of the natural world (Wilson *et al.*, 1996).

Research has identified many benefits to time outdoors for young children. The outdoor environment tends to foster resourcefulness, imagination, initiative, language, socialization, and even literacy (Frost, 1992; Quinn, 1996; Striniste and Moore, 1989). Children's play also differs in relation to outdoor and indoor settings. Outdoors, boys tend to engage in more dramatic play and girls in more constructive play (Johnson *et al.*, 1987). The opposite is true for indoor play. Children from impoverished homes also seem to engage in more dramatic play outdoors than they do indoors. Outdoor play also tends to be more creative, active, adventuresome, socially interactive and carefree than indoor play (Quinn, 1996). In addition, 'children in well designed, extensively equipped, balanced play environments engage in less unoccupied and onlooker behavior and are less frequently involved in behavior problems than children in traditional sterile playgrounds' (Frost, 1992, pp. 9–10). For children to realize these benefits of outdoor play, however, they need the necessary time, place and adult support to facilitate the process.

Characteristics of quality outdoor environments

Some work has been carried out to identify the characteristics of a quality outdoor environment for young children (Quinn, 1996; Winter *et al.*, 1994). A selection of these characteristics in relation to developmentally appropriate learning activities is presented in Figure 12.1.

Opportunities for children	*Elements of the physical environment*
• healthy risk taking	• loose parts
• graduated challenges	• promote a variety of play types
• open-ended play	• safety and health features
• decision making	• messiness
• social interactions	• variety of play surfaces
	• natural elements (plants, animals)
	• complexity
	• variety
	• accessible

Figure 12.1 Characteristics of a quality outdoor environment for young children

For children with special needs, Winter and colleagues (1994) outline four major principles for creating safe, inclusive, outdoor play environments. These four principles focus on safety, developmentally appropriate practice, full inclusion and the interplay of the prior principles. They state, 'Safe inclusion of children with special needs [in outdoor play environments] requires safety, developmentally appropriate practices and full inclusion to function in unison' (p. 31).

Traditional playgrounds generally do not offer these characteristics; nor do they meet the diverse needs of many young children sufficiently, especially children with disabilities. As described by Joe Frost (1992), many playgrounds are actually bad for children-they are developmentally sterile and they are hazardous. Numerous studies have shown that traditional playgrounds are dangerous to the health and safety of young children. Between half and two-thirds of serious injuries to children occur in playgrounds. Such injuries include broken bones, concussion, brain damage, and sometimes even result in death (Taylor and Morris, 1996).

Young children with special needs tend be at greater risk of injuries in the playground than their typically developing peers. Balance problems, seizures, impulsivity and limited skills in anticipating results are some of the reasons that place them at greater risk. Social isolation and long periods of unoccupied or onlooker behaviour are also concerns relating to young children with special needs in the outdoor environment. Attention to such concerns, however, can make the outdoor environment especially conducive to growth and development. There follows a discussion of how to attend to some of these concerns.

Safety concerns

A safe environment not only reduces accidents and injuries, but also fosters feelings of security. Children will be more likely to explore their environment if they feel safe and secure in doing so. Many young children with disabilities are faced with situations that make them more at risk of accidents and injuries than their typically developing peers. Such situations include problems with balance and motor control, seizure disorders, vision and hearing impairments, and hyperactivity.

At times, parents and educators working with children with disabilities try to create environments that are devoid of all risks. This is not a good idea. An environment that is free of risk limits children's opportunities for novel experiences. Children need such experiences to stimulate exploration and, at times, to learn from their mistakes. Since risk taking plays an important role in learning new skills, teachers must be able to make informed decisions about what constitutes constructive risk versus what arrangements present undue danger.

Children with sensory disabilities (e.g. hearing and vision impairments) tend to be left on the sidelines during outdoor activities rather than being 'in the thick of things'. They are also at greater risk of injury. A good practice for children with hearing impairments is for an adult to remain in the child's field of vision so that it is easier to attract the child's attention if necessary. The child with a hearing impairment should receive special instruction regarding safety rules. He or she should be instructed to always pay visual attention when on the playground, since certain equipment (e.g. swings and climbing structures) and activities (running and batting balls) can be dangerous. The other children in the class should also be aware of the child's need for visual versus verbal clues to alert him or her to danger.

For children with visual impairments, tactile markers may be used to define the location of certain equipment and activity areas. Sound features may also be added to help orient the child and make the play environment more interesting. Examples of sound features include wind chimes and bells.

Independence and accessibility concerns

While we cannot make all aspects of the outdoor environment totally accessible to children with disabilities, there is much we can do to improve accessibility. The first step in improving accessibility for children with special needs is to recognize the barriers. If barriers are not identified and attended to, children with disabilities tend to be onlookers versus active participants during outdoor play. Gravel as ground cover, for example, can restrict the manoeuvrability of children in wheelchairs and children wearing leg braces. Wood shavings are a better alternative. Wood shavings are also impact absorbent, making the environment safer if children should fall. Outdoor dramatic play areas (such as play houses and theatres) should also be accessible for children who use wheelchairs or rely on adaptive equipment.

Children with physical disabilities should also have access to playground equipment. Bucket seats or straps can make swings more accessible for children with posture and balance difficulties. As illustrated in Figure 12.2, there are also swings that accommodate a child in a wheelchair. A fold-up ramp on this swing allows wheelchair access to the platform. Clamps then hold the wheelchair in place as the entire platform swings back and forth. Figure 12.3 depicts a slide designed for children with disabilities. By embedding the slide into an incline of the yard, children are not faced with the barrier of steps and are much less likely to be hurt in a fall.

Figure 12.2 Platform swing

Figure 12.3 Slide embedded in yard

Additional modifications for children with motor impairments include straps on tricycle pedals, rails on climbing equipment, and ramps over barriers and uneven surfaces. An elevated sandbox and elevated garden represent other welcome adaptations for children in wheelchairs (see Figure 12.4).

In addition to being free of physical barriers, outdoor environments for young children should also be 'psychologically accessible'. This means that they should be 'attractive, secure, and understandable to the children who use the environments' (Moore *et al.*, 1987).

Social interaction concerns

While early childhood professionals generally recognize the value of outdoor play for enhancing the physical development of young children with disabilities, time outdoors tends to be underused in terms of fostering social development and inclusion. There may be several reasons for this. Four reasons that have been identified in the literature (Nabors *et al.*, 2001) are as follows: (1) teachers commonly view time outdoors as 'free play' and thus tend to be less involved in implementing interventions to foster inclusive play; (2) the unstructured, fast-paced nature of interactions in the outdoor setting may make it more difficult for children with special needs to enter play groups and become engaged in ongoing play; (3) children with disabilities may not be able to physically access some areas that are

Figure 12.4 Elevated garden

optimal spaces for co-operative play; and (4) children with special needs may not have as much experience with 'outdoor games' as the other children, as they may have had fewer opportunities for outdoor play outside of the school setting.

There are several interventions that can be used to make outdoor play time more productive in fostering the social development and inclusion of young children with special needs. These interventions include environmental arrangements and teacher-mediated activities. Environmental interventions involve changes in space and materials, group composition and activities (Nabors *et al.*, 2001). Moving classroom activities and centres to the playground represents one type of environmental intervention. Learning centres are often used to organize toys and materials around the idea of social interaction. As these centres have proven successful indoors, it may be expected that they will also be effective in promoting social interaction outdoors. Centre materials that can be moved easily from the classroom to the playground include blocks, art materials, sand, water and dramatic play accessories.

Teacher-mediated activities may also be used to facilitate co-operative interactions between children with and without special needs in the playground. At times, this may mean adding structure to a play activity. At other times, it may take the form of simplifying a social activity. In teacher-mediated play, teachers generally do not lead or direct play. Their primary role is to facilitate child-to-child interaction. Thus teachers may suggest activities or the direction of a play episode so as to include a child with special needs. For example, if several children are making 'roads' in the sandbox, the teacher may suggest that a child with SEN use sticks to make a bridge.

The outdoor play setting is also ideal for incidental teaching. Nabors and colleagues (2001) provide a description and an example of incidental teaching on the playground. They describe incidental teaching as occurring when teachers capitalize on naturally occurring situations that allow a particular skill to be taught or reinforced. They provide the following as an example of using incidental teaching to explain the behaviour of a child with special needs to a typically developing peer. Jamal is a preschool boy with cerebral palsy. He grabs a playmate's arm for balance as he tries to get on the tyre swing. The teacher explains this intent to the playmate. She explains that Jamal is not trying to pull the other child off and asks, 'Can you let him hold your arm so he can get on?'

Rich sensory stimulation

Outdoor spaces for young children should have a variety of surfaces, textures, shapes, colours, sounds and scents. Such variety engages the senses and invites children to attend and explore. Grass, wood and sand are good choices for surfaces. Paved surfaces may also be used for pushing or riding wheeled toys, but should not be used under climbing equipment or places where children run, crawl or roll. Natural materials can add a rich variety of textures to outdoor settings. Such materials include smooth, round boulders, coarse bark, soft pine needles, and other types of vegetation. Natural materials are also excellent sources of colour, sound and scent. Brightly colored flowers, birds around a feeder or bird-bath, and blossoms on bushes and trees all add sensory delight and interest to an outdoor setting.

Pathways through the play space may be constructed with different types of surface: cobblestone, dirt, half logs, wood rounds, coloured brick and so on. Lawn umbrellas, banners, windsocks and awnings may also be used to add colour to the outdoor environment. Wind chimes and a small waterfall may be added for sound. Banners, flags and branches make wind audible. Some programmes have even included homemade musical instruments into the outdoor setting. In addition to adding sound, these musical instruments also enhance children's opportunities for direct interaction with the environment. Musical instruments for outdoors may be made out of 'junk' materials. Look for materials that can make sounds by striking, blowing, plucking and shaking.

Cultivating a garden is one of the best ways to add opportunities for taste. Some vegetables that work well in gardens for young children include peas, beans, potatoes, tomatoes, cabbages, carrots and sweet corn. For a herb garden (rich in taste and smell), thyme and peppermint tend to be popular choices.

Opportunities for discovery and learning

Because young children learn through hands-on manipulation, a stimulating outdoor environment will include 'loose parts' that children can actually manipulate. The traditional playground, equipped with slides, swings and climbers, usually offers little that children can move about or rearrange. There might be balls, riding toys and an assortment of sandbox tools, but there is usually little variety in the types of material children can use when playing in a typical playground. This static quality can be easily remedied by providing an array of loose parts. Natural materials make great loose parts. They tend to be readily available, inexpensive and interesting to children. Some of the natural materials that might be used include seed pods, stems, stones, pine-cones, 'waxy' leaves, shells, moss, sticks, grasses, eggshells and flowers. Other loose parts that lend themselves to outdoor play include buckets, boxes, old bicycle tyres, boards, cups, pots and watering cans. Books, art materials and puppets may also be brought outdoors to enhance learning.

Water is one of the most frequently requested additions to an outdoor play space. When asked what they wanted in a playground, young children have requested a pond with fish and frogs, a waterfall and a sprinkler. Providing a bucket, hose and sprinkler is one easy way to add water to an outdoor play space. Water tables, suitably equipped with cups, sponges and paintbrushes, work well too. Elevated waterways have also been used. Wooden, metal or plastic troughs mounted on 'legs' provide water in motion.

Quiet restoration

In addition to providing a stage for active learning, outdoor environments should also provide spaces for quiet restoration – that is, places where children can go when they need a rest from more active play or a break from the intensity of large group activity. Many children also choose small secluded places to spend time with a special friend.

Children's gardens

Some communities, in response to the need for better outdoor play spaces for children, have constructed elaborate play structures. Some of these are designed to represent a type of 'magical kingdom'. While impressive, such structures are quite expensive and tend to be limited in terms of learning potential.

A welcome alternative is the idea of a children's garden or play garden. In the past, playgrounds and gardens claimed their separate spaces and individual agendas. Gardens were designed for beauty and harvest, and rarely invited the active engagement of young children. In fact, 'don't touch' was usually the unwritten rule when it came to young children. Playgrounds, on the other hand, were designed for rough-and-tumble games, encouraging children to run, jump, swing and slide. Such a design is also limited in learning potential.

There are different forms of children's gardens. Some focus almost entirely on the process of gardening and are designed specifically to help children learn about the world of nature – its beauty, interconnections and fragility. Others are designed more for a variety of play and learning activities within a garden setting. The play garden is of the latter kind. Its primary purpose is to provide a safe, nature-oriented play environment that supports and encourages children's growth and development. A well-designed play garden offers children the incentives and opportunities to explore and practise activities that stimulate their curiosity and promote independence, spontaneity and creativity. Such play spaces foster growth in the physical, cognitive, social and sensory realms. An added – and important – benefit of children's gardens is the nurturing of a love and respect for the world of nature.

Children's gardens are about teaching children to be comfortable in the garden – letting kids touch, stretch, sniff, and be surprised and full of wonder (Rushing, 1999). Such gardens often feature child-size mazes and statues, themes and characters from popular children's books, giant-size models of butterflies, and opportunities for a variety of hands-on activities. Such hands-on activities might include floating leaves or pieces of bark in a shallow stream of water, arranging small stones around a flower bed, digging for worms in a pile of dirt, watering flower and vegetable plants, rolling down a grassy hill, climbing over bridges, and playing hide-and-seek in a hedge maze.

At one time, school gardening programmes were considered essential for teaching real-life skills and fostering the overall development of the child. In fact, in the early 1900s, children's school gardening was recognized by leading educators as an important factor in the health and education of the whole child. One of the most successful school garden programmes operated from 1900 to 1975 in Cleveland, Ohio (USA). The fact that Cleveland still has one of the highest per capita expenditures on garden supplies in North America reflects the programme's long-lived success. Maria Montessori strongly encouraged the use of gardening with young children to stimulate their learning and imagination. The Montessori tradition still maintains this position. For the most part, however, by the 1950s, interest in school gardening was greatly diminished.

Recently, thousands of schools in Great Britain and North America have decided to reintroduce gardening into the curriculum, often with the goal of fostering environmental understandings and an environmental ethic. Gardening, along with other types of school yard naturalization projects, are designed to bring nature back into the daily lives of children. Such contact is considered crucial for the long-term conservation and protection of the natural environment (Moore and Wong, 1997; Nabhan and Trimble, 1994; Sobel, 1996).

Children's gardens need not be elaborate. A tomato plant growing in a broken bucket could be the beginning of a special garden for a child who has never watched a plant grow to fruition. A row of tulips or zinnias might be a special garden to a group of kindergarten children who grow flowers for their friends in a nearby nursing home. Both provide valuable learning experiences and a sense of joy and accomplishment for children who are involved in the nurturing of these simple gardens.

While the principle of starting simple has great merit, a look at some 'remarkable gardens' for children can offer insights and inspiration for continued development of gardening efforts with children. The following description of one 'special garden' is offered, not as a blueprint of what should be done, but as an 'idea starter' of what might be included in a play garden for young children. Located at the Howard A. Rusk Institute of Rehabilitation Medicine in New York City, the Rusk Children's PlayGarden offers a special place for preschool children with disabilities. While landscape architects designed the PlayGarden, they did so with the participation of a team of physical, occupational and horticultural therapy staff and the teachers from the paediatric unit at Rusk.

The Rusk Children's PlayGarden offers a safe space for a full range of motor-planning and physical movement activities. A range of topography, surfaces and custom-designed play components invites children to run, crawl, climb, bend, jump and turn. Gently curving pathways aid in orientation as the children climb over bridges and under arbours. The PlayGarden also offers rich sensory stimulation, with many opportunities for children to discriminate between a wide variety of qualitative aspects of the environment. Children can feel the breezes through the grasses and leaves, see the visual patterns and forms presented by such natural elements as flowers and rocks, and explore the differing textures of natural materials such as bark, sand and water. Scented herbs, bright flowers, running water and wind chimes all contribute to the children's experience of a full range of sensory stimulation. The diverse tree, shrub and plant collections were selected to encourage children to explore nature's sensory richness, to provide materials for environmental education lessons, and to attract a wide range of exciting wildlife and insect life.

One of the most unique experiences for the children in this PlayGarden is the opportunity to interact with rainbows. A prism sculpture 'Over the Rainbow' rotates gently in the wind currents and projects moving rainbows throughout the PlayGarden space. In this 'special garden', young children have rich opportunities to explore, to socialize, to rest and to experience joy.

Exceptionality appropriate practices

Exceptionality appropriate practices may be defined in several different ways. They may be defined as practices that provide the appropriate adaptations for children with disabilities. They may also be defined as specific adaptations for specific areas of disability. It is this second definition that forms the basis for this section of the chapter.

While special education is based on the principle of individualization (i.e. individualizing the programme to the unique needs of each child), there are some guidelines related to adaptations for specific areas of disability. Thus knowing the nature of a child's disability suggests the appropriateness of certain adaptations. These adaptations can form part of the child's individualized education plan.

Some suggestions for meeting the needs of children with various types of disability have already been presented, particularly in Chapters 4 to 7. Additional suggestions are presented below. These suggestions are offered as examples of exceptionality appropriate practices. There is some overlap between the areas.

For children with disabilities in the area of communication

- Provide frequent visual cues (e.g. gestures, pictures, objects) to reinforce clarity/comprehension.
- Use specific terminology (e.g. use the names of things versus such pronouns as 'it', 'them').
- Expand on what the child says (e.g. 'Ball. You want this big ball').
- Model the correct language usage and pronunciation versus correcting the child's 'mistakes'.
- Keep directions and explanations simple.
- Speak clearly and face the children when talking.

For children with motor difficulties

- Organize the physical space to accommodate wheelchairs and other special equipment as needed.
- Use elevated working areas that can accommodate children in wheelchairs.
- Use bolsters or other supports for floor activities.
- Use adaptive equipment, as needed, for positioning, support and therapy goals.

- Use adaptive tools (e.g. scissors, spoons, pencils) as needed.
- Keep materials on open shelves which can be reached easily by children who are unable to stand and/or who are in wheelchairs.
- Provide adaptive seating to ensure that children will be at the same height as their peers.
- Avoid isolating children in their wheelchairs. Provide additional seating and positioning options (e.g. beanbag chair, corner chair).
- Make playground equipment and outdoor play activities accessible.
- Provide adequate time for completion of tasks.
- Arrange activities and instructional tasks so that minimal movements by the child produce effects on the environment.
- Be alert to subtle responses which indicate that the child is learning and communicating. Such responses might include smiling, changes in breathing, eye or head movements.
- Organize the classroom to allow for privacy during change of clothing, toileting and so on.
- Make sure the child's adaptive equipment is in good working order.
- Use a TV tray or large cookie sheet with sides to provide boundaries for loose materials.

For children with mental retardation and/or developmental delays

- Sequence learning activities and other tasks into small steps.
- Establish goals in relation to the child's developmental level.
- Provide frequent positive feedback.
- Allow extra time for learning and completion of tasks.
- Encourage interaction with and imitation of typically developing peers.
- Keep directions simple, sequenced and organized.

For children with attention problems

- Provide visual cues.
- Offer only a limited number of choices.
- Provide positive reinforcement for sustained attention.
- Introduce 'calming' activities after vigorous play.
- Provide support during transition times (i.e. arrival, departure and change of activities).
- Seat the child away from distractions (e.g. the classroom door, windows). Seat the child next to 'good workers'.
- Give only one direction at a time. Be specific and brief. Ask the child to repeat the direction to ensure that he or she understands.
- Establish and maintain a daily routine.

- Use interactive teaching styles and techniques. Encourage comments and questions. Move about the room. Provide opportunities for active involvement.

For children with social/emotional problems

- Help the child learn to express feelings in appropriate ways (e.g. using words instead of actions).
- Provide extra structure to activities and use of materials (e.g. define physical space for activities).
- Allow a reluctant child to observe group activities until ready to participate.
- Help an aggressive child control behaviour through consistent enforcement of rules.

For children with hearing impairments

- Use vision as a primary input source. Provide visual clues (e.g. pictures, gestures, symbols) and remove visual barriers.
- Demonstrate (versus just talking about) new activities or tasks and use of new materials.
- Obtain the child's attention before speaking.
- Teach the child to watch the speaker's face.
- Position the child close to the speaker, the source of music and other relevant sounds.
- Learn some sign language and teach signing to the whole class.
- Reduce the noise level of the room.

For children with vision impairments

- Attend to the child's safety at all times without being too protective.
- Provide a variety of tactile, manipulative and auditory experiences. Include objects that the child can feel – objects of different shapes, textures, pliability and so on. Use actual objects rather than representations of objects. Use toys that make sounds (e.g. music box, train with a whistle).
- Introduce the child to changes in the environment verbally and through touch.
- Inform the child of what will happen next.
- Use hand-over-hand guidance when necessary so that the child knows what is expected.
- Teach skills in the context of their natural occurrence (e.g. teach feeding skills at mealtimes while seated at the table).
- Present materials against a contrasting background (e.g. present light-coloured materials on a dark surface).

- Make the child aware of your presence before touching him or her.
- Use the child's name when addressing him or her.
- Use the child's body as a reference point (e.g. 'The book is on the floor by your foot').
- Develop a 'buddy' system.
- Keep materials at the child's level.
- Encourage the child to examine materials tactily.
- Provide adequate lighting.
- Keep child's personal items in an organized storage unit that is easily accessible to the child.
- Keep walkways free of clutter.
- Teach the child to localize sounds.
- Provide familiar routines.
- Help the child to get comfortable with movement in space. Ensure his or her comfort and safety while moving or being moved. Provide motivation and physical guidance as needed.
- Discourage self-stimulatory behaviour (e.g. rubbing eyes, shaking parts of the body) by keeping the child involved in fun and meaningful activities.
- Use a TV tray or large cookie sheet with sides to provide boundaries for loose materials.

Of special note

Much has been said about modifying the environment to foster independence and exploration on the part of children with disabilities. A word of caution, however, is in order. This caution relates to the message we give to children when we do things for them or exercise control over their environment. As already stated in various ways, children need to learn that they can affect the environment through their own efforts. Once children learn this, they will be more likely to interact with the environment with zest and joy.

Because children need to be encouraged to take initiative and responsibility for their own learning and experiences, they should be given opportunities to modify the environment in ways that work for them. Modifications to the environment should not always be external to the child (i.e. designed by adults). For children to be independent (and to develop feelings of competence and self-esteem), they must encounter the world as it is and learn strategies to solve the problems they encounter. If modifications are required, changes can be made in either the physical or social situation or the children's own behaviour. Children should have a say in whether or not their environment is modified and in what way. Sometimes, children's voices can be heard through what they say; at other times it may be through what they do.

Professionals and parents should thus be cautious about intervening too quickly and too often to modify the physical and social environment. Rather than promoting independence, such modifications may serve as a 'hidden dependency trap' (Lang and Deitz, 1990) and lead to 'learned helplessness'. 'If parents or professionals always modify the environment for the children, the children never learn how to control their environment' (Lang and Deitz, 1990, p. 3).

The extent and types of adaptation to be made should always be determined on an individual basis. The following are several questions that may be useful in deciding when to modify an environment and when to refrain from doing so.

- Is this adaptation necessary?
- How will this adaptation benefit the child?
- Is this adaptation age appropriate?
- Is this adaptation the least intrusive way to accomplish the purpose?
- Does this adaptation preserve the dignity of the child?
- What does this adaptation say to others about children with disabilities?
- Does this adaptation generalize to the natural environment – i.e. does it maintain its usefulness across settings and over time?
- Have the wishes and ideas of the child been considered in deciding whether or not – and in what way – to modify the environment?
- Does this adaptation say to the child, 'You are not able'?

Inappropriate and useless adaptations and modifications deny the dignity of an individual by reinforcing society's belief that people who are disabled are incompetent (Lang and Deitz, 1990). Environmental adaptations that are imposed from without can easily interfere with the development of feelings of self-esteem and personal effectiveness. These two variables – i.e. self-esteem and personal effectiveness – must be carefully considered when attempting to create environments and provide experiences that facilitate independence.

Some adaptations and modifications are needed to enable young children with disabilities to experience success in the regular classroom setting. Teachers, however, must consider the potential dangers associated with the overuse of adaptations. They need to know that pervasive, long-term structuring of the physical or social environment conveys a negative message about children. Over-protection – or inappropriate and unnecessary adaptations – suggests that children with disabilities are unable to deal effectively with the world as it is. Rather than promoting independence and development, unnecessary adaptations tend to nurture dependent behaviour (Wilson, 2000b).

Teachers who work with children with disabilities need to be aware of the physical barriers that such children face in interacting with the environment. They also need to be aware, however, of more subtle barriers that exist in certain language and social conventions that suggest to children that they are incompetent. The success of an intervention programme should be judged, not in relation to how many adaptations were made, but in relation to how truly independent the child has become.

GLOSSARY

Adaptation A change made to better meet the needs of an individual.

Age appropriate Experiences and/or learning environments that support predictable growth and development for typically developing children at specific chronological ages.

Arena assessment The process of one professional interacting with a child to conduct an assessment, while other team members (including the family) observe and contribute.

Assessment The collection of information through different types of procedures to better understand an individual, often in terms of development and learning.

Assistive device Any specific aid, tool or piece of equipment used to assist an individual with a disability.

At risk A condition that results in an individual having a greater chance of experiencing developmental, social and/or academic difficulties.

Atypical development Development that is outside the range of normalcy.

Augmentative communication Any method of communicating without speech, such as using gestures, signs, picture boards and electronic devices.

Bolster A cylindrical piece of equipment (often made of foam) on which a young child is placed to help with positioning and to foster the development of muscle strength, balance and protective reactions.

Cerebral palsy Disorder of posture, muscle tone and movement resulting from brain damage.

Child-initiated activity An activity selected by a child with little or no intervention by another child or adult.

Chromosomal abnormality A genetic disorder caused by too few or too many chromosomes, or by chromosomes with extra or missing pieces.

Chronological age A child's actual age in years and/or months.

Collaboration Working towards and sharing a common goal.

Communication board An assistive device that allows individuals to point to pictures or symbols to communicate a message.

Community collaboration Different agencies within a community working together to provide more effective services.

Compensatory programme A type of intervention programme designed to offset poverty conditions experienced at home.

Conductive hearing loss A hearing loss caused by an obstruction in the auditory canal; partially or totally prevents sound waves from reaching the inner ear.

Congenital Presumed to be present at birth.

Criterion-referenced tests Evaluation tools which are constructed specifically to evaluate a person's performance level in relation to some standard (i.e. criteria).

Curriculum-based assessment An assessment of a child's abilities or behaviours in the context of a predetermined sequence of curriculum objectives.

Developmental Having to do with the typical steps or stages in human growth and development before the age of 18.

Developmental age The age at which a child is functioning; based on assessment of the child's skills and comparison of those skills to the age at which they are considered typical.

Developmental delay A classification for children who perform significantly behind developmental norms.

Developmentally appropriate The extent to which a programme and/or activity is appropriate for the age span of the children involved and is implemented with attention to the different needs, interests and developmental levels of individual children.

Developmentally appropriate practices (DAP) Curriculum which is appropriate to the age and individual needs of children.

Diagnosis An effort to find the cause of a problem by observing the child and considering the results of tests.

Disability An inability to perform certain tasks because of an impairment in some area of functioning.

Early intervention Services for young children with special needs or who are at risk.

Eligibility Determination of whether a child meets the criteria to receive services.

Engagement The amount of time spent in developmentally and contextually appropriate behaviours.

Environmental assault Conditions in the environment which put children at risk of developmental delay. Examples include toxic pollutants in the air, water and food.

Evaluation A comprehensive term which includes screening, assessment and monitoring activities.

Exceptionality appropriate practices Specific adaptations for specific areas of disabilities.

Exosystem A network of societal structures, such as public and private service agencies, advocacy groups and churches, which contribute to an individual's total environment.

Expansion A language stimulation technique in which adults expand a child's utterance by stating the child's idea in a longer phrase or sentence.

Expectations The level of behaviour, skills and participation expected of an individual. Expectations often vary from one setting to another.

Expressive language What is said or written to communicate an idea or question.

Family systems perspective The family is viewed as an interactive unit; includes the understanding that what affects one member affects all.

Fine motor skills Skills that involve small muscles, such as working with the fingers and hands.

Functional skills Skills that will be immediately useful to the child and that will be used relatively frequently in the child's typical environment.

Generalization The integration of newly acquired information and skills and the application of these skills to new situations.

Gross motor skills Skills that use large muscles, such as when running, climbing, throwing and jumping.

Handicap A problem which an individual with a disability encounters when attempting to function and interact in the environment.

Hypertonic A condition in which muscles are tense and stretched; often related to spasticity.

Hypotonic Low muscle tone; usually characterized by weakness, 'floppiness', poor posture and hypermobile joints.

Incidental teaching Providing instruction in the context of play and other informal activities.

Inclusion The practice of including all children in the regular programme.

Individual appropriateness Experiences that match each child's unique pattern of growth, personality, learning style and family/cultural background.

Individualized objectives Specify critical developmental skills to be taught; based on an individual's current level of functioning.

Integration The practice of bringing together different groups which previously have been segregated (e.g. children with special needs and typically developing children).

Interagency Between agencies.

Interdisciplinary A model of team organization characterized by professionals from several disciplines who work together to design, implement and document goals for an individual child. With this model, all members assess and/or provide direct services to the child.

Learned helplessness A belief held by an individual that he or she lacks control over life's events.

Least restrictive environment The most integrated placement in which a child may function successfully.

Legal blindness A condition where an individual's visual acuity is 20/200 or less in the best eye with correction and/or his or her peripheral field of vision is 20 degrees or less.

Macrosystem Cultural and legislative contexts in which other components of one's environment operate.

Mainstreaming The placement of a child with a disability in a programme designed for children without disabilities.

Maturation The universal sequence of biological changes that occur as one ages.

Mesosystem The relationships among the components of an individual's microsystem. For young children with special needs, this usually includes the relationships between parents and teacher, therapist and physician. It also includes the relationships between professions involved in serving the child.

Microsystem The setting in which individuals spend most of their time. For young children this usually includes the child's home, the homes of relatives and friends, and childcare centre or family daycare home.

Morphology Rules for changing the form of individual words (e.g. from singular to plural).

Multidisciplinary A model of team organization characterized by professionals from several disciplines working independently who relate information to each other but do not co-ordinate, practice or design a total educational programme together.

Neonatal The period from birth to 28 days of age.

Neurological Refers primarily to the nervous system.

Non-discriminatory Not prejudicial. A non-discriminatory test, for example, would not be prejudicial against a particular group of people (e.g. minority, disabled).

Norm-referenced tests Tests that compare the performance of an individual against a group average or norm.

Normal curve A bell-shaped curve which represents the theoretical frequency distribution of human characteristics (e.g. cognitive ability).

Normalization A belief and practice based on the understanding that individuals with disabilities should experience patterns of life and conditions of everyday living that are as close as possible to the regular ways of life.

Open-ended materials Materials which offer a wide range of opportunities for exploration.

Orientation An awareness of spatial aspects of the environment, especially in relation to one's own body position in space.

Orthopaedic Refers primarily to bones and joints.

Otitis media Inflammation of the middle ear; often results in a temporary fluctuating hearing loss.
Perinatal The period around the time of birth.
Phonemic awareness Ability to detect rhyme, separate sounds in words and beginning sounds.
Phonology The sound systems of speech and language.
Positioning Placing an individual in certain positions in an attempt to promote symmetrical body alignment, normalize muscle tone and promote functional skills.
Pragmatics The rules and conventions that govern how language is used for communication in different situations.
Prenatal The period before birth.
Prevention Efforts to prevent a problem from occurring or from getting worse.
Prompt An intervention technique involving a suggestion or command.
Receiving programme The programme into which the child will be going.
Receptive language The receiving of messages; language that is understood.
Reliability A measure of whether a test consistently measures what it was designed to measure.
Residual hearing The hearing ability remaining to an individual with a hearing impairment.
Residual vision The visual ability remaining to an individual with a vision impairment.
Responsivity The quality of being responsive; responding readily.
Role release Mutual sharing of knowledge and expertise by professionals on a team which enables each team member to carry out responsibilities traditionally assigned to another member of the team.
Screening A process of identifying children who may need further assessment to determine special needs.
Secondary handicap A handicap that develops in response to the challenges faced by having a disability; for example, a child who is deaf is likely to have communication and social deficits as well.
Semantics The meaning of words.
Sending programme The programme the child is leaving.
Sensory impairments Impairments related to the senses (e.g. hearing, vision).
Social toxicity Harmful aspects of the social environment (e.g. violence, poverty).
Spasticity The tendency to have sudden, involuntary contractions of the muscles.
Standard deviation A term used to describe how far a score is from the mean.

Standardized tests Tests which include a fixed set of items carefully developed to evaluate a child's skills and to allow comparison against a group average or norm.

Survival skills Those skills needed to be successful in the child's current and/or next environment.

Syntax Rules determining correct word order in sentences.

Teachable moment A situation that arises naturally in unstructured or semi-structured situations which provide a special opportunity for teaching a concept or skill within the context of what just occurred.

Teacher-directed activity An activity in which the adult initiates and continues to supervise what children do.

Total communication A combination of methods to communicate effectively in a given situation (e.g. sign language combined with oral expression).

Transdisciplinary A model of team organization characterized by professionals from several disciplines mutually sharing knowledge and expertise which enables each team member to carry out responsibilities traditionally assigned to another member of the team.

Typically developing child A child who is not identified as having a disability.

Validity A measure of whether test items measure what they were designed to do.

Visual acuity Sharpness of vision.

Walking ropes Ropes running horizontally to assist people who are blind to move safely from one place to another.

REFERENCES

Abramowitz, A.J., Eckstrand, D., O'Leary, S.G. and Dulcan, M.K. (1992) ADHD children's response to stimulant medication in two intensities of a behavioral intervention program. *Behavior Modification*, 16, 193–203.

Adeola, F.O. (1994) Environmental hazards, health, and racial inequity in hazardous waste distribution. *Environment and Behavior*, 26(1), 99–126.

Ainsworth, M.D.S. (1973) The development of infant–mother attachment. In B.M. Caldwell and H.N. Ricciuti (eds), *Review of Child Development Research: Child Development and Social Policy*. Chicago, IL: University of Chicago Press (pp. 1–94).

Ainsworth, M.D.S., Bell, S.M. and Stayton, D.J. (1972) Individual differences in the development of some attachment behaviors. *Merrill-Palmer Quarterly*, 18, 123–143.

Ainsworth, M.D.S., Blehar, M.D., Waters, E. and Wall, S. (1978) *Patterns of Attachment: A Psychological Study of the Strange Situation*. Hillsdale, NJ: Erlbaum.

Allen, E.A., and Marotz, L. (1989) *Developmental Profiles: Birth to Six*. Albany, NY: Delmar.

American Psychiatric Association (APA) (1987) *Diagnostic and Statistical Manual of Mental Disorders* (3rd edn). Washington, DC: APA.

American Psychiatric Association (APA) (1994) *Diagnostic and Statistical Manual of Mental Disorders* (4th edn). Washington, DC: APA.

American Psychological Association and American Academy of Pediatrics (1999) *Raising Children to Resist Violence: What You Can Do*. Washington, DC: Author.

Andrews, K.B. (1999) Attention-deficit hyperactivity disorder: the implication for early childhood educators. *Early Childhood Education Journal*, 27(2), 115–117.

Appl, D.J. (2000) Clarifying the preschool assessment process: traditional practices and alternative approaches. *Early Childhood Education Journal*, 27(4), 219–225.

Atwater, J.B., Orth-Lopes, L., Elliott, M., Carta, J.J. and Schwartz, I.S. (1994) Completing the circle: planning and implementing transitions to other programs. In M. Wolery and J.S. Wilbers (eds), *Including Children with Special Needs in Early Childhood Programs*. Washington, DC: National Association for the Education of Young Children (pp. 167–188).

Aylward, G.P. (1990) Environmental influences on the developmental outcome of children at risk. *Infants and Young Children*, 2(4), 1–9.

Bailey, D.B. (1991) Issues and perspectives on family assessment. *Infants and Young Children*, 4(1), 26–34.

REFERENCES

Bailey, D.B. (1994) Working with families of children with special needs. In M. Wolery and J.S. Wilbers (eds), *Including Children with Special Needs in Early Childhood Programs*. Washington, DC: National Association for the Education of Young Children (pp. 23–44).

Bailey, D.B. and Wolery, M. (1992) *Teaching Infants and Preschoolers with Handicaps* (2nd edn). Columbus, OH: Merrill.

Barkley, R.A. (1990) *Attention Deficit Hyperactivity Disorder: A Handbook for Diagnosis and Treatment*. New York: Guilford Press.

Barone, F.J. (1997). Bullying in school: it doesn't have to happen. *Phi Delta Kappan*, pp. 80–82.

Batshaw, M.L. and Perret, Y.M. (1992) *Children with Disabilities: A Medical Primer* (3rd edn). Baltimore, MD: Paul H. Brookes.

Bellamy, C. (1998) *The State of the World's Children*. New York: Oxford University Press.

Bigge, J.L. (1991) *Teaching Individuals with Physical and Multiple Disabilities* (3rd edn). Columbus, OH: Macmillan.

Blahna, D.J. and Toch, M.F. (1993) Environmental reporting in ethnic magazines: implications for incorporating minority concerns. *Journal of Environmental Education*, 24(2), 22–29.

Bowlby, J. (1982) *Attachment and Loss: Attachment* (2nd edn). New York: Basic Books.

Bowman, B.T. (1992) Who is at risk for what and why. *Journal of Early Intervention*, 16(2), 101–108.

Bredekamp, S. and Copple, C. (eds) (1997) *Developmentally appropriate practice in early childhood programs* (revised edn). Washington, DC: National Association for the Education of Young Children.

Bricker, D. (1989) *Early Intervention for At-risk and Handicapped Infants, Toddlers, and Preschool Children* (2nd edn). Palo Alto, CA: VORT.

Bronfenbrenner, U. (1979) *The Ecology of Human Development*. Cambridge, MA: Harvard University Press.

Brown, M.S., Bergen, D., House, M., Hittle, J. and Dickerson, T. (2000) An observational study: examining the relevance of developmentally appropriate practices, classroom adaptations, and parental participation in the context of an integrated preschool program. *Early Childhood Education Journal*, 28(1), 51–56.

Brown, N. and Kalbli, J. (1997) Facilitating the socialization of children with autism. *Early Childhood Education Journal*, 24(3), 185–189.

Bruder, M.B. (1994) Working with members of other disciplines: collaboration for success. In M. Wolery and J.S. Wilbers (eds), *Including Children with Special Needs in Early Childhood Programs*. Washington, DC: National Association for the Education of Young Children (pp. 45–70).

Bruder, M.B. (2000) Renewing the inclusion agenda: attending to the right variables. *Journal of Early Intervention*, 23(4), 223–230.

Bruer, J.T. (1998) Brain science, brain fiction. *Educational Leadership*, 56(3), 14–18.

Bullard, R.D. (1994) Grassroots flowering. *The Amicus Journal*, spring, 32–37.

Burgener, G.W. (1980) Voice amplification and its effects on test taking performance (Doctoral dissertation, Southern Illinois University at Carbondale, 1980). *Dissertation Abstracts International*, 41, 08A 3485.

Burgess, D.M. and Streissguth, A.P. (1992) Fetal alcohol syndrome and fetal alcohol effects: principles for educators. *Phi Delta Kappan*, 1, 24–30.

Buysse, V. and Bailey, D.B. (1993) Behavioral and developmental outcomes in young children with disabilities in integrated and segregated settings: a review of comparative studies. *Journal of Special Education*, 26, 434–461.

Carpenter, B. (ed.) (1997) *Families in Context: Emerging Trends in Family Support and Early Intervention*. London: David Fulton.

Chavis, F.F. (1992) Race, justice and the environment. *Nature Conservancy*, September/October, 38.

Cioni, G., Paolicelli, P.B., Sordi, C. and Vinter, A. (1993) Sensorimotor development in cerebral palsied infants assessed with the Uzgiris-Hunt scales. *Developmental Medicine and Child Neurology*, 35, 1055–1066.

Clay, M. (1966) Reading: emergent reading behavior. Unpublished Doctoral dissertation, University of Auckland, New Zealand.

Collin, R.W. (1993) Environmental equity and the need for government intervention: two proposals. *Environment*, 35(9), 41–43.

Cook, R.E., Tessier, A. and Klein, M.D. (1996) *Adapting Early Childhood Curricula for Children in Inclusive Settings*. Columbus, OH: Merrill.

Council for Exceptional Children (1988) Does early intervention help? *ERIC Digest* (#455). Reston, VA: Author.

Cross, K.L., Bazron, B.J., Dennis, K.W. and Issacs, M.R. (1989) *Towards a Culturally Competent System of Care: A Monograph on Effective Services for Minority Children who are Severely Emotionally Disturbed*. Washington, DC: Child and Adolescent Service System Program, Georgetown University Child Development Center.

Davis, M.D., Kilgo, J.L. and Gamel-McCormick, M. (1998) *Young Children with Special Needs*. London: Allyn & Bacon.

Daw, N.W. (1995) *Visual Development*. New York: Plenum Press.

Daycare Trust (1999) *Listening to Children: Young Children's View on Childcare: A Guide for Parents*. London: Daycare Trust.

Denham, S.A. (2001) Dealing with feelings: foundations and consequences of young children's emotional competence. *Early Education and Development*, 12(1), 5–9.

Department for Education and Employment (DfEE) (1999) *Social Inclusion: Pupil Support* (Circular 10/99). London: DfEE.

Department for Education and Skills (DfES) (2001a) *Special Educational Needs Code of Practice*. London: DfES.

Department for Education and Skills (DfES) (2001b) *SEN Toolkit: Enabling Pupil Participation*. London: DfES.

Drecktrah, M. and Blaskowski, L. (2000) Bullying: the problem and how to deal with it. *Early Childhood News*, 12(5), 40–42, 44–45.

Duckworth, E. (1987) *The Having of Wonderful Ideas*. London: Teachers College Press.

Dunst, C.J. (2000) Revisiting "Rethinking Early Intervention". *Topics in Early Childhood Special Education*, 20(2), 95–103.

Dunst, C.J., Mahoney, G. and Buchan, K. (1996) Promoting the cognitive competence of young children with or at risk for developmental disabilities. In S.L. Odom and M.E. McLean (eds), *Early Intervention/Early Childhood Special Education*. Austin, TX: PRO-ED (pp. 159–196).

Elkind, D. (1987) *Miseducation: Preschoolers at Risk*. New York: Knopf.

Environmental Protection Agency (1992) *Environmental Equity: Reducing Risk for all Communities*. Washington, DC: Author.

Erwin, E.J. and Schreiber, R. (1999) Creating supports for young children with disabilities in natural environments. *Early Childhood Education Journal*, 26(3), 167–171.

European Commission Childcare Network (n.d) *Quality in Services for Young Children*. Author.

Failla, S. and Jones, L. (1991) Families of children with developmental disabilities: an examination of family hardiness. *Research in Nursing and Health*, 14, 41–50.

Fewell, R.R. (2000) Assessment of young children with special needs: foundations for tomorrow. *Topics in Early Childhood Special Education*, 20(1), 38–42.

Ford, F.R. (1966) *Diseases of the Nervous System in Infancy, Childhood and Adolescence* (5th edn). Springfield, IL: Thomas.

Frost, J. (1992) Reflections on research and practice in outdoor play environments. *Dimensions of Early Childhood*, 20(4), 6–10.

Fuchs, D. and Fuchs, L.S. (1994) Inclusive school movement and the radicalization of special education. *Exceptional Children*, 60, 294–309.

Garbarino, J. (1997) Educating children in a socially toxic environment. *Educational Leadership*, 54(7), 12–16.

Gardner, H. (1983) *Frames of Mind: The Theory of Multiple Intelligences*. New York: Basic Books.

Gardner, H. (1997) *Education, Information and Transformation*. New York: Prentice-Hall.

Gardner, P. (2001) *Teaching and Learning in Multicultural Classrooms*. London: David Fulton.

Garner, P.W. and Estep, K.M. (2001). Emotional competence, emotion socialization, and young children's peer-related social competence. *Early Education and Development*, 12(1) 29–46.

Goldman, J. and Gardner, H. (1989) Multiple paths to educational effectiveness. In D. Kerzner and A. Gartner (eds), *Beyond Separate Education*. Baltimore, MD: Paul H. Brookes.

Goldstein, H., Kaczmarek, L.A. and Hepting, N.H. (1996) Indicators of quality in communication intervention. In S.L. Odom and M.E. McLean (eds), *Early Intervention/Early Childhood Special Education*. Austin, TX: PRO-ED (pp. 197–221).

Goleman, D. (1995) *Emotional Intelligence*. New York: Bantam Books.

Goss, J.L. (2001) Brainworks: the aggression component. *Early Childhood News*, 13(4), 36–42.

Graves, M.F., Juel, C. and Graves, B.B. (2001) *Teaching Reading in the 21st Century* (2nd edn). Boston: Allyn & Bacon.

Guralnick, M.J. (1990) Social competence and early intervention. *Journal of Early Intervention*, 14, 3–14.

Guralnick, M.J. (1994) Social competence with peers: outcome and process in early childhood special education. In P.L. Safford (ed.), *Early Childhood Special Education*. New York: Teachers College Press.

Guralnick, M.J. (2000) An agenda for change in early childhood inclusion. *Journal of Early Intervention*, 23(4), 213–222.

Haines, A.H., Fowler, S.A. and Chandler, L.K. (1988) Planning school transitions:

family and professional collaboration. *Journal of the Division for Early Childhood*, 12, 108–115.

Halford, J.M. (1998) Brain-based policies for young children. *Educational Leadership*, 56(3), 85.

Hanline, M.F. (1993) Inclusion of preschoolers with profound disabilities: an analysis of children's interactions. *Journal of the Association for the Severely Handicapped*, 18, 28–34.

Hanson, M.J. (1992) Ethnic, cultural, and language diversity in intervention settings. In E.W. Lynch and M.J. Hanson (eds), *Developing Cross-cultural Competence: A Guide for Working with Young Children and Their Families*. Baltimore, MD: Paul H. Brookes (pp. 3–18).

Hanson, M.J. (1996) Early interactions: the family context. In M.J. Hanson (ed.), *Atypical Infant Development*. Austin, TX: PRO-ED (pp. 235–272).

Hanson, M. and Gilkerson, D. (1999) Portfolio assessment: more than ABCs and 123s. *Early Childhood Education Journal*, 27(2), 81–86.

Hanson, M.J. and Lynch, E.W. (1995) *Early Intervention*. Austin, TX: PRO-ED.

Harrington, M. and Meyers, H.W. (1992) Preschool programs for the hearing impaired: young children with hearing disabilities deserve special attention. *Principal*, 34–36.

Hemmeter, M.L. (2000) Classroom-based interventions: evaluating the past and looking forward to the future. *Topics in Early Childhood Special Education*, 20(1), 56–60.

Hemphill, S.A. (1996) Characteristics of conduct disordered children and their families: a review. *Australian Psychologist*, 31, 109–118.

Hilliard, A.G. (1991/92) Why we must pluralize the curriculum. *Educational Leadership*, December/January, 12–31.

Hoon, A.H. (1991) Visual impairments in children with developmental disabilities. In A.J. Capute and P.J. Accardo (eds), *Developmental Disabilities in Infancy and Early Childhood*. Baltimore, MD: Paul H. Brookes (pp. 395–411).

Horn, E., Lieber, J., Shouming, L. Sandall, S. and Schwartz, I. (2000) Supporting young children's IEP goals in inclusive settings through embedded learning opportunities. *Topics In Early Childhood Special Education*, 20(4), 208–223.

Howard, V.F., Williams, B.F., Port, P.D. and Lepper, C. (1997) *Very Young Children with Special Needs*. Columbus, OH: Merrill.

Howard, V.F., Williams, B.F., Port, P.D. and Lepper, C. (2001) (2nd edn) *Very Young Children with Special Needs*. Columbus, OH: Merrill.

Howes, C. (1980) Peer play scale as an index of complexity of peer interaction. *Developmental Psychology*, 16, 371–372.

Hunt, J.M. (1961) *Intelligence and Experience*. New York: John Wiley & Sons.

Johnson, D. and Johnson, R. (1986) Mainstreaming and cooperative learning strategies. *Exceptional Children*, 52(6), 553–561.

Johnson, J.E., Christie, J.F. and Yawkey, T.D. (1987) *Play and Early Childhood Development*. Glenview, IL: Scott, Foresman.

Johnson, R.A. (1981) A review of existing programs and their relationship to a theoretical model for young language-impaired children with recurrent otitis media. Masters thesis, Bowling Green State University, Ohio.

Johnson, R.A. and Mandell, C.J. (1984) *Individualizing Parent and Professional Partnerships*. Bowling Green, OH: Bowling Green State University.

Johnson, R.A. and Mandell, C.J. (1988) A social observation checklist for preschoolers. *Teaching Exceptional Children*, winter, 18–21.

Kagan, S.L. (1991) *United We Stand: Collaboration for Child Care and Early Childhood Services*. New York: Teachers College Press.

Kalyanpur, M., Harry, B. and Skrtic, T. (2000) Equity and advocacy expectations of culturally diverse families' participation in special education. *International Journal of Disability, Development and Education*, 47(2), 119–133.

Kaufeldt, M. (1999) *Begin with the Brain – Orchestrating the Learner-Centered Classroom*. Tuscon, AZ: Zephyr Press.

Kemple, K.M. and Hartle, L. (1997) Getting along: how teachers can support children's peer relationships. *Early Childhood Education Journal*, 24(3), 139–146.

Kirchner, C. (1988) National estimates of prevalence and demographics of children with visual impairments. In M.D. Wang, M.D. Reynolds and H.J. Walberg (eds), *Handbook of Special Education: Research and Practice* (Vol. 3). Elmsford, NY: Pergamon Press (pp. 135–153).

Kitzinger, S. and Kitzinger, C. (1990) *Talking with Children about Things that Matter*. London: Pandora.

Klein, M.D., Cook, R.E.; and Richardson-Gibbs, A.M. (2001) *Strategies for Including Children with Special Needs in Early Childhood Settings*. Albany, NY: Delmar.

Kohler, F.W., Anthony, L.J., Steighner, S.A. and Hoyson, M. (2001) Teaching social interaction skills in the integrated preschool: an examination of naturalistic tactics. *Topics in Early Childhood Special Education*, 21(2), 93–113.

Kostelnik, M.J., Soderman, A.K. and Whiren, A.P. (1999) *Developmentally Appropriate Curriculum*. Columbus, OH: Merrill.

Krull, S. (2000) Early empathy development. *Early Childhood News*, 12(5), 8.

Lane, M. (1984) Reaffirmations: speaking out for children. A child's right to the valuing of diversity. *Young Children*, 39(6), 76.

Lang, M.A. and Deitz, S. (1990) Creating environments that facilitate independence: the hidden dependency trap. *Children's Environments Quarterly*, 7(3), 2–6.

Learning and Skills Council (LSC) (2002) *The Special Educational Needs and Disability Act 2001*. London: LSC.

LeDoux, J. (1996) *The Emotional Brain*. New York: Simon & Schuster.

Lewis, J. (2000) Let's remember the 'education' in inclusive education. *British Journal of Special Education*, 27(4), 202.

Lewis, M. (1984) Developmental principles and their implications for at-risk and handicapped infants. In M.J. Hanson (ed.), *Atypical Infant Development*. Austin, TX: PRO-ED (pp. 3–24).

Linder, T.W. (1990) *Transdisciplinary Play-based Assessment: A Functional Approach to Working with Young Children*. Baltimore, MD: Paul H. Brookes. Revised edn 1993.

Linn, M.I., Goodman, J.F. and Lender, W.L. (2000) Played out? passive behavior by children with Down syndrome during unstructured play. *Journal of Early Intervention*, 23(4), 264–278.

Linton, G. (1995) The effects of sound field amplification on the academic readiness of kindergarten students. Doctoral dissertation, Bowling Green State University, Bowling Green, Ohio.

Lussier, B.J., Crimmins, D.B. and Alberti, D. (1994) Effects of three adult interaction styles on infant engagement. *Journal of Early Intervention*, 18, 12–24.

Lyons-Ruth, K., Alpern, L. and Repacholi, B. (1993) Disorganized infant attachment classification and maternal psychosocial problems as predictors of hostile-aggressive behavior in preschool children. *Child Development*, 64, 572–585.

McCracken, J.B. (1993) *Valuing Diversity: The Primary Years*. Washington, DC: National Association for the Education of Young Children (NAEYC).

McEvoy, M.A. and Odom, S.L. (1996) Strategies for promoting social interaction and emotional development of infants and young children with disabilities and their families. In S.L. Odom and M.E. McLean (eds), *Early Intervention/Early Childhood Special Education*. Austin, TX: PRO-ED (pp. 223–244).

McGee, G.G., Daly, T., Izeman, S.G., Mann, L.H. and Fisley, T.R. (1991) Use of classroom materials to promote preschool engagement. *Teaching Exceptional Children*, summer, 44–47.

McGeehan, J. (2001) Brain-compatible learning. *Green Teacher*, 64, 7–13.

McLean, M.E. and Odom, S.L. (1996) Establishing recommended practices in early intervention/early childhood special education. In S.L. Odom and M.E. McLean (eds), *Early Intervention/Early Childhood Special Education*. Austin, TX: PRO-ED, pp. 1–22.

McWilliam, R.A. (1991) Targeting teaching at children's use of time. *Teaching Exceptional Children*, summer, 42–43.

Mahoney, G., Kaiser, A., Girolametto, L., MacDonald, J., Robinson, C., Safford, P. and Spiker, D. (1999) Parent education in early intervention: a call for a renewed focus. *Topics in Early Childhood Special Education*, 19(3), 131–140.

Mandell, C. and Johnson, R.A. (1985) Individualizing parent participation. Unpublished paper, Bowling Green State University, Bowling Green, Ohio.

Marion, M. (1995) *Guidance of Young Children* (3rd edn). New York: Macmillan.

Mettler, R. (1987) Blindness and managing the environment. *Journal of Visual Impairment and Blindness*, 81, 476–481.

Meyer, L.H. (2001) The impact of inclusion on children's lives: multiple outcomes and friendship in particular. *International Journal of Disability, Development and Education*, 48(1), 15–29.

Miller, P.S. and Stayton, V.D. (1996) Personnel preparation in early education and intervention: recommended preservice and inservice practices. In S.L. Odom and M.E. McLean (eds), *Early Intervention/Early Childhood Special Education*. Austin, TX: PRO-ED (pp. 329–358).

Moore, R.C. and Wong, H.H. (1997) *Natural Learning*. Berkeley, CA: MIG Communications.

Moore, R.C., Goltsman, S.M. and Iacofano, D.S. (1987) *Play for all Guidelines*. Berkeley, CA: MIG Communications.

Morse, M. (1991) Visual gaze behaviors: considerations in working with visually impaired and multiply handicapped children. *Review*, 23(1), 5–15.

Most, T. Al-Yagon, M., Tur-Kaspa, H. and Margalit, M. (2000) Phonological awareness, peer nominations and social competence among preschool children at risk for developing learning disabilities. *International Journal of Disability, Development and Education*, 47(1), 89–105.

Musselwhite, C.R. (1986) *Adaptive Play for Special Needs Children*. Toronto, Ont: Little, Brown & Co.

Nabhan, G.P. and Trimble, S. (1994) *The Geography of Childhood: Why Children Need Wild Places*. Boston, MA: Beacon Press.

Nabors, L., Willoughby, J. and McMenamin, S. (2001) Promoting inclusion for young children with special needs on playgrounds. *Journal of Developmental and Physical Disabilities*, 13(2), 179–190.

National Association for the Education of Young Children and the National Association of Early Childhood Specialists in State Departments of Education (NAEYC and NAECS/SDE) (1991) Guidelines for appropriate curriculum content and assessment in programs serving children ages 3 through 8. *Young Children*, 46(3), 21–38.

National Society for the Prevention of Cruelty to Children (NSPCC) (1995) *A Child's View of School – Consulting Pupils to Create a Listening and Responsive School*. London: NSPCC.

Neisworth, J.T. and Bagnato, S.J. (1996) Assessment for early intervention: emerging themes and practices. In S.L. Odom and M.E. McLean (eds), *Early Intervention/Early Childhood Special Education*. Austin, TX: PRO-ED (pp. 23–57).

Nelson, C.A. and Bloom, F.W. (1997) Child development and neuroscience. *Child Development*, 68(5), 970–987.

Nickse, R.S. (1990) *Family and Intergenerational Literacy Programs: An Update of the Noises of Literacy*. Columbus, OH: ERIC Information Series no. 342.

Niemeyer, J.A., Caddisy, D.J., Collins, E. and Taylor, B. (1999) Facilitating individual planning for young children with disabilities in developmentally appropriate classrooms. *Early Childhood Education Journal*, 26(4), 255–262.

Noonan, M.J. and McCormick, L. (1993) *Early Intervention in Natural Environments*. Pacific Grove, CA: Brookes/Cole Publishing.

Northern, J. and Downs, M. (1984) *Hearing in Children* (3rd edn). Baltimore, MD: Williams & Wilkins.

Odom, S.L. (2000) Preschool inclusion: what we know and where we go from here. *Topics in Early Childhood Special Education*, 20(1), 20–26.

Odom, S.L. and McLean, M.E. (1996) *Early Intervention/Early Childhood Special Education*. Austin, TX: PRO-ED.

Odom, S.L., McConnell, S.R., McEvoy, M.A., Peterson, C., Ostrosky, M., Chandler, L.K., Spicuzza, R.J., Skellenger, A., Creighton, M. and Favazza, P.C. (1999) Relative effects of interventions supporting the social competence of young children with disabilities. *Topics in Early Childhood Special Education*, 19(2), 75–92.

Osborn, J.J., Graves, L. and VonderEmbse, D.R. (1992) Project MARCS. Putnam County Schools, Putnam County, Ohio, unpublished raw data.

Parten, M.B. (1932) Social participation among preschool children. *Journal of Abnormal and Social Psychology*, 27, 243–269.

Perrone, V. (1991) On standardized testing. An ACEI position paper. *Childhood Education*, 67, 132–142.

Peterson, N.L. (1987) *Early Intervention for Handicapped and At-risk Children*. London: Love Publishing.

Portwood, M. (1996) *Developmental Dyspraxia*. Durham: Durham County Council.

Qualifications and Curriculum Authority (QCA) (2000) *Curriculum Guidance for the Foundation Stage*. London: QCA.

Quinn, M. (1996) The development and application of design criteria for outdoor play environments for child care centers in Iowa. Masters thesis, Iowa State University.

Raver, S.A. (1991) *Strategies for Teaching At-risk and Handicapped Infants and Toddlers*. New York: Macmillan.

Ray, H., Sarff, L.S. and Glassford, F.E. (1986) Project MARRS. Walbash and Ohio Valley Special Education District, Norris City, Illinois, unpublished raw data.

Report of Consensus Conferences (1987) *Access to Prenatal Care: Key to Preventing Low Birthweight*. Kansas City, MO: American Nurses' Association.

Robinson, R.D., McKenna, M.C. and Wedman, J.M. (2000) *Issues and Trends in Literacy Education* (2nd edn). Boston, MA: Allyn & Bacon.

Roffey, S. and O'Keirdan, T. (2001) *Young Children and Classroom Behaviour*. London: David Fulton.

Rogue, J.A. (1993) Environmental equity: reducing risk for all communities. *Environment*, 35(5), 25–28.

Rothbart, M.K. (1996) Social development. In M.J. Hanson (ed.), *Atypical Infant Development*. Austin, TX: PRO-ED.

Rowe, K. and Rowe, K. (1992) Impact of antisocial, inattentive and restless behaviours on reading. In J. Elinds and J. Izard (eds), *Student Behavior Problems: Context, Initiatives, Programs*. Hawthorne, Victoria: Australian Council for Educational Research (pp. 47–76).

Schweinhart, L.J., Barnes, H.V. and Weikart, D.P. (1993) *Significant Benefits: The High/Scope Perry Preschool Study Through age 27*. Monographs of the High/Scope Educational Research Foundation No. 10. Ypsilanti, MI: High/Scope Educational Research Foundation.

Sestini, E. (2001) Early Years Development and Childcare Partnerships (EYCDPs) in England: policy and implementation. *International Journal of Early Childhood*, 32(2), 32–39.

Sheridan, S. (2001) Quality evaluation and quality enhancement in preschool: a model of competence development. *Early Childhood Development and Care*, 166, 7–27.

Sherman, A. (1997) Five year olds' perception of why we go to school. *Children and Society*, 11(2): 117–128.

Shields, A., Dickstein, S., Seifer, R., Giusti, L., Magee, K.D. and Spritz, B. (2001) Emotional competence and early school adjustment: a study of preschoolers at risk. *Early Education and Development*, 12(1), 73–90.

Skeels, H.M. (1966) *Adult Status of Children with Contrasting Early Life Experiences*. Monographs of the Society for Research in Child Development, 31(3), Serial No. 105.

Skeels, H.M. and Dye, H.B. (1939) A study of the effects of differential stimulation on mentally retarded children. *Proceedings and Addresses of the American Association on Mental Deficiency*, 44, 114–136.

Sobel, D. (1996) *Beyond Ecophobia: Reclaiming the Earth in Nature Education*. Great Barrington, MA: Orion Society.

Spalding, B. (2000) The contribution of a 'Quiet Place' to early intervention strategies for children with emotional and behavioural difficulties in mainstream schools. *British Journal of Special Education*, 27(3), 129–134.

Spitz, R.A. (1965) *The First Year of Life: A Psychoanalytic Study of Normal and Deviant Development of Object Relations*. New York: International Universities Press.

Stafford, I. (2000) Children with movement difficulties. *British Journal of Special Education*, 27(2), 81–86.

Stephenson, J., Linfoot, K., and Martin, A. (2000) Behaviors of concern to teachers in the early years of school. *International Journal of Disability, Development and Education*, 47(3), 225–235.

Stile, S.W. (1996) Early childhood education of children who are gifted. In S.L. Odom and M.E. McLean (eds), *Early Intervention/Early Childhood Special Education*. Austin, TX: PRO-ED (pp. 309–328).

Strain, P.S. and Danko, C.D. (1995) Caregivers' encouragement of positive interaction between preschoolers with autism and their siblings. *Journal of Emotional and Behavioral Disorders*, 3(1), 2–12.

Strain, P.S., Danko, C.D. and Kohler, F. (1995) Activity engagement and social interaction development in young children with autism: an examination of 'free' intervention effects. *Journal of Emotional and Behavioral Disorders*, 3(2), 108–123.

Striniste, N.A. and Moore, R.C. (1989) Early childhood outdoors: a literature review related to the design of childcare environments. *Children's Environments Quarterly*, 6(4), 25–31.

Sugden, D.A. and Keogh, J.F. (1990) *Problems in Movement Skill Development*. Columbia: University of South Carolina Press.

Sylwester, R. (1995) *A Celebration of Neurons: An Educator's Guide to the Human Brain*. Alexandria, VA: Association for Supervision and Curriculum Development.

Taylor, S.I. and Morris, V.G. (1996) Outdoor play in early childhood education settings: is it safe and healthy for children? *Early Childhood Education Journal*, 23(3), 153–157.

Teicher, M.H. (2000) Wounds that time won't heal: the neurobiology of child abuse. *Cerebrum*, 2(4), 50–67.

The Blade (1997) Parents give up child with genetic disorder. 30 March.

UNICEF (1997) *The State of the World's Children*. Oxford: Oxford University Press.

Thommessen, M., Kase, B.F., Riis, G. and Heiberg, A. (1991) The impact of feeding problems on growth and energy intake in children with cerebral palsy. *European Journal of Clinical Health*, 45, 479–487.

Uttig, D. (ed.) (1998) *Children's Services, Now and in the Future*. London: National Children's Bureau.

van Ijzendoorn, M.H., Juffer, R. and Duyvesteyn, M.G. (1995) Breaking the intergenerational cycle of insecure attachment: a review of the effects of attachment-based interventions on maternal sensitivity and infant security. *Journal of Child Psychology and Psychiatry*, 36, 225–248.

Vincent, L.J. and McLean, M.E. (1996) Family participation. In S.L. Odom and M.E. McLean (eds), *Early Intervention/Early Childhood Special Education*. Austin, TX: PRO-ED (pp. 59–76).

Wardle, F. (2000) Emergent literacy. *Early Childhood News*, 12(3), 12–17.

Weiner, L. and Morse, B.A. (1988) FAS: clinical perspectives and prevention. In I.J. Chasnoff (ed.), *Drugs, Alcohol, Pregnancy and Parenting*. Lancaster: Kluwer Academic (pp. 127–148).

Williams, R. (1992) *Nobody Nowhere*. New York: Times Books.

Wilson, R.A. (1988) The effect of sound field amplification paired with teacher training as an approach to language stimulation with Head Start children. Doctoral dissertation, University of Toledo, Ohio.

Wilson, R.A. (1991) Unpublished research data. Bowling Green State University, Bowling Green, OH.

Wilson, R.A. (2000a) Emergent literacy. *Early Childhood News*, 12(3), 6–8.

Wilson, R.A. (2000b) Children with special needs: adaptations and a sense of independence. *Early Childhood News*, 12(2), 41–42, 44.

Wilson, R.A. (2002) Bridging invisible boundaries: the physically present, socially absent child. *Early Childhood News*, 14(2), 32–40.

Wilson, R.A., Kilmer, S. and Knauerhase, V. (1996) Developing an environmental outdoor play space. *Young Children*, 51(6), 56–61.

Winter, S.M., Bell, M.J. and Dempsey, J.D. (1994) Creating play environments for children with special needs. *Childhood Education*, 28–32.

Wolery, M. (1994a) Designing inclusive environments for young children with special needs. In M. Wolery and J.S. Wilbers (eds), *Including Children with Special Needs in Early Childhood Programmmes*. Washington, DC: National Association for the Education of Young Children (pp. 97–118).

Wolery, M. (1994b) Assessing children with special needs. In M. Wolery and J.S. Wilbers (eds), Including children with special needs in early childhood programs. Washington, DC: National Association for the Education of Young Children (pp. 71–96).

Wolery, M. and Sainato, D.M. (1996) General curriculum and intervention strategies. In S.L. Odom and M.E. McLean (eds), *Early Intervention/Early Childhood Special Education*. Austin, TX: PRO-ED (pp. 125–158).

Wolery, M. and Wilbers, J.S. (eds) (1994) *Including Children with Special Needs in Early Childhood Programmes*. Washington, DC: National Association for the Education of Young Children.

Wolfe, P. and Brandt, R. (1998) What do we know from brain research? *Educational Leadership*, 56(3), 8–13.

Wolfendale, S. (ed.) (1997) *Working with Parents of SEN Children After the Code of Practice*. London: David Fulton.

Wolfendale, S. (1998)(2nd edn) *All About Me*. Nottingham: NES-Arnold.

Wolfendale, S. (ed.) (2000) *Special Needs in the Early Years – Snapshots of Practice*. London: RoutledgeFalmer.

World Health Organization (WHO) (1992) *The ICD-10 Classification of Mental and Behavioural Disorders: Clinical Descriptions and Diagnostic Guidelines*. Geneva: WHO.

Zirpoli, T.J. (1995) *Understanding and Affecting the Behavior of Young Children*. Englewood Cliffs, NJ: Prentice Hall.

INDEX